Nutshell Series
Hornbook Series
and
Black Letter Series
of
WEST PUBLISHING COMPANY
P.O. Box 64526
St. Paul, Minnesota 55164–0526

Accounting

FARIS' ACCOUNTING AND LAW IN A NUTSHELL, 377 pages, 1984. Softcover. (Text)

Administrative Law

GELLHORN AND LEVIN'S ADMINISTRATIVE LAW AND PROCESS IN A NUTSHELL, Third Edition, 479 pages, 1990. Softcover. (Text)

Admiralty

MARAIST'S ADMIRALTY IN A NUTSHELL, Second Edition, 379 pages, 1988. Softcover. (Text)

SCHOENBAUM'S HORNBOOK ON ADMIRALTY AND MARITIME LAW, Student Edition, 692 pages, 1987 with 1989 pocket part. (Text)

Agency—Partnership

REUSCHLEIN AND GREGORY'S HORNBOOK ON THE LAW OF AGENCY AND PARTNERSHIP, Second Edition, 683 pages, 1990. (Text)

STEFFEN'S AGENCY-PARTNERSHIP IN A NUTSHELL, 364 pages, 1977. Softcover. (Text)

American Indian Law

CANBY'S AMERICAN INDIAN LAW IN A NUTSHELL, Second Edition, 336 pages, 1988. Softcover. (Text)

Antitrust—see also Regulated Industries, Trade Regulation

GELLHORN'S ANTITRUST LAW AND ECONOMICS IN A NUTSHELL, Third Edition, 472 pages,

Antitrust—Continued
1986. Softcover. (Text)

HOVENKAMP'S BLACK LETTER ON ANTITRUST, 323 pages, 1986. Softcover. (Review)

HOVENKAMP'S HORNBOOK ON ECONOMICS AND FEDERAL ANTITRUST LAW, Student Edition, 414 pages, 1985. (Text)

SULLIVAN'S HORNBOOK OF THE LAW OF ANTITRUST, 886 pages, 1977. (Text)

Appellate Advocacy—see Trial and Appellate Advocacy

Art Law
DUBOFF'S ART LAW IN A NUTSHELL, 335 pages, 1984. Softcover. (Text)

Banking Law
BANKING LAW: SELECTED STATUTES AND REGULATIONS. Softcover. 263 pages, 1991.

LOVETT'S BANKING AND FINANCIAL INSTITUTIONS LAW IN A NUTSHELL, Second Edition, 464 pages, 1988. Softcover. (Text)

Civil Procedure—see also Federal Jurisdiction and Procedure

CLERMONT'S BLACK LETTER ON CIVIL PROCEDURE, Second Edition, 332 pages, 1988. Softcover. (Review)

FRIEDENTHAL, KANE AND MILLER'S HORNBOOK ON CIVIL PROCEDURE, 876 pages, 1985. (Text)

KANE'S CIVIL PROCEDURE IN A NUTSHELL, Third Edition, 303 pages, 1991. Softcover. (Text)

KOFFLER AND REPPY'S HORNBOOK ON COMMON LAW PLEADING, 663 pages, 1969. (Text)

SIEGEL'S HORNBOOK ON NEW YORK PRACTICE, Second Edition, Student Edition, 1068 pages, 1991. Softcover. (Text)

Commercial Law
BAILEY AND HAGEDORN'S SECURED TRANSACTIONS IN A NUTSHELL, Third Edition, 390 pages, 1988. Softcover. (Text)

HENSON'S HORNBOOK ON SECURED TRANSACTIONS UNDER THE U.C.C., Second Edition, 504 pages, 1979, with 1979 pocket part. (Text)

NICKLES' BLACK LETTER ON COMMERCIAL PAPER, 450 pages, 1988. Softcover. (Review)

SPEIDEL'S BLACK LETTER ON SALES AND SALES FINANCING, 363 pages, 1984. Softcover. (Review)

STOCKTON'S SALES IN A NUT-

Commercial Law—Continued

SHELL, Second Edition, 370 pages, 1981. Softcover. (Text)

STONE'S UNIFORM COMMERCIAL CODE IN A NUTSHELL, Third Edition, 580 pages, 1989. Softcover. (Text)

WEBER AND SPEIDEL'S COMMERCIAL PAPER IN A NUTSHELL, Third Edition, 404 pages, 1982. Softcover. (Text)

WHITE AND SUMMERS' HORNBOOK ON THE UNIFORM COMMERCIAL CODE, Third Edition, Student Edition, 1386 pages, 1988. (Text)

Community Property

MENNELL AND BOYKOFF'S COMMUNITY PROPERTY IN A NUTSHELL, Second Edition, 432 pages, 1988. Softcover. (Text)

Comparative Law

GLENDON, GORDON AND OSAKWE'S COMPARATIVE LEGAL TRADITIONS IN A NUTSHELL. 402 pages, 1982. Softcover. (Text)

Conflict of Laws

HAY'S BLACK LETTER ON CONFLICT OF LAWS, 330 pages, 1989. Softcover. (Review)

SCOLES AND HAY'S HORNBOOK ON CONFLICT OF LAWS, Student Edition, approximately 1100 pages, November 1991 Pub. (Text)

SIEGEL'S CONFLICTS IN A NUTSHELL, 470 pages, 1982. Softcover. (Text)

Constitutional Law—Civil Rights

BARRON AND DIENES' BLACK LETTER ON CONSTITUTIONAL LAW, Third Edition, 440 pages, 1991. Softcover. (Review)

BARRON AND DIENES' CONSTITUTIONAL LAW IN A NUTSHELL, Second Edition, 483 pages, 1991. Softcover. (Text)

ENGDAHL'S CONSTITUTIONAL FEDERALISM IN A NUTSHELL, Second Edition, 411 pages, 1987. Softcover. (Text)

MARKS AND COOPER'S STATE CONSTITUTIONAL LAW IN A NUTSHELL, 329 pages, 1988. Softcover. (Text)

NOWAK AND ROTUNDA'S HORNBOOK ON CONSTITUTIONAL LAW, Fourth Edition, approximately 1275 pages, August, 1991 Pub. (Text)

VIEIRA'S CONSTITUTIONAL CIVIL RIGHTS IN A NUTSHELL, Second Edition, 322 pages, 1990. Softcover. (Text)

Constitutional Law—Civil Rights—Continued

WILLIAMS' CONSTITUTIONAL ANALYSIS IN A NUTSHELL, 388 pages, 1979. Softcover. (Text)

Consumer Law—see also Commercial Law

EPSTEIN AND NICKLES' CONSUMER LAW IN A NUTSHELL, Second Edition, 418 pages, 1981. Softcover. (Text)

Contracts

CALAMARI AND PERILLO'S BLACK LETTER ON CONTRACTS, Second Edition, 462 pages, 1990. Softcover. (Review)

CALAMARI AND PERILLO'S HORNBOOK ON CONTRACTS, Third Edition, 1049 pages, 1987. (Text)

CORBIN'S TEXT ON CONTRACTS, One Volume Student Edition, 1224 pages, 1952. (Text)

FRIEDMAN'S CONTRACT REMEDIES IN A NUTSHELL, 323 pages, 1981. Softcover. (Text)

KEYES' GOVERNMENT CONTRACTS IN A NUTSHELL, Second Edition, 557 pages, 1990. Softcover. (Text)

SCHABER AND ROHWER'S CONTRACTS IN A NUTSHELL, Third Edition, 457 pages, 1990. Softcover. (Text)

Copyright—see Patent and Copyright Law

Corporations

HAMILTON'S BLACK LETTER ON CORPORATIONS, Second Edition, 513 pages, 1986. Softcover. (Review)

HAMILTON'S THE LAW OF CORPORATIONS IN A NUTSHELL, Third Edition, 518 pages, 1991. Softcover. (Text)

HENN AND ALEXANDER'S HORNBOOK ON LAWS OF CORPORATIONS, Third Edition, Student Edition, 1371 pages, 1983, with 1986 pocket part. (Text)

Corrections

KRANTZ' THE LAW OF CORRECTIONS AND PRISONERS' RIGHTS IN A NUTSHELL, Third Edition, 407 pages, 1988. Softcover. (Text)

Creditors' Rights

EPSTEIN'S DEBTOR-CREDITOR LAW IN A NUTSHELL, Fourth Edition, 401 pages, 1991. Softcover. (Text)

NICKLES AND EPSTEIN'S BLACK LETTER ON CREDITORS' RIGHTS AND BANKRUPTCY, 576 pages, 1989. (Review)

Criminal Law and Criminal Procedure—see also Corrections, Juvenile Justice

ISRAEL AND LaFAVE'S CRIMINAL PROCEDURE—CONSTITUTIONAL LIMITATIONS IN A NUTSHELL, Fourth Edition, 461 pages, 1988. Softcover. (Text)

LaFAVE AND ISRAEL'S HORNBOOK ON CRIMINAL PROCEDURE, Second Edition, Student Edition, approximately 1200 pages, December, 1991 Pub. (Text)

LaFAVE AND SCOTT'S HORNBOOK ON CRIMINAL LAW, Second Edition, 918 pages, 1986. (Text)

LOEWY'S CRIMINAL LAW IN A NUTSHELL, Second Edition, 321 pages, 1987. Softcover. (Text)

LOW'S BLACK LETTER ON CRIMINAL LAW, Revised First Edition, 443 pages, 1990. Softcover. (Review)

Domestic Relations

CLARK'S HORNBOOK ON DOMESTIC RELATIONS, Second Edition, Student Edition, 1050 pages, 1988. (Text)

KRAUSE'S BLACK LETTER ON FAMILY LAW, 314 pages, 1988. Softcover. (Review)

KRAUSE'S FAMILY LAW IN A NUTSHELL, Second Edition, 444 pages, 1986. Softcover. (Text)

MALLOY'S LAW AND ECONOMICS: A COMPARATIVE APPROACH TO THEORY AND PRACTICE, 166 pages, 1990. Softcover. (Text)

Education Law

ALEXANDER AND ALEXANDER'S THE LAW OF SCHOOLS, STUDENTS AND TEACHERS IN A NUTSHELL, 409 pages, 1984. Softcover. (Text)

Employment Discrimination—see also Gender Discrimination

PLAYER'S FEDERAL LAW OF EMPLOYMENT DISCRIMINATION IN A NUTSHELL, Second Edition, 402 pages, 1981. Softcover. (Text)

PLAYER'S HORNBOOK ON EMPLOYMENT DISCRIMINATION LAW, Student Edition, 708 pages, 1988. (Text)

Energy and Natural Resources Law—see also Oil and Gas

Environmental Law—see also Energy and Natural Resources Law; Sea, Law of

FINDLEY AND FARBER'S ENVIRONMENTAL LAW IN A NUTSHELL, Second Edition, 367

Human Rights—see International Law

Immigration Law

WEISSBRODT'S IMMIGRATION LAW AND PROCEDURE IN A NUT-SHELL, Second Edition, 438 pages, 1989, Softcover. (Text)

Indian Law—see American Indian Law

Insurance Law

DOBBYN'S INSURANCE LAW IN A NUTSHELL, Second Edition, 316 pages, 1989. Softcover. (Text)

KEETON AND WIDISS' INSUR-ANCE LAW, Student Edition, 1359 pages, 1988. (Text)

International Law—see also Sea, Law of

BUERGENTHAL'S INTERNATIONAL HUMAN RIGHTS IN A NUTSHELL, 283 pages, 1988. Softcover. (Text)

BUERGENTHAL AND MAIER'S PUBLIC INTERNATIONAL LAW IN A NUTSHELL, Second Edition, 275 pages, 1990. Softcover. (Text)

FOLSOM, GORDON AND SPA-NOGLE'S INTERNATIONAL BUSI-NESS TRANSACTIONS IN A NUT-SHELL, Third Edition, 509 pages, 1988. Softcover. (Text)

Interviewing and Counseling

SHAFFER AND ELKINS' LEGAL IN-TERVIEWING AND COUNSELING IN A NUTSHELL, Second Edition, 487 pages, 1987. Softcover. (Text)

Introduction to Law—see Legal Method and Legal System

Introduction to Law Study

HEGLAND'S INTRODUCTION TO THE STUDY AND PRACTICE OF LAW IN A NUTSHELL, 418 pages, 1983. Softcover. (Text)

KINYON'S INTRODUCTION TO LAW STUDY AND LAW EXAMINA-TIONS IN A NUTSHELL, 389 pages, 1971. Softcover. (Text)

Judicial Process—see Legal Method and Legal System

Juvenile Justice

FOX'S JUVENILE COURTS IN A NUTSHELL, Third Edition, 291 pages, 1984. Softcover. (Text)

Labor and Employment Law—see also Employment Dis-crimination, Workers' Com-pensation

LESLIE'S LABOR LAW IN A NUT-SHELL, Second Edition, 397 pages, 1986. Softcover. (Text)

Labor and Employment Law—
Continued

NOLAN'S LABOR ARBITRATION LAW AND PRACTICE IN A NUTSHELL, 358 pages, 1979. Softcover. (Text)

Land Finance—Property Security—see Real Estate Transactions

Land Use

HAGMAN AND JUERGENS-MEYER'S HORNBOOK ON URBAN PLANNING AND LAND DEVELOPMENT CONTROL LAW, Second Edition, Student Edition, 680 pages, 1986. (Text)

WRIGHT AND WRIGHT'S LAND USE IN A NUTSHELL, Second Edition, 356 pages, 1985. Softcover. (Text)

Legal Method and Legal System—see also Legal Research, Legal Writing

KEMPIN'S HISTORICAL INTRODUCTION TO ANGLO-AMERICAN LAW IN A NUTSHELL, Third Edition, 323 pages, 1990. Softcover. (Text)

REYNOLDS' JUDICIAL PROCESS IN A NUTSHELL, Second Edition, approximately 310 pages, 1991. Softcover. (Text)

Legal Research

COHEN'S LEGAL RESEARCH IN A NUTSHELL, Fourth Edition, 452 pages, 1985. Softcover. (Text)

COHEN, BERRING AND OLSON'S HOW TO FIND THE LAW, Ninth Edition, 716 pages, 1989. (Text)

Legal Writing and Drafting

SQUIRES AND ROMBAUER'S LEGAL WRITING IN A NUTSHELL, 294 pages, 1982. Softcover. (Text)

Legislation—see also Legal Writing and Drafting

DAVIES' LEGISLATIVE LAW AND PROCESS IN A NUTSHELL, Second Edition, 346 pages, 1986. Softcover. (Text)

Local Government

MCCARTHY'S LOCAL GOVERNMENT LAW IN A NUTSHELL, Third Edition, 435 pages, 1990. Softcover. (Text)

REYNOLDS' HORNBOOK ON LOCAL GOVERNMENT LAW, 860 pages, 1982, with 1990 pocket part. (Text)

Mass Communication Law

ZUCKMAN, GAYNES, CARTER AND DEE'S MASS COMMUNICATIONS LAW IN A NUTSHELL, Third Edition, 538 pages, 1988. Softcover. (Text)

Medicine, Law and

HALL AND ELLMAN'S HEALTH CARE LAW AND ETHICS IN A NUTSHELL, 401 pages, 1990. Softcover (Text)

JARVIS, CLOSEN, HERMANN AND LEONARD'S AIDS LAW IN A NUTSHELL, 349 pages, 1991. Softcover. (Text)

KING'S THE LAW OF MEDICAL MALPRACTICE IN A NUTSHELL, Second Edition, 342 pages, 1986. Softcover. (Text)

Military Law

SHANOR AND TERRELL'S MILITARY LAW IN A NUTSHELL, 378 pages, 1980. Softcover. (Text)

Mortgages—see Real Estate Transactions

Natural Resources Law—see Energy and Natural Resources Law, Environmental Law

Office Practice—see also Computers and Law, Interviewing and Counseling, Negotiation

HEGLAND'S TRIAL AND PRACTICE SKILLS IN A NUTSHELL, 346 pages, 1978. Softcover (Text)

Oil and Gas—see also Energy and Natural Resources Law

HEMINGWAY'S HORNBOOK ON THE LAW OF OIL AND GAS, Third Edition, Student Edition, approximately 700 pages, Aug., 1991 Pub. (Text)

LOWE'S OIL AND GAS LAW IN A NUTSHELL, Second Edition, 465 pages, 1988. Softcover. (Text)

Partnership—see Agency— Partnership

Patent and Copyright Law

MILLER AND DAVIS' INTELLECTUAL PROPERTY—PATENTS, TRADEMARKS AND COPYRIGHT IN A NUTSHELL, Second Edition, 437 pages, 1990. Softcover. (Text)

Products Liability

PHILLIPS' PRODUCTS LIABILITY IN A NUTSHELL, Third Edition, 307 pages, 1988. Softcover. (Text)

Professional Responsibility

ARONSON AND WECKSTEIN'S PROFESSIONAL RESPONSIBILITY IN A NUTSHELL, Second Edition, approximately 500 pages, 1991. Softcover. (Text)

ROTUNDA'S BLACK LETTER ON PROFESSIONAL RESPONSIBILITY, Second Edition, 414 pages, 1988. Softcover. (Review)

WOLFRAM'S HORNBOOK ON

Professional Responsibility—
Continued

MODERN LEGAL ETHICS, Student Edition, 1120 pages, 1986. (Text)

Property—see also Real Estate Transactions, Land Use, Trusts and Estates

BERNHARDT'S BLACK LETTER ON PROPERTY, Second Edition, approximately 375 pages, 1991. Softcover. (Review)

BERNHARDT'S REAL PROPERTY IN A NUTSHELL, Second Edition, 448 pages, 1981. Softcover. (Text)

BURKE'S PERSONAL PROPERTY IN A NUTSHELL, 322 pages, 1983. Softcover. (Text)

CUNNINGHAM, STOEBUCK AND WHITMAN'S HORNBOOK ON THE LAW OF PROPERTY, Student Edition, 916 pages, 1984, with 1987 pocket part. (Text)

HILL'S LANDLORD AND TENANT LAW IN A NUTSHELL, Second Edition, 311 pages, 1986. Softcover. (Text)

Real Estate Transactions

BRUCE'S REAL ESTATE FINANCE IN A NUTSHELL, Third Edition, approximately 270 pages, 1991. Softcover. (Text)

NELSON AND WHITMAN'S BLACK LETTER ON LAND TRANSACTIONS AND FINANCE, Second Edition, 466 pages, 1988. Softcover. (Review)

NELSON AND WHITMAN'S HORNBOOK ON REAL ESTATE FINANCE LAW, Second Edition, 941 pages, 1985 with 1989 pocket part. (Text)

Regulated Industries—see also Mass Communication Law, Banking Law

GELLHORN AND PIERCE'S REGULATED INDUSTRIES IN A NUTSHELL, Second Edition, 389 pages, 1987. Softcover. (Text)

Remedies

DOBBS' HORNBOOK ON REMEDIES, 1067 pages, 1973. (Text)

DOBBYN'S INJUNCTIONS IN A NUTSHELL, 264 pages, 1974. Softcover. (Text)

FRIEDMAN'S CONTRACT REMEDIES IN A NUTSHELL, 323 pages, 1981. Softcover. (Text)

O'CONNELL'S REMEDIES IN A NUTSHELL, Second Edition, 320 pages, 1985. Softcover. (Text)

Sea, Law of

SOHN AND GUSTAFSON'S THE LAW OF THE SEA IN A NUTSHELL, 264 pages, 1984. Softcover. (Text)

Securities Regulation

HAZEN'S HORNBOOK ON THE LAW OF SECURITIES REGULATION, Second Edition, Student Edition, 1082 pages, 1990. (Text)

RATNER'S SECURITIES REGULATION IN A NUTSHELL, Third Edition, 316 pages, 1988. Softcover. (Text)

SECURITIES REGULATION, SELECTED STATUTES, RULES, AND FORMS. Softcover. 1331 pages, 1991.

Sports Law

SCHUBERT, SMITH AND TRENTADUE'S SPORTS LAW, 395 pages, 1986. (Text)

Tax Practice and Procedure

MORGAN'S TAX PROCEDURE AND TAX FRAUD IN A NUTSHELL, 400 pages, 1990. Softcover. (Text)

Taxation—Corporate

SCHWARZ AND LATHROPE'S BLACK LETTER ON CORPORATE AND PARTNERSHIP TAXATION, Approximately 500 pages, September, 1991 Pub. Softcover. (Review)

WEIDENBRUCH AND BURKE'S FEDERAL INCOME TAXATION OF CORPORATIONS AND STOCKHOLDERS IN A NUTSHELL, Third Edition, 309 pages, 1989. Soft-

cover. (Text)

Taxation—Estate & Gift—see also Estate Planning, Trusts and Estates

MCNULTY'S FEDERAL ESTATE AND GIFT TAXATION IN A NUTSHELL, Fourth Edition, 496 pages, 1989. Softcover. (Text)

Taxation—Individual

HUDSON AND LIND'S BLACK LETTER ON FEDERAL INCOME TAXATION, Third Edition, 406 pages, 1990. Softcover. (Review)

MCNULTY'S FEDERAL INCOME TAXATION OF INDIVIDUALS IN A NUTSHELL, Fourth Edition, 503 pages, 1988. Softcover. (Text)

POSIN'S HORNBOOK ON FEDERAL INCOME TAXATION, Student Edition, 491 pages, 1983, with 1989 pocket part. (Text)

ROSE AND CHOMMIE'S HORNBOOK ON FEDERAL INCOME TAXATION, Third Edition, 923 pages, 1988, with 1989 pocket part. (Text)

Taxation—International

DOERNBERG'S INTERNATIONAL TAXATION IN A NUTSHELL, 325 pages, 1989. Softcover. (Text)

BISHOP AND BROOKS' FEDERAL

Taxation—International—Continued

PARTNERSHIP TAXATION: A GUIDE TO THE LEADING CASES, STATUTES, AND REGULATIONS, 545 pages, 1990. Softcover. (Text)

SCHWARZ AND LATHROPE'S BLACK LETTER ON CORPORATE AND PARTNERSHIP TAXATION, Approximately 500 pages, September, 1991 Pub. Softcover. (Review)

Taxation—State & Local

GELFAND AND SALSICH'S STATE AND LOCAL TAXATION AND FINANCE IN A NUTSHELL, 309 pages, 1986. Softcover. (Text)

Torts—see also Products Liability

KIONKA'S BLACK LETTER ON TORTS, 339 pages, 1988. Softcover. (Review)

KIONKA'S TORTS IN A NUTSHELL: INJURIES TO PERSONS AND PROPERTY, 434 pages, 1977. Softcover. (Text)

MALONE'S TORTS IN A NUTSHELL: INJURIES TO FAMILY, SOCIAL AND TRADE RELATIONS, 358 pages, 1979. Softcover. (Text)

PROSSER AND KEETON'S HORNBOOK ON TORTS, Fifth Edition, Student Edition, 1286 pages, 1984 with 1988 pocket part. (Text)

Trade Regulation—see also Antitrust, Regulated Industries

MCMANIS' UNFAIR TRADE PRACTICES IN A NUTSHELL, Second Edition, 464 pages, 1988. Softcover. (Text)

SCHECHTER'S BLACK LETTER ON UNFAIR TRADE PRACTICES, 272 pages, 1986. Softcover. (Review)

Trial and Appellate Advocacy—see also Civil Procedure

BERGMAN'S TRIAL ADVOCACY IN A NUTSHELL, Second Edition, 354 pages, 1989. Softcover. (Text)

GOLDBERG'S THE FIRST TRIAL (WHERE DO I SIT? WHAT DO I SAY?) IN A NUTSHELL, 396 pages, 1982. Softcover. (Text)

HEGLAND'S TRIAL AND PRACTICE SKILLS IN A NUTSHELL, 346 pages, 1978. Softcover. (Text)

HORNSTEIN'S APPELLATE ADVOCACY IN A NUTSHELL, 325 pages, 1984. Softcover. (Text)

JEANS' HANDBOOK ON TRIAL ADVOCACY, Student Edition, 473 pages, 1975. Softcover.

Advisory Board

LABOR LAW
IN A NUTSHELL

By

DOUGLAS L. LESLIE
Charles O. Gregory Professor of Law,
University of Virginia

THIRD EDITION

ST. PAUL, MINN.
WEST PUBLISHING CO.
1992

COPYRIGHT © 1979 WEST PUBLISHING CO.
COPYRIGHT © 1986 DOUGLAS L. LESLIE
COPYRIGHT © 1992 By WEST PUBLISHING CO.
                        50 West Kellogg Boulevard
                        P.O. Box 64526
                        St. Paul, MN 55164–0526

Library of Congress Cataloging-in-Publication Data

Leslie, Douglas L., 1942–
   Labor law in a nutshell / by Douglas L. Leslie. — 3rd ed.
    p.   cm. — (Nutshell series)
   Includes index.
   ISBN 0–314–92205–9

   1. Labor laws and legislation—United States. 2. Trade-unions-
-Law and legislation—United States. 3. Collective labor
agreements—United States. I. Title. II. Series.
KF3369.3.L39 1992
344.73'01—dc20
[347.3041]   91–35300
                                                                CIP

ISBN 0–314–92205–9

OUTLINE

TABLE OF CASES

TABLE OF CASES

*

LABOR LAW
IN A NUTSHELL

*

CHAPTER I

EARLY REGULATION BY LAW AND A STATUTORY OVERVIEW

A. Judicial Control of Union Activity Prior to the Wagner Act

In the 1800's, many courts considered concerted activities by workers, such as strikes, picketing and refusals to deal with certain employers, to be common law criminal conspiracies. In one of the earliest reported cases, Commonwealth v. Pullis (Philadelphia Mayor's Court, 1806), workers were convicted of criminal conspiracy for refusing to work except at a specified wage rate and for attempting to prevent others from working at a lower rate. Other cases in the nineteenth century held that union efforts to improve wages and working conditions violated the criminal law.

Subjecting workers to criminal sanctions drew public criticism and in 1842 the celebrated case of Commonwealth v. Hunt (Mass.1842) marked a shift from criminal to civil liability as the tool for controlling union activity. Workers had refused to work for employers who paid their employees less than union scale. The court dismissed a criminal indictment and permitted the use of an economic weapon by a group of workers to prevent other workers from entering into individual employment contracts inconsistent with the group's interest. The court adopted an ends/means test: The finding of a criminal conspiracy required proof of either an illegal purpose or the use of illegal means.

After *Hunt,* the ends/means test was used most often in state court civil suits for injunctions and damages against concerted worker activity. One arm of the ends/means test was articulated in the prima facie tort doctrine: The intentional infliction of economic harm is a tort unless justified by a legitimate purpose. Assessing the legitimacy of a union's purpose was left to the lower courts. Some judges were prepared to uphold union economic activity on a showing that it was taken in the union's self-interest, but many others undertook to weigh the respective interests involved in a labor dispute—those of the workers, the employer and the public. In the absence of identifiable standards or of an established common law tradition, each case tended to be decided in accordance with the judge's individual notions of what constituted good and bad union conduct. Results were ad hoc and unpredictable.

During this period federal courts were also staking out a role in the judicial regulation of labor-management relations. Jurisdiction was asserted by virtue of diversity of citizenship or by application of the Sherman Antitrust Act. The prima facie tort doctrine was one substantive ground for

outlawing union activity, but the antitrust laws
proved even more useful. The Sherman Act's prohibition of "restraint of trade" could be applied to
most union tactics involving organizing and economic pressure. In the *Danbury Hatters* case,
Loewe v. Lawlor (U.S.1908), the Supreme Court
found a Sherman Act violation when a union insti-
gated a boycott of retail stores that sold hats produced by a struck manufacturer. The union was
subjected to treble damages. Congress attempted
to diminish unions' exposure to antitrust liability
by passing the Clayton Act in 1914, but the Supreme Court in Duplex Printing Press Co. v. Deering (U.S.1921) gave a narrow reading to Clayton
Act provisions protecting labor activity.

Because of certain procedural problems and the
difficulty of finding union assets to satisfy federal
court damage awards, employers often sought the
relatively quick relief of the injunction to thwart
union activity. Many later observers considered
the cases disgraceful. Marked by standardized
"form pleadings" and vaguely worded affidavits,
injunctions were often issued *ex parte* and tended
to be cast in broad terms. While a full hearing on
the appropriateness of continuing the injunction
would eventually be held, usually this came too
late to help the union, whose strike, boycott or
other activity had been effectively "broken."

Public pressure intervened and in 1932 Congress
passed the Norris–LaGuardia Act. Norris–La-
Guardia specifically withdraws the power of the

federal courts to issue either temporary or permanent injunctions in nonviolent labor disputes. Certain activities, such as picketing and refusals to work, are specifically immunized from injunctions. If union conduct falls within the statute's coverage, federal courts are powerless to enjoin even a clear violation of substantive law. Even where injunctions are permitted to prevent violence, specified procedures must be observed. But Norris–LaGuardia accomplished more than the withdrawal of a remedy; it declared that federal courts were not to be in the business of formulating rules to govern labor policy—the government was to be neutral, and this was expected to permit union growth.

B. Wagner Act

Passage of the Wagner Act (National Labor Relations Act) in 1935 marked the beginning of affirmative support of unionization and collective bargaining by the federal government. The key provision is § 7, a declaration of employee rights. As originally enacted, it read: "Employees shall have the right to self-organization, to form, join or assist labor organizations, to bargain collectively through representatives of their own choosing, and to engage in concerted activities for the purpose of collective bargaining or other mutual aid or protection." Section 7 is enforced by § 8, which lists employer unfair labor practices. Section 8(a)(1) (originally § 8(1)) prohibits employer interference with the rights guaranteed in § 7. Section 8(a)(2) outlaws employer-formed or dominated "company unions." Section 8(a)(3) forbids discrimination by employers on account of union activity in hiring, firing and other means of employment; § 8(a)(4) prohibits such discrimination against employees on account of their testifying or giving charges before the agency charged with implementing the statute. Section 8(a)(5) requires employers to bargain collectively with the duly established representatives (unions) of their employees.

Section 9 of the Wagner Act describes the procedures, primarily the secret ballot election in an "appropriate bargaining unit," by which employees can choose whether they want a particular union to represent them.

The Wagner Act establishes an administrative agency, the National Labor Relations Board (NLRB or Board) to administer and interpret the unfair labor practice and representation provisions of the Act. With respect to unfair labor practice cases, the members of the NLRB were originally designated to serve both prosecutorial and adjudicatory functions. They issued complaints alleging violations, prosecuted them through Board staff, and then ruled on their merits. Judicial review in specified courts of appeals was established by § 10. The Wagner Act contained no restrictions on the activities of unions.

C. Taft–Hartley Act

Unions enjoyed a considerable growth in membership and economic power following the passage of the Wagner Act. In some instances, unions were thought to be abusing their new strength. By 1947 Congress was in the mood to forbid certain union "bad practices," and also to change some of the Act's procedures. Over President Truman's veto, Congress passed the Taft–Hartley Act (Labor–Management Relations Act). Taft–Hartley amended § 8 of the NLRA by prohibiting union activities that are specified in § 8(b). Forbidden are secondary boycotts, jurisdictional strikes over work assignments, and strikes to force an employer to discharge an employee on account of his or her union affiliation, or lack of it. Section 7 was amended to include the right to *refrain* from engaging in concerted activities. The office of the General Counsel of the NLRB was established to handle the Board's unfair labor practice prosecutorial functions. Section 301 of the Taft–Hartley Act makes collective bargaining agreements enforceable in federal district court, and § 303 provides a civil damage remedy to private parties injured by secondary boycotts. The statute thus marks a shift away from a federal policy encouraging unionization to a more neutral posture, while continuing the right of employees to be free from employer coercion.

D. Landrum–Griffin Act

In the 1950s, congressional committee hearings uncovered evidence of looting of some union treasuries and denials of fundamental rights to members in a few unions. In 1959 the Landrum–Griffin Act (Labor–Management Reporting and Disclosure Act) was passed. It contains a bill of rights for union members, requires certain financial disclosures by unions, prescribes procedures for the election of union officers, and provides civil and criminal remedies for financial abuses by union officers. At the same time, employer interest groups were able to secure passage of amendments to the National Labor Relations Act broadening the coverage of the secondary boycott provisions and partially restricting the right of unions to picket in order to obtain representation rights.

CHAPTER II

NLRB STRUCTURE AND PROCEDURE

A. Structure of the NLRB

The principal components of the National Labor Relations Board are five Board members, a General Counsel, regional directors, and administrative law judges (formerly called "trial examiners"). The five Board members are appointed by the President, with the advice and consent of the Senate. They serve five-year, staggered terms. One member is designated Chairman. Routine cases are decided by panels of three Board members, but cases of particular importance are decided by the entire Board. The Board members and their supporting staffs are housed in Washington, D.C.

The General Counsel is also appointed by the President, with the advice and consent of the Senate. The General Counsel is responsible for overseeing the investigation and prosecution of unfair labor practice charges. The General Counsel also represents the NLRB in the courts. Most unfair labor practice case work is done in the field, through regional offices. There are over thirty regional offices scattered throughout the country and each is headed by a regional director appoint-

8

ed by and responsible to the General Counsel in Washington. The General Counsel is supported by considerable staff in Washington.

The regional directors, in addition to their responsibility for prosecuting unfair labor practice cases, have been delegated considerable authority to act for the Board in representation cases—cases involving a decision of whether to designate a particular union as the exclusive bargaining representation for a group of employees.

While the Board has statutory jurisdiction over all enterprises whose activities "affect" interstate commerce, the Board in its discretion has refused to assert jurisdiction over employers not meeting a minimum volume of business. For example, before the Board will assert jurisdiction over a non-retail business, the business must have a minimum annual volume measured by inflow or outflow, direct or indirect, of at least $50,000 across state lines. In the Landrum–Griffin Act of 1959, Congress added § 14(c)(1) to the NLRA which has the effect of prohibiting the Board from declining to assert jurisdiction over any labor dispute over which it would have asserted jurisdiction under the standards prevailing on August 1, 1959. Thus, the Board can expand, but can no longer contract, its jurisdiction. In cases falling outside of the Board's jurisdictional standards, the states are permitted to act.

B. Procedures in Unfair Labor Practice Cases

Each NLRB case, whether it involves an unfair labor practice or a matter of representation, must be initiated by a private party. In recent years the number of such cases of all types filed each year has been over 50,000. Of these, close to 40,000 were unfair labor practice charges. An unfair labor practice case is initiated when a private party (called the "charging party") files a "charge" that an unfair labor practice has been committed. The regional office where the charge is filed is responsible for investigating it, although in practice some regional offices are so clogged with cases that they do no more than demand that the charging party produce sufficient evidence to indicate a meritorious case. After investigation, the regional director decides whether to issue a "complaint" in the case. Only if a complaint is issued will the case be prosecuted and heard by the Board. Many factors may influence the choice of whether to issue a complaint, such as the strength of the evidence, the seriousness of the activity under attack, the case load of the regional office, and the clarity of Board precedent on the substantive issues raised. While an internal appeal to the General Counsel's office in Washington can be taken if the regional director refuses to issue a complaint, such appeals are almost always denied. No appeal to Board members or to the courts can be taken from the refusal to issue a complaint; the General Counsel's discretion is unreviewable. Ordinarily over 70 percent of the unfair labor practice charges filed are either dismissed by the regional director or are withdrawn by the charging party upon being advised by the regional director that no complaint would be issued.

If the regional director issues the unfair labor practice complaint, an attorney from the regional office will prosecute the case for the charging party. Most complaints (over 80 percent) are settled by the regional office prior to any hearing. Information is often exchanged during settlement discussions but the Board neither requires nor has any mechanisms allowing pre-hearing discovery in unfair labor practice cases. The Supreme Court ruled in NLRB v. Robbins Tire & Rubber Co. (U.S.1978) that witnesses' statements in pending unfair labor practice proceedings are exempt from Freedom of Information Act disclosure at least until completion of the hearing.

If an unfair labor practice hearing is necessary, a regional staff attorney representing the General Counsel will control the case, but the charging party may intervene and present evidence. An unfair labor practice case is tried before an administrative law judge (ALJ). ALJs are selected by the Civil Service Commission and are housed in either Washington or San Francisco. They travel throughout the country to take evidence in unfair labor practice cases. After taking evidence and receiving briefs, an ALJ issues a recommended decision and order. These recommended decisions routinely recite the evidence in considerable detail, make credibility resolutions when necessary, and discuss applicable Board precedent. The recommended order will either set out the appropriate remedy or dismiss the complaint.

If no party (respondent, General Counsel or charging party) files exceptions to this recommended decision and order, it automatically becomes final as an order issued by the Board. If exceptions are filed, the case file is transferred to the Board in Washington, briefs are filed (oral argument is very rare), and the Board issues a written decision and order. Thus the Board members hear no evidence, see no witnesses; in that sense, they are similar to an appellate tribunal. Board members have a large case load and rely heavily upon their staff in routine cases.

A Board order is not self-enforcing; that is, the Board has no coercive power to compel adherence to its order. Section 10(e) of the NLRA provides that the Board may petition specified United States Courts of Appeals for enforcement of a Board order. In addition, § 10(f) provides that any person aggrieved by a final Board order granting or denying relief sought may petition a Court of Appeals for review of the order. Both sections provide that the "findings of the Board with respect to questions of fact if supported by substantial evidence on the record considered as a whole shall be conclusive." In Universal Camera Corp. v. NLRB (U.S.1951), the Supreme Court construed this standard of review to mean that the courts of appeals have authority to assess not only those facts supporting the Board's result, but also those pointing to an opposite conclusion. The findings of the ALJ are deemed a part of the record of which the Board is to take account; and the ALJ's findings may be given weight by the Court of Appeals: "Evidence supporting a [Board] conclusion may be less substantial when an impartial experienced [Administrative Law Judge] who has observed the witnesses and lived with the case has drawn conclusions different from the Board's...."

Generally Board cases in unfair labor practice proceedings have been affirmed in whole or in part by Courts of Appeals at a rate of over 80 percent. A party who fails to comply with a Court of Appeals enforcement order risks a contempt citation. A final review possibility is a writ of certiorari from the United States Supreme Court.

Delay is a major problem in prosecuting unfair labor practice cases. In recent years it has taken on the average 48 days to complete the investigative stage of an unfair labor practice case, and an average of 94 days from the close of an unfair labor practice hearing to receipt of the ALJ's decision. After receipt of the ALJ's decision, it took on the average 116 days for the Board to issue its order.

C. Procedures in Representation Cases

A major responsibility of the NLRB is to determine whether employees should be represented by a union. The hallmark of this selection process is free employee choice consistent with certain employer interests in the proper functioning of its business.

Unions normally engage in campaigns for the allegiance of company employees prior to initiating NLRB representation procedures. A petition for an NLRB representation election can be filed by unions, employers, or by the employees themselves. A union petition alone is not sufficient to initiate the Board's election process; the petition must be supported by a substantial number of employees, currently required to be at least 30 percent of the employees in the bargaining unit designated by the petition. Support is usually shown by signed, dated cards authorizing the union to represent the signer in collective bargaining ("authorization cards"). This "showing of interest" is submitted to the regional director whose staff investigates and authenticates the cards. The employer is not permitted to see the cards, nor to challenge the results of this administrative investigation.

An employer can file an election petition only if a union has claimed to represent a majority of its employees and/or has sought to bargain with the employer on behalf of the workers. A petition by the employer is not warranted merely because a union is campaigning among the employees. Otherwise, the employer might thwart an organizing attempt by forcing a premature election.

Once a petition has been filed, the regional director will first investigate whether the NLRB asserts jurisdiction over an employer of this sort and whether there are any bars to the election. If there are no obstacles to holding the election, the regional director will attempt to secure the agreement of the union (or unions) and the employer to the holding of a consent election. The union may not be seeking an election over every non-supervisory employee of the employer. In order to obtain a representation election the union must be seeking to represent all the employees in an "appropriate bargaining unit." If the regional director is unable to secure an agreement for a consent election, the director will order a representation hearing to be conducted by an employee of the regional office. At that hearing interested parties will litigate all issues relating to the appropriateness of holding the election, the identification of a proper bargaining unit, and the determination of which employees are eligible to vote. This hearing is labeled non-adversarial: the rules of evidence are relaxed, and the hearing officer makes no credibility resolutions. In practice, the hearings are often highly adversarial.

If the regional director orders the election to be held, it will be conducted by a secret ballot by a representative of the regional office. Following the election and tabulation of the result, the losing party may file objections contending that some error in the election process, or misconduct by the winning party, should cause the NLRB to set the election aside. The regional director will determine whether a hearing is necessary to resolve these objections and either with or without a hearing will render a decision on whether the election results are valid.

In the early 1960s, the Board delegated to regional directors with respect to election petitions the power to determine whether there is a properly raised question concerning representation, the appropriateness of the requested bargaining unit, and the validity of challenged ballots and election objections. The Board itself only hears these matters on a discretionary, case-by-case basis. A regional director's decision on these matters is final and binding unless discretionary review is sought and obtained on one of several grounds. These include that a substantial question of law or policy is raised; that the regional director's decision on a substantial factual issue is erroneous and such error prejudicially affects the rights of a party; that error in the conduct of a hearing or any ruling made in connection with the hearing has resulted in prejudicial error; or that there are compelling reasons for reconsideration of an important Board rule or policy.

CHAPTER III

SELECTING A BARGAINING REPRESENTATIVE

A. The Meaning of Exclusivity

When a union is designated by the NLRB as the representative of a group of employees, or when an employer privately accords the union such recognition, the union enjoys the exclusive right to represent those employees. Section 9(a) of the NLRA states this exclusivity principle in general terms. Shortly after its passage, the NLRA was alleged to be unconstitutional because its effect was to interfere with the right of individual employees, and minority groups, to contract with employers on their own behalf. In upholding the constitutionality of the NLRA and the Railway Labor Act in NLRB v. Jones & Laughlin Steel Corp. (U.S.1937) and Virginian Railway Co. v. System Federation (U.S.1937), the Court avoided this issue by holding that the effect of the statutes was merely to prohibit the negotiation of labor contracts by anyone acting as the agent or representative of employees other than one duly authorized under the statutes but that the statutes did not preclude "such individual contracts as [the employer] may elect to make directly with individual employees."

17

The full import of this language was not long to survive, however. In J.I. Case Co. v. NLRB (U.S.1944), the employer, prior to any union campaign, offered individual employment contracts to its employees. These contracts were not mandatory, and not every employee signed one, but those that did found their wage rates and certain other benefits maintained in return for a promise to serve the employer and comply with company rules. While those contracts were in effect a union was designated by the NLRB as exclusive bargaining representative for the company's production and maintenance employees. The company was unsuccessful before the Board in urging the individual contracts as a bar to the union's designation as employee representative. However, when the union requested the employer to bargain over wages, hours and other working conditions, the employer refused, again relying on the preclusive effect of the individual contracts.

The NLRB held that the employer's refusal violated the duty to bargain section (now § 8(a)(5)) of the NLRA and ordered the employer to cease giving effect to the individual contracts. The Supreme Court, analogizing collective bargaining agreements first to tariffs and then to third party beneficiary contracts, held that individual employees cannot waive the benefits of collective bargaining agreements by agreeing with their employer to accept less. Individual contracts regardless of their circumstances may not defeat or delay NLRA representation procedures, nor may they exclude employees from the duly ascertained bargaining group or forestall or limit collective bargaining. While refusing to rule that an individual employment contract containing terms better than the bargaining agreement negotiated by the group is always unenforceable, the Court noted that such individually negotiated benefits would often be thought by the group to have been obtained at the group's expense. The Court said that the employer and the union were always free to negotiate a bargaining agreement that set minimum terms only, leaving open the possibility of individual employees negotiating more favorable terms. In the 1980s and 1990s, students of sports will recognize this arrangement in major league baseball and basketball. Players' unions represent the athletes and negotiate (lucrative) minimum salaries; but individual players and their agents are permitted to obtain salaries in excess of the minimums, and many do.

An employee need not vote for union representation but even the dissenting employee will be bound by the vote of the majority. It is obvious that the will of the majority may disadvantage particular employees or employee groups that have higher levels of skill than the average employee. One protection against a union excessively disadvantaging relatively skilled employees is that the NLRB will designate the union as the exclusive representative only in an appropriate bargaining unit, which to some extent guarantees that employees share a community of interest. Also, an employer can bargain with the union to maintain the right to pay individual employees higher rates and better benefits than those given to the majority. Another doctrine giving employees some protection is that the union must fairly represent all employees in the unit (see Chapter 9, D).

The concept of exclusivity also means that the employer may not avoid the union and deal directly with employees, even if the employees initiate the dealings. Medo Photo Supply Corp. v. NLRB (U.S.1944). If under all the circumstances the employer is deemed to have sought to deal with employees individually in an attempt to undermine the union and establish individual bargaining, it will be found to have violated § 8(a)(5) and 8(a)(1).

The importance of the exclusivity principle is demonstrated by Emporium Capwell Co. v. Western Addition Community Organization (U.S.1975). The employer's department store employees were represented by a union and the collective bargaining agreement contained a clause prohibiting employment discrimination by reason of race, color, creed, national origin, sex, or age. The agreement had a no-strike clause and a grievance and arbitration procedure for processing claims of breach of the agreement. A group of employees presented the union with a list of grievances claiming that the company was discriminating on the basis of race in making assignments and promotions. The union began to process these grievances but denied the request of the employees that the union authorize picketing of the employer. The processing of the grievances was not proceeding in a manner satisfactory to the complaining employees and, after the president of the company refused to discuss the matter with them, they denounced the store publicly and picketed, calling for a consumer boycott of the store. After a warning, the employer discharged them.

Discharging an employee for engaging in concerted activity for mutual aid and protection as defined by § 7 of the NLRA is a violation of § 8(a)(1) of the Act. In *Emporium Capwell*, however, the NLRB held that there was no NLRA violation because the actions of the complaining employees amounted to a demand on the employer to bargain with them, circumventing the union, and that such demands for direct bargaining do not enjoy NLRA protection because they are inconsistent with the exclusivity principle. Separate bargaining with the complaining employees would undermine union efforts at bettering working conditions, the Board reasoned, and would put the employer between potentially conflicting demands of the protesters on the one hand and of the collective bargaining agreement with the other. The Court of Appeals reversed, holding that the principle of exclusivity must be accommodated with the national policy against racial discrimination in employment. It held that minority group activities deserve § 7 protection unless the union is actually remedying the racial discrimination to the fullest

extent possible, by the most expedient and effica-
cious means.

The Supreme Court agreed with the NLRB. The
protesting employees first argued that their activity was protected by a proviso to § 9(a) of the
NLRA, which gives individual employees and
groups of employees the right to present grievances
to their employer and to have such grievances
adjusted without the intervention of the union so
long as any adjustment is not inconsistent with the
applicable collective bargaining agreement. The
Court held that this proviso merely permits the
employees to present such a grievance and the
employer to consider it without subjecting the employer to § 8(a)(5) liability for circumventing the
exclusive bargaining representative; the employer
need not listen to such a grievance and the proviso
is not to be interpreted to authorize a grieving
employee to resort to economic coercion.

The Court then turned to consideration of the
exclusivity principle. Noting the central position
of the exclusivity principle in the NLRA, the Court
described the rights of minority interests as being
protected in three ways: the power of the employee majority is limited to an appropriate bargaining
unit; dissenting employees are guaranteed certain
democratic rights within the union by virtue of the
Landrum–Griffin Act of 1959; and the union is
charged with the responsibility, enforceable by law,
of representing all employees fairly and in good
faith. The issue is whether considerations of na-

tional policy against racial discrimination outweigh the exclusivity principle. Relying on the processes of the collective bargaining agreement, here deemed adequate, the Court rejected the argument that the separate protest of the dissidents was necessary to eliminate racial discrimination. Conflicting claims on an employer can make resolution of issues difficult. Separate bargaining may divide and conquer both union and minority group interests, and the employer is in the intractable position of being presented with demands by dissidents potentially inconsistent with promises in his collective bargaining agreement.

B.   Bars to Elections and the Determination of Appropriate Bargaining Units

In some circumstances a union will be denied a right to be designated as a bargaining representative for a group of employees. Under the Board's contract-bar rules, an election among employees currently covered by a valid collective bargaining agreement will usually be denied. A rival union, for instance, will not be granted an election during the contract-bar period. To operate as a contract-bar, a bargaining agreement must be in writing, properly signed and binding on the parties, and of a definite duration of no more than three years. It must also contain substantive provisions not inconsistent with the policies of the NLRA. To serve as a bar, the agreement must be signed before a rival union petition is filed.

When a collective bargaining agreement with a duly designated union is nearing expiration, dual policy considerations come into play. Negotiations for a new bargaining agreement should not completely bar the possibility of a rival union petition lest repeated bargaining agreements forever bar a rival's challenge. On the other hand, the employer and the incumbent union should be free to bargain for a new agreement without the pressure created by the possibility that negotiations will be halted by a rival union petition. Thus the Board has ruled that the rival union may not file a petition more than 90 days prior to or less than 60 days prior to the expiration of an outstanding bargaining agreement. The last 60 days of a valid contract constitute an insulated period; and if the incumbent union and the employer reach agreement on a new or amended contract, the rival petition will be barred during the duration of that contract. If the parties reach the termination date of the bargaining agreement without executing a new agreement, the rival union will then be permitted to file its petition.

In American Seating Co. (NLRB 1953), the Board held that a bargaining agreement of excessive duration did not bar the designation of a rival union as the new bargaining representative. Moreover, because the newly designated union would not be bound by the terms of the old agreement, the employees would have no incentive to select a new bargaining representative in order to escape an unfavorable agreement. Since it may be that an incumbent union is bound by a bargaining agreement of too long a duration to act as a contract-bar against a rival union, the practical effect of the Board's contract-bar rules and the *American Seating* doctrine has been the establishment of a period of three years maximum duration for collective bargaining agreements.

Section 9(c)(3) of the NLRA provides that no election will be directed in a bargaining unit in which a valid election has been held during the preceding 12–month period. An election within the past twelve months in a particular bargaining unit will preclude another election in that unit or in any smaller unit which is a part of it; it will not, however, preclude an election in a larger unit even though some of the employees in that larger unit may have voted in the election within the past year. The effect of § 9(c)(3) is that if the employer wins a valid election, it will enjoy a twelve-month period free of the possibility of another union representation election, and that a union winning a valid election will be free from rival challenges during the first twelve months. If the union has won the election but the employer refuses to bargain in order to test the validity of the election, the Board has held that the union's twelve months of protection begins only when the employer actually starts bargaining. Lamar Hotel (NLRB 1962). If an employer lawfully recognizes a union without demanding a Board-conducted election ("voluntary recognition"), this recognition will bar a rival union's election petition for a "reasonable time," which may be substantially shorter than one year. Keller Plastics Eastern, Inc. (NLRB 1969).

A union can be certified as the bargaining representative of a group of employees only if those employees constitute an appropriate bargaining unit. ("Certified" means designation by the Board as a bargaining representative after a valid representation election.) Decisions as to the appropriateness of proposed bargaining units are a major determination of union power. For example, if a union seeks an election for a group consisting of 25 percent of the company's employees—the shipping department, for instance—the employer may assert that these employees are not an appropriate unit and that the only appropriate unit is one comprised of all the employer's nonsupervisory employees. If the employer prevails on that issue, the union's election petition will be dismissed.

A union is not required to seek an election in the *most* appropriate bargaining unit, but it must request an election in *an* appropriate unit. Where two unions seek overlapping and mutually exclusive units, the Board must choose which is the better unit and direct an election in it. In determining whether a proposed bargaining unit is appropriate, the general inquiry is whether the employees share a community of interest. The following is a list of factors sometimes relied on by the Board:

1.   Similarity of pay and method of computing pay.

2.   Similarity of benefits.

3.   Similarity of hours worked.

4.   Similarity of kind of work performed.

5.   Similarity of qualifications, skills, and training.

6.   Physical proximity and frequency of contact and transfers.

7.   Functional integration of the firm.

8.   The firm's supervisory and organizational structure, especially with respect to labor relations.

9.   Bargaining history.

10.   Employee desires.

11.   Extent of union organization within the firm.

Bargaining unit appropriateness is also a critical issue when a union seeks to sever a group of employees from an existing bargaining unit represented by an incumbent union. This has occurred most often when a union seeking to represent a group of craftsmen has sought to separate them from a larger unit. The history of the Board's treatment of such attempts illustrates the importance of the bargaining unit issue. The Board views the severance question as involving "the need to balance the interest of the employer and the total employee complement in maintaining the industrial stability and the resulting benefits of an historical plantwide bargaining unit as against the interest of a portion of such complement in having an opportunity to break away from the historical unit by a vote for separate representation." Mallinckrodt Chemical Works (NLRB 1966).

The Board reasons that while craft employees may be able to show that their separate unit is appropriate, granting representation in that unit tends to diminish the collective strength of the group as a whole, and is often inconsistent with the interests of the public and the employer in maintaining industrial labor relations stability and reducing strikes. In the early American Can Co. (NLRB 1939) decision, the Board refused to allow craft severance in the face of a bargaining history in a broader unit. Congress responded in 1947 by amending the NLRA to add § 9(b), which states "the Board shall ... not ... decide that any craft unit is inappropriate on ... the ground that a different unit has been established by a prior Board determination, unless a majority of the employees in the proposed craft unit vote against separate representation." Shortly thereafter, the Board held that amendment did not preclude the Board from considering bargaining history in a broader unit as one factor in determining the appropriateness of a proposed craft unit. The Board declared that it would look at a variety of factors, such as the history in the industry and the basic nature of the duties performed by the craft employees as compared with those performed by employees in the broader unit, bearing on the appropriateness of the proposed craft unit. National Tube Co. (NLRB 1948).

The Board reversed itself, however, in American Potash and Chemical Corp. (NLRB 1954). That case held that the Board would not inquire into a variety of factors in determining whether to grant craft severance but would only consider whether the employees requesting severance constitute a true craft or departmental group, and whether the union seeking to carve out that group is one which has traditionally devoted itself to the special problems of the group involved.

Finally, in the *Mallinckrodt* case, the Board reversed *American Potash* and returned to a multi-factored analysis. Relevant inquiries are now identified as: whether the group proposing severance constitutes a craft; the history of bargaining at this plant and other plants of the employer with emphasis on whether past bargaining has produced stable labor relations and whether those stable labor relations are likely to be disrupted by severance; the extent to which employees in the proposed unit have maintained their separate identity during the period of inclusion in the broader unit and the extent of their participation in existing representation; the history and pattern of bargaining in the industry; the degree of integration of the employer's production processes, including the extent to which a strike by the proposed unit employees would shut down the employer; and the qualifications of the union seeking to represent the craft unit. While purporting to consider these factors on a case by case basis, the Board gives only lip service to the factors listed in *Mallinckrodt*. Since that case was decided, the Board has almost never permitted a craft unit to be severed. The history of the Board's treatment of craft severance highlights the political nature of Board decisions.

Where the employer's workers have never been represented by a union and an industrial union seeks an election in a broad production and maintenance unit at the same time that a craft union seeks an election among craftsmen, the Board will apply most of the *Mallinckrodt* factors to determine whether the craftsmen can establish a separate unit. If the factors are evenly balanced, the Board may hold a separate vote among the craft employees. This is called a "*Globe*" election, the name coming from Globe Machine and Stamping Co. (NLRB 1937). If a majority of the craftsmen vote for the craft union, they will be separately represented; but if they vote against the craft union, their votes will be pooled with the employees voting in the overall unit. In recent years, the Board has never found the other factors evenly balanced and thus has not conducted *Globe* elections.

Other groups of employees are also given special consideration in representation matters. Sections 9(b)(1) and (3) of the NLRA require that special treatment be given to professional employees and guards.

The hearing that establishes the bargaining unit will also dispose of matters of employee exclusions from the unit and of rival union intervention. The Board must exclude certain groups of employees: for example, supervisors and independent contractors. Whether a given employee is a supervisor or not is likely to be a contested issue. The positions of the employer and the union on that issue may depend on their predictions as to which way an employee will vote.

A rival union can secure a place on the election ballot by showing the support of just a single employee; but if the rival union wants full intervention in the representation hearing (so as to block a consent election and force a hearing, for example), the rival union must demonstrate a 10 percent showing of interest. If the rival union seeks a unit substantially different from that described in the petitioning union's petition, it must produce a 30 percent showing of interest from the unit that it seeks.

Many employers conduct their business at several different geographical locations and this can introduce a difficult factor into Board unit consideration. Two often litigated examples in Board history have been retail chain stores and insurance companies with many district offices. The union's bargaining unit strategy is likely to be dictated by the extent of its employee support: it will seek the largest bargaining unit in which it is confident of winning a representation election. The employer's strategy is more complex. Suppose union support at a particular geographical location is strong but it is relatively weak at other geographical locations. If the employer can persuade the Board that the single location is the only appropriate unit, then the employer will have to bargain with the union only with respect to a small group of his employees. But the employer might wish to take the position that only an enterprise-wide bargaining unit is appropriate, hoping that the pro-union group at one geographical location will be outnumbered by the anti-union vote at the other locations, thus freeing the employer from any bargaining obligation whatsoever. In determining the appropriateness of multi-location units, the Board considers: bargaining history, geographical location, centralization of management decision making (especially with respect to labor relations), employee and equipment interchange between locations, functional interdependence of the enterprise, the union's desires and the breadth of the union's employee support. As with the craft severance issue, these factors have proved capable of manipulation by the Board over time and with respect to particular industries. Section 9(c)(5) of the NLRA precludes the Board from giving controlling weight to the extent of organization in determining whether a unit is appropriate but extent of organization can still be a factor.

There are certain economic and tactical advantages to multiemployer bargaining (that is, bargaining between a union on the one side and a group of employers on the other, all attempting to reach a single bargaining agreement). Those advantages will be discussed *infra*. Consider here the implications of multiemployer bargaining for the procedures for gaining representative status. Multiemployer bargaining is consensual, neither an employer nor a union may insist that the other commence or continue multiemployer bargaining. If a union seeks a unit consisting of more than one employer and those employers have no history of unionization on a multiemployer basis, the unit will be held inappropriate absent the consent of those employers. But where a union has achieved representative status with respect to a single employer who thereafter bargains with the union's consent on a multiemployer basis, a startling development occurs. If the employer continues in the multiemployer bargaining group, the Board is likely to rule that the unit has been transformed into a multiemployer unit and that any rival union seeking new representation rights must petition for all the employees encompassed by the multiemployer group. Yet if the employer makes a timely withdrawal from multiemployer bargaining, the rival union's petition will be proper. Thus the employer has some power to assist or thwart a rival union by defining the unit on the basis of his continuing consent to multiemployer bargaining.

Similarly, where units of separate locations of a single employer have been individually unionized but have a history of bargaining together, the unit will be treated by the Board as employer-wide.

Consider, for example, the position of employees at a newly established manufacturing facility of a national automobile manufacturer. The union may persuade the employees that union representation can be to their advantage and that it is at least worth a try. Some employees may vote for the union on the basis of, "we'll try it and see if we like it." But once the union is voted in, this production facility may be included in national bargaining with the manufacturer. If so, the Board is likely to rule that the unit at this facility has been submerged in the nation-wide bargaining unit. While it was easy for these employees to select the union as their bargaining representative, they may only be able to rid themselves of the union by persuading all of the manufacturer's United States employees to vote against the union—an impossible task. The question is whether industrial stability warrants these rules.

C. Judicial Review of Board Representation Procedures

Section 10(f) of the NLRA permits "a person aggrieved by a final order of the Board" to petition for review of that order in a court of appeals. While the finding of an unfair labor practice and the dismissal of an unfair labor practice complaint qualify as final orders, neither the certification of a union nor a refusal to certify constitutes a final order. AFL v. NLRB (U.S.1940). However, an employer can obtain indirect review. Where the

Board certifies a union and the employer objects to the certification (on the grounds of union pre-election misconduct, or bargaining unit inappropriateness, for example), the employer may refuse to bargain with the union.   A § 8(a)(5) complaint alleging an unlawful refusal to bargain will issue against the employer and will be adjudicated by summary judgment.   If the employer refuses to comply with the Board's bargaining order, this will force the case to the court of appeals where the employer will defend by raising the representation issues.   Issues such as bargaining unit appropriateness and other questions pertinent to representation are deemed by the court of appeals particularly subject to NLRB expertise and the Board will often be the beneficiary of substantial deference. Nevertheless, by such a procedure, the employer has its day in the court of appeals on the representation issues.   When a union is denied certification there is no way for it to gain court of appeals review.

In some cases, pre-election conduct is alleged to amount to an unfair labor practice and also to warrant setting aside an election victory.   If the regional director decides to issue a complaint on the unfair labor practice charge, the complaint and the election objections will be consolidated in one proceeding before an ALJ.   On review of the ALJ's recommended decision, the Board will decide both whether an unfair labor practice has been committed and whether the election is to be set aside. The unfair labor practice order is reviewable by the court of appeals but the representation issue is not. Therefore, even if the court of appeals reverses the Board on the unfair labor practice issue, involving the same facts as the election objection and consolidated in the same proceeding, it will not interfere with the Board's determination of whether to order a rerun election.

In Leedom v. Kyne (U.S.1958), the Supreme Court permitted district court review of a representation issue in a case where the Board had held appropriate a bargaining unit consisting of both professional and non-professional employees. Professional employees sued in district court to set aside the certification and the district court's jurisdiction was upheld. The Supreme Court deemed this case as "not one to 'review' ... a decision of the Board made within its jurisdiction.... Rather it is one to strike down an order of the Board made in excess of its delegated powers and contrary to a specific prohibition in the Act. Section 9(b)(1) [prohibiting such a mixed unit] is clear and mandatory." The case has seldom been used successfully by either employers or unions to gain district court scrutiny of Board representation decisions. In Boire v. Greyhound Corp. (U.S.1964), the Court denied the jurisdiction of the district court to hear a challenge to a Board finding in a representation case that two companies were joint employers. "The *Kyne* exception is a narrow one, not to be extended to permit plenary district court review of Board orders in certification proceedings whenever it can be said that an erroneous assessment of the particular facts before the Board has led it to a conclusion which does not comport with the law."

D. The Protection of Property

Section 8(a)(1) makes it an unfair labor practice for an employer to interfere with employees exercising the right guaranteed them by § 7 to act in concert for mutual aid and protection. The section says nothing about employer property rights nor the employer's interest in managing its business. It has never been seriously contended, however, that these employer interests can be ignored in determining the parameters of § 8(a)(1).

In NLRB v. Babcock & Wilcox Co. (U.S.1956), the employer refused to permit non-employee union organizers onto company parking lots to distribute union literature. he NLRB found that the organizers had no pr   alternative to entering company property t   h   ill employees because the plant's physical   ion made solicitation from public property   up ible. The employer defended its refusal on   rounds that its rule against permitting stra   on the property had been consistently app ied   nd that distribution would litter its propert   he Board held that the employer violated §   ) because the union's alternative opportuni ies   reach the employees—personal contact in   ommunity or at home, telephones, letters o   rtised meetings—were much less effective th n   mmunications at the work site. Since no   yees were engaged in the solicitation, it was not the employees' § 7 right to speak that was at issue, but their § 7 right to hear. The Board balanced the right to hear against the employer's property right to secure its plant from strangers. The Supreme Court reversed the Board.

In the Court's view, the Board had not taken into account that different balances should be struck depending on whether employees or non-employees wish to communicate with the workers. The Court held: "[An] employer may validly post his property against non-employee distribution of union litera-ture if reasonable efforts by the union through other available channels of communication will enable it to reach the employees with its message and if the employer's notice or order does not discriminate against the union by allowing other distribution." Had the employer's restriction been on the employees' right to speak, the balance would have been different: "No restriction may be placed on the employees' right to discuss self-orga-nization among themselves, unless the employer can demonstrate that a restriction is necessary to maintain production or discipline."

After *Babcock,* unions argued that their organiz-ers should have access to company premises if solicitation on public property near the plant was impractical and if employee homes were scattered throughout a large metropolitan area. The NLRB has ruled against a right of access for union orga-nizers in these circumstances. Monogram Models, Inc. (NLRB 1971).

A standard such as whether reasonable efforts will enable the union to carry its message to employees leaves the Board with considerable discretion. Consider the union's attempt to organize retail store employees in Dexter Thread Mills, Inc. (NLRB 1972). The employer's property was accessible only by means of a public highway with a speed limit of 60 m.p.h. running adjacent to the parking lot. A ten-foot wide, tree-filled public easement separated company property from this highway. The union challenged the employer's refusal to permit organizers to distribute handbills on the company parking lot and showed that efforts to obtain employee names and addresses and to make home visits had been very unsuccessful. The Board nonetheless upheld the employer's right to exclude the organizers: "[i]t would have been relatively easy and safe for the union organizers to stand on the public easement between the lot and the highway and copy the license numbers of cars entering the lot. From this, and a greater utilization of sympathetic employees, the union could have obtained a fairly complete list of employees for direct home contact or for distribution of literature through the mails." It appears from *Dexter* and similar decisions that the Board will not permit access to company property by outside organizers unless the employees live on the property. If that is so, it raises several issues. Does the Board have expertise as to what constitutes a reasonable attempt by a union? Does it have expertise as to what can be accomplished by copying the license numbers of cars pulling into a company parking lot from a four-lane highway, or by using employee spies? Should a court of appeals substitute its notion of what constitutes a "reasonable effort" on the facts of *Dexter?* Finally, is the Board's decision, especially if part of a pattern of similar Board cases, faithful to the *Babcock & Wilcox* decision and, if not, does that warrant court of appeals intervention?

For several years it appeared that First Amendment free speech considerations played an important role in the ability of some employers to deny access to their properties. It is familiar learning in constitutional law that freedom of speech is guaranteed by the First Amendment only against infringement by government. In Amalgamated Food Employees Union Local 590 v. Logan Valley Plaza, Inc. (U.S.1968), the union picketed inside a large shopping center. Its target was a tenant of the shopping center, a retail store employing a non-union staff. The pickets carried signs complaining that the retail store's employees were not receiving union wages and other union benefits. A state court enjoined picketing inside the shopping center. The Supreme Court held that sufficient state action was involved so as to render the First Amendment applicable. The Court relied on its prior decision in Marsh v. Alabama (U.S.1946) in which the Court had held that a town in Alabama that was completely owned by a private corporation had all the characteristics and functions of any other American town. Thus, the First Amendment precluded the town from preventing the distribution of religious literature on its sidewalk without a license. In *Logan Valley,* the Court found that the shopping center was the "functional equivalent" of the business district of the company town involved in *Marsh,* thus giving union members a free speech right to picket there.

Four years later, however, in Lloyd Corp., Ltd. v. Tanner (U.S.1972), the Court refused to apply the First Amendment when a group of young people entered a shopping center to distribute handbills protesting the ongoing military operations in Viet Nam. A substantial portion of the Court's opinion in *Lloyd* was devoted to distinguishing it from *Logan Valley,* noting particularly that in the latter case the communications specifically related to a store in the shopping center and that the pickets had no other reasonable opportunity to reach their intended audience.

In Hudgens v. NLRB (U.S.1976), another case of union picketing at a shopping center store, the Court overruled *Logan Valley* on the extraordinary rationale that although the *Lloyd* decision had gone at some length to distinguish *Logan Valley,* the two cases were incompatible and that the last one decided was controlling. "It matters not that some members of the Court may continue to believe that the *Logan Valley* case was rightly decided. Our institutional duty is to follow until changed the law as it now is, not as some members of the Court wish it to be." It is clear, however, that on the merits a majority of the Court were persuaded that *Logan Valley* had been wrongly decided. The two prior cases were incompatible, in the Court's view, because the presence or absence of state action cannot depend on judicial scrutiny of the content of the speech subject to regulation. The shopping center picketing had to be tested under the NLRA, free of any First Amendment considerations. The Court did not decide the NLRA issue, but did note several respects in which the case differed from *Babcock & Wilcox. Hudgens* involved lawful economic strike activity rather than organizational activity, and was carried on by employees (although not employees of the shopping center store) rather than outsiders. Finally, the infringed-upon property interests were not those of the targeted employer but of another.

Several variables might bear upon an employer's right to oust pickets from a shopping center. The pickets themselves may be employees or nonemployees of the targeted company; the audience at which the picketing is directed may be employees, strike replacements, suppliers, or the public (consumers); the picket's message may be economic (employer wages are too low) or organizational or the union may be protesting an unfair labor practice; and the property interests may be that of the targeted employer or of a third party. In Jean Country (NLRB 1988), the Board adopted a balancing test that seems to treat all these factors as relevant and to apply them on a case-by-case basis. Such a rule is at once commendable for considering all relevant policy factors, and defective because applications are unpredictable in advance of a Board decision.

However, a rule may be multifactored as stated, but its applications may yield predictable results. This appears to be the case with the rule of *Jean Country*. The Board there permitted union access to a shopping center with characteristics of many open-air malls. The union's purpose was to urge consumers not to patronize Jean Country, a non-union retailer. The Board rejected the company's argument that the union could effectively target customers of Jean Country by picketing at mall entrances. Owners of malls will find *Jean Country* difficult to distinguish.

E. Solicitation and Distribution of Literature

The Board has adopted rules stating the presumptive validity or invalidity of employer restrictions on employees' right to solicit orally and to distribute literature at their place of employment. The employer may restrict oral solicitations during the working time of the particular employees to whom the restriction is applied. Because of the special difficulties with litter that distribution often creates, an employer can restrict the distribution of literature in working areas of the plant both on and off the employees' working time. These rules will be applied to test the legality of an employer's restrictions in the absence of a showing of special circumstances at the particular plant involved.

The adoption of such general rules received Supreme Court approval in Republic Aviation Corp. v. NLRB (U.S.1945). In that case the employer had adopted, well before the commencement of any union activity at the plant, a prohibition of solicitations of any kind on the premises. An employee was discharged for breaking the rule and three other employees were discharged for wearing union buttons in the plant. The Board held that enforcement of the solicitation rule by the employer violated § 8(a)(1) and that the discharge of the employees violated § 8(a)(3) and (1). The employer contended that the Board should be required to show that the particular employer restraints involved actually interfered with employee attempts to organize. The employer also argued that a no-solicitation rule should not be found to violate the Act in the absence of a showing that alternative means of communication are unavailable.

Section 8(a)(3) states "it shall be an unfair labor practice for an employer by discrimination in regard to hire or tenure of employment ... to encourage or discourage membership in any labor organization...." The word "discrimination" presumably means to treat people or things differently, but what does "to encourage or discourage membership" mean? It could mean that only those acts of discrimination that actually result in an encouragement or discouragement violate

§ 8(a)(3), or it could mean that an intent by the employer to encourage or discourage will make out a violation, or the section could be construed to require both effect and intent. No showing was made in *Republic Aviation* that the employer's rule actually precluded the union from organizing, but the Court upheld the Board's conclusion that enforcement of the rule violated § 8(a)(3) when it resulted in an employee discharge. The Court's discussion of the meaning of § 8(a)(3) was cryptic: "It seems clear ... that if a rule against solicitation is invalid as to union solicitation on the employer's premises during the employees' own time, a discharge because of violation of that rule discriminates within the meaning of § 8(a)(3) in that it discourages membership in a labor organization."

Republic Aviation was an opportunity for the Court to deal with the difficult issues of what employer intent, if any, is required under § 8(a)(3) and 8(a)(1), and whether the broader prohibition of § 8(a)(1) permits the finding of a violation even though the challenged conduct does not fall within the narrow prohibition of § 8(a)(3). These questions are not answered in *Republic Aviation* although the case is useful in that it establishes the Board's power to set out general principles respecting employee solicitation. This power was later reaffirmed in Eastex, Inc. v. NLRB (U.S.1978).

The Board's rules with respect to solicitation and distribution of literature will be applied in the absence of some special showing by the employer that a broader rule was necessary for the sake of discipline or because of some other special circumstances in his work place. No actual interference with an attempt to organize need be shown; indeed, even an employer showing that the rule had no effect whatsoever on the union organizing drive will be of no avail. As the Board stated in Cooper Thermometer Co. (NLRB 1965): "Interference, restraint and coercion under § 8(a)(1) of the Act does not turn on the employer's motive or on whether it succeeded or failed. The test is whether the employer engaged in conduct which, it may reasonably be said, tends to interfere with the free exercise of employee rights under the Act."

Even an otherwise valid employer restriction on employee solicitation and distribution is unlawful if it is promulgated for antiunion reasons. A rule that is promulgated at the beginning of a union organizing drive will not necessarily be unlawful, however, because the employer is permitted to foresee that the solicitations and distributions accompanying a union organizing drive may create disruptions of a magnitude not previously experienced, although the Board has vacillated on this issue. An otherwise lawful restriction applied only to union solicitation and distribution will be held unlawful.

Do the *Republic Aviation* rules protect union distributions of literature regardless of the literature's content? The Supreme Court dealt with

that issue in Eastex, Inc. v. NLRB (U.S.1978).
Among other items, the union newsletter called for
employee opposition to a proposed state right to
work law, and urged members to register to vote in
light of a recent presidential veto of minimum
wage legislation. The employer, which refused to
permit distribution of the newsletter by employees
on company property in nonworking areas, argued
that the distribution request was not, in § 7 language, "concerted ... for the purpose of ... mutual aid or protection," because the newsletter's content did not relate to a specific dispute between the
employees and the employer over an issue which
the employer had the right or power to effect.

The Court rejected the argument. First, since
the term "employees" is defined broadly in § 2(3),
the Court found a Congressional intent to protect
employees when they engage in concerted activities in support of employees or employers other
than their own. Second, the Court declined to give
§ 7 a narrow scope; concerted activity is protected
even though the employees resort to "channels
outside the immediate employee-employer relationship." The opinion stated that at some point the
relationship between the employees' interest as
employees and the content of the literature may
become so attenuated that an activity cannot fairly
be deemed to come within § 7. But determining
that point is for the Board in the first instance and
it had not erred in its determination in this case.

Eastex also reaffirmed the distinction between
Republic Aviation and *Babcock & Wilcox*. Absent

a no-solicitation ban shown necessary to maintain plant discipline or production, the *Republic Aviation* rule obtains "even though the employees [do not show] that distribution off the employer's property would be ineffective;" the balance is between § 7 rights and the right of employers to maintain discipline. In a *Babcock & Wilcox* situation, the balance is between § 7 rights and an employer's right to keep trespassers off its property, a property interest rather than a management interest.

A Supreme Court case of uncertain impact put into some doubt the Board's power to adopt general rules specifying the sorts of employer conduct that will be deemed to violate § 8(a). In NLRB v. United Steelworkers [Nutone and Avondale Mills] (U.S.1957), the employers had promulgated no-solicitation rules valid on their face but had not applied the rules to antiunion solicitation by supervisors. The Board found this to be discriminatory enforcement and held that the rules violated § 8(a)(1) and that discharges pursuant to the rules violated § 8(a)(3).

The Supreme Court began with two premises not seriously open to dispute. The employer's rules respecting solicitation were not overbroad, and employers and their supervisors can engage in antiunion solicitation without violating the NLRA. Employer solicitation is protected by the employer free speech provision of § 8(c). But from those premises confusing conclusions were reached, and three different tests are set out at various points in the opinion. First, the Board is directed to look into whether the employers' conduct "to any considerable degree created an imbalance in the opportunities for organizational communication." Second, the Court complained that "no attempt was made in either of these cases to make a showing that the no-solicitation rules truly diminished the ability of the labor organizations invoked to carry their messages to the employees." Third, the Court stated that "if, by virtue of the location of the plant and of the facilities and resources available to the union, the opportunities for effectively reaching the employees with a pro-union message, in spite of a no-solicitation rule, are at least as great as the employer's ability to promote the legally authorized expression of his antiunion views, there is no basis for invalidating these 'otherwise valid' rules." As support for the conclusion that the Board must look at the facts and circumstances of the particular case in applying one or all of these tests, the opinion cites both *Republic Aviation* and *Babcock & Wilcox*. Ignored is the fact that while such a test was directed for nonemployee organizers in the *Babcock & Wilcox* context, the Board was clearly permitted in *Republic Aviation* to establish general principles about the appropriateness of solicitations at the workplace, etc.

While the precise holding on the facts of *Nutone* has probably survived, its implications for the propriety of Board rules of general application should not be taken at face value. Requiring a case-by-case determination of the validity of employer no-solicitation rules is costly. When a rule requires case-by-case application, liability often cannot be predicted. It is true that the liability exposure to employers is limited. Perhaps a company's no-solicitation rule will not be challenged; or if it is challenged, the company can drop it with no cost, or defend it by the expenditure of legal fees. The ultimate risk is a cease and desist order, and so there is no liability exposure beyond the firm's attorney fees, unless an employee is discharged for violating the rule and gains the back pay remedy. While a union may not have a great deal at stake in challenging a particular employer's no-solicitation rule (except for freedom from the rule's restraints in the long run), if the union challenges the rule the General Counsel will prosecute the charge at no expense to the union. Board litigation expense is reduced by a rule of general application, while the ability of employers and unions to predict the effect of particular employer rules is increased. Finally, in some cases where it is claimed that a state court is preempted from acting in a labor dispute because the NLRB's unfair labor practice jurisdiction takes precedence, the state court is required to predict how the NLRB would rule in a particular case. Without NLRB rules of general application, prediction is often impossible.

One series of cases illustrates how the Board members are split over the effect of *Nutone.* Employers in retail stores have been permitted by the Board to ban union solicitation in selling areas of a store both during employees' working and nonworking time, a ban that absent special circumstances would be invalid. The Board reasons that union solicitation in the presence of customers in these areas might have an adverse affect on business. In May Dept. Stores Co. (NLRB 1962), the union was subjected to this unusually broad rule and the employer made noncoercive antiunion speeches to assemblies of employees on department store property while refusing a union's request for equal time and access. A majority of the Board held that the combined effect of the broad no-solicitation rule and the captive audience speech violated 8(a)(1). Responding to the company's reliance on *Nutone,* the majority opinion discussed in general the advantages that companies have in presenting their views during working time while they relegate the union to other methods of communication. The opinion spoke in terms of "an imbalance in opportunities for organizational communication," and did not look at the facts of this particular case to see whether the union had difficulty in reaching the employees. A dissenting Board member stated, "I do not think ... a true diminution can be established merely by showing that as a general proposition department store employees can be more easily reached through the avenues of communication open to their employer than through the avenues open to a union." The Court of Appeals ultimately refused to enforce the Board's order (6th Cir.1963).

Unions sometimes attempt to bargain away (waive) the § 7 rights of employees whom they represent to engage in solicitation and distribution of literature. The Board has held that a union will not be permitted to waive the rights of employees wishing to solicit against the incumbent union or to distribute antiunion literature and that an employer rule prohibiting such distribution thus violates § 8(a)(1). Gale Products Co. (NLRB 1963). The Supreme Court approved an extension of this rationale to encompass literature supporting the union in NLRB v. Magnavox Co. (U.S.1974). The Court found the place of work to be uniquely appropriate for the dissemination of views concerning the union and bargaining issues, and held that employees supporting the union should have as great a § 7 right to distribute literature as those opposed to the union. Thus a union attempt to waive those rights will be invalid and an overly broad employer rule will still be subject to § 8(a)(1) scrutiny.

F. Campaign Propaganda

Unions have a much easier time organizing employees when employers are neutral with regard to union representation than when managers oppose unionization. Initially the NLRB took the position that the Wagner Act required employers to stay neutral when employees were faced with the decision of whether to designate a bargaining agent—the employers were deemed to have no legitimate interest in whether their employees chose a union. In 1947, Congress passed § 8(c), intending to reverse the Board's position and ensure that employers could exercise free speech, which included vigorous opposition to unions. A remaining issue is whether the Board should impose bounds on the kinds of preelection statements that can be made by employers and unions. The Board has developed a "laboratory conditions" test for deciding whether campaign tactics should overturn the results of a completed representation election. The theory is that notwithstanding whether conduct might amount to an unfair labor practice, it may show a faulty election environment, suggesting that the election result has been fatally infected and requires a rerun election. Since the Board has held that § 8(c) is applicable only in unfair labor practice cases and not in representation cases, General Shoe Corp. (NLRB 1948), the question of the propriety of Board regulation of campaign propaganda has turned more on notions of sound administrative policy than of technical statutory interpretation.

For many years the Board would set aside an election victory where the winner had made certain kinds of factual misrepresentations in its campaign propaganda. Under the standards developed in Hollywood Ceramics Co. (NLRB 1962), the Board would set aside an election where challenged conduct involved a substantial departure from the truth at a time which prevented the other party from making an effective reply, so that the representation, whether or not deliberate, may reasonably be expected to have had significant impact on the election.

The Board reconsidered and reversed this doctrine in Shopping Kart Food Market (NLRB 1977). On the eve of the election the union had misrepresented to employees the employer's profits during the past year. Two members of the Board announced that they were prepared to overrule *Hollywood Ceramics* in its entirety and to stop policing campaign literature for misrepresentation. These Board members made several criticisms of Board scrutiny of campaign propaganda: (1) the time spent by Board staff in reviewing extensive campaign propaganda; (2) the restriction on the right of free speech; (3) variances in applications of the Board's tests in particular cases, or the lack of a manageable norm; and (4) the resulting decrease in the finality of election results. Policing for misrepresentation is uniquely subjective, in the view of these Board members. Further, an empirical study of NLRB representational actions suggests that in the majority of campaigns the votes of employees could be correctly predicted from their precampaign intent and their attitudes toward working conditions and unions in general, thus suggesting that campaign propaganda affected the results in only a small percentage of the cases. For these two Board members, the Board should intervene only where a party has engaged in such deceptive campaign practices as to improperly involve the Board and its processes, or where the use of forged documents has rendered voters unable to recognize propaganda for what it is.

A concurring Board member also voted to overrule *Hollywood Ceramics* but she would still set aside elections "where a party makes an egregious mistake of fact" but then only "in the most extreme situations." Two members of the Board would not have overturned the election result in this case, and dissented from the overruling of *Hollywood Ceramics.*

The dissenters disagreed with the majority's reliance on the empirical study of voters' behavior in representation elections. Not only were 22 percent of the studied voters aware of the content of union claims, but a significant percentage of the voters admitted changing their minds during the campaign on how they would vote. Also, although Board elections now number in excess of 10,000 per year, objections based on misrepresentation average only between 3 and 4½ percent of such elections. Rerun elections were only directed in about 25 elections per year under the *Hollywood Ceramics* standard, not a substantial investment of Board time.

The dissenters also argued that the presence of the *Hollywood Ceramics* rule served to promote responsibly conducted election campaigns. Nor were the dissenters convinced that the differing results reached by the Board and the courts of appeals in particular cases demonstrated a difficulty with the *Hollywood Ceramics* standards as such.

Rather, the differences were the product of disagreements on the strictness with which the standard should be applied.

No rules come to mind that have been less stable than the Board's rules respecting campaign propaganda. *Shopping Kart* was overruled in General Knit of Calif., Inc. (NLRB 1978). *General Knit* was itself overruled in Midland National Life Insurance Co. (NLRB 1982). The empirical study discussed in *Shopping Kart* has been sharply criticized on methodological and interpretative grounds in law journals. The *Hollywood Ceramics* standards no longer apply to representation elections. It is unclear how this affects union representation efforts. Unions have opposed repeal of the *Hollywood Ceramics* rule, but one unhappy effect of that rule was that an employer determined to avoid its bargaining duty as long as possible used objections to union campaign propaganda as the excuse for his refusal to bargain. Apparently unions believe that some other excuse for refusing to bargain is always available to employers who want to delay their legal obligations, and that policing employer statements that violate the *Hollywood Ceramics* standards helps protect union election efforts. In light of the mild sanction for a violation of that rule, it is sometimes hard to see how this controversy is worth the candle.

The Board also polices representation elections for threats and for promises of reward. It has received Supreme Court guidance on the applicable

standards in this area. The leading case is NLRB
v. Gissel Packing Co. (U.S.1969). In response to a
union election campaign the employer repeatedly
expressed worry that the union would strike if
they won the election and that this would lead to
the plant's closing. The Board found that the
statements tended to convey a threat to employees
and thus violated § 8(a)(1). The Board also found
that the statements interfered with a free election
and it overturned the employer's election victory.
In the Supreme Court, the employer argued that
its campaign had been pure speech and was thus
protected by the First Amendment. The Court
affirmed an employer's right to communicate its
views to its employees on unionism and construed
§ 8(c) of the NLRA as implementing this First
Amendment right. But the employer's right of
expression must be analyzed in the context of its
labor relations setting. Balanced against the employer's right to speak is the employees' right to
associate freely as embodied in § 7 and protected
by § 8(a)(1). Such a balance "must take into account the economic dependence of the employees
on their employers, and the necessary tendency of
the former, because of that relationship, to pick up
intended implications of the latter that might be
more readily dismissed by a more disinterested
ear." The employer, then, is free to communicate
its general views about unionism but is not free to
issue threats or promises of benefit. "[The employ-
er] may even make a prediction as to the precise
effects he believes unionization will have on his

company. In such a case, however, the prediction must be carefully phrased on the basis of objective fact to convey an employer's belief as to demonstrably probable consequences beyond his control or to convey a management decision already arrived at to close the plant in case of unionization.... If there is any implication that an employer may or may not take action solely on his initiative for reasons unrelated to economic necessities and known only to him, the statement is no longer a reasonable prediction based on available facts but a threat of retaliation based on misrepresentation and coercion, and as such without the protection of the First Amendment."

On the facts of the instant case, the Court found that the Board was reasonable in concluding that the import of the employer's message was not a prediction that unionization would inevitably cause plant closure, but was a threat to throw employees out of work without regard for economic realities. The employer had no support for its assertion that the union would have to strike for its demands or that plant closing, the ultimate industrial tragedy for employees, was inevitable.

Gissel by no means provides the answer to every case of employer speech. Consider some typical examples presenting policy choices for the Board. The employer makes a speech noting that the law requires good faith bargaining but not the granting of a single economic benefit, and then states that the employees may not come out of collective bargaining with as many benefits as they enjoyed before bargaining. Another employer truthfully states that it intends to test the validity of a potential union election victory in the Court of Appeals, a process that might take several years. A third employer notes the competitive disadvantage that it will suffer if it is unionized and is forced to raise wages while its competitors remain nonunion.

The *Gissel* Court's suggestion that the employer could convey "a management decision already arrived at to close the plant in case of unionization" is disquieting. Surely the Court is not suggesting that if an employer has gone through the formalities of making such a decision prior to the representation election balloting, it is foreclosed from reconsidering its decision if the union wins the election.

Upon being presented with a union claim of majority status and a request to bargain, an employer might want to investigate whether the union actually represents a majority of the employees. The Board has grappled in several cases with whether employer questioning, or polling, of employees necessarily coerces employees. In Blue Flash Express (NLRB 1954), the Board adopted the general criteria of whether under all the circumstances the interrogation reasonably tends to restrain, coerce, or interfere with guaranteed rights. It implemented the standard by holding in Strucksnes Const. Co. (NLRB 1967) that, absent unusual circumstances, polling of employees by an owner or supervisor violates § 8(a)(1) unless: "(1) the purpose of the poll is to determine the truth of a union's claim of majority, (2) this purpose is communicated to the employees, (3) assurances against reprisal are given, (4) the employees are polled by secret ballot, and (5) the employer has not engaged in unfair labor practices or otherwise created a coercive atmosphere." Obviously, requirement (4) is the key protection; employees whose ballots are secret have much less to fear from employer retaliation. In Rossmore House (NLRB 1984) the Board reversed prior precedent and held that the questioning of a known union adherent, in the absence of threats or promises, was presumptively lawful.

Employers usually act through their supervisors, and the Board considers supervisors to be agents of their employer with respect to election interference unless the supervisor's activity is minor and not clothed with apparent authority. The acts of persons unconnected with the employer, such as involvement by public and private groups in the community, are difficult to lay at an employer's feet absent a showing of actual collaboration. With no showing of agency, the employer cannot be subjected to unfair labor practice liability; but if the acts of outsiders create a sufficiently hostile environment to union organizing and a free election, an employer election victory will be set aside by the Board.

G. Certification as a Remedy for Employer Misconduct

Prior to seeking a Board conducted secret ballot representation election, unions almost invariably attempt to secure from a majority of employees signed cards that authorize the union to represent the employee for the purposes of collective bargaining. At a minimum, these cards will be used for the 30 percent showing of interest needed to secure a Board election. In NLRB v. Gissel Packing Co. (U.S.1969), the Court was asked to decide the worth of these authorization cards as a route to union representation status. It was also asked to decide the propriety of NLRB reliance on employer preelection misconduct as a justification for a bargaining order absent a union election victory.

In the several cases decided under the *Gissel* caption, the unions had secured signed authorization cards from a majority of employees. Their demands for employer recognition, however, were refused on the ground that the employers deemed the cards to be inherently unreliable. Thereafter the employers engaged in antiunion campaigns during which they committed unfair labor practices. As a result of the antiunion campaigns, one union gave up on filing a representation election, believing the employer campaign to have rendered an election futile; another blocked its own election petition by filing an unfair labor practice charge against the employer and requesting that the Board process the charge before conducting any election; a third went ahead with the representation election but lost it to the employer. In each instance the Board found that prior to the employer's campaign the union had secured authorization cards from a majority of the employees, and that the employer's refusal to recognize the union was motivated not by a good faith doubt as to the union's majority status but by a desire to delay representation in order to engage in unfair labor practices. The Board, however, took a different position at oral argument before the Supreme Court than it had taken in prior written decisions.

The Board had previously ruled that an employer can refuse union recognition on the basis of authorization cards only if it has a good faith doubt as to the union's majority status. Board cases found the lack of a good faith doubt, and ordered the employer to bargain, on a showing that the employer had engaged in independent unfair labor practices during the election campaign (the unfair labor practices were deemed to show that the employer's motive was only to gain time and was not the product of a doubt of majority status), or that the employer had come forward with no reasons for doubting the union's majority status. Subsequent Board opinions qualified this: the employer need not come forward with a reason for its good faith doubt other than a mistrust of authorization cards, and some unfair labor practices were not significant enough to justify the conclusion that the employer had refused to bargain in order to gain time to engage in misconduct. At oral argument before the Supreme Court, Board counsel announced the Board's current position to be that the employer's good faith was largely irrelevant; the propriety of a bargaining order would turn solely on whether the employer had engaged in substantial unfair labor practices interfering with the union's election efforts. The employer would be able to insist upon a secret ballot election even in the face of a union majority card showing except in two unusual circumstances: where an employer, through a poll for instance, knew that a majority of its employees supported the union; or where the employer refused recognition initially because of a challenge to the appropriateness of the requested bargaining unit and later claimed a doubt of the union's employee support.

The employers in *Gissel* challenged the use of authorization cards as a basis for a bargaining order on several grounds: (1) the employer may have no chance to campaign and present its views to the employees prior to the union's solicitation of card support; (2) absent a secret ballot election, employees will succumb to group pressure to sign cards, or will be coerced into doing so; and (3) too often union authorization cards are obtained by misrepresentation and coercion. The Court rejected all three arguments. While a Board conducted secret ballot election is the preferable statutory route to bargaining status, other routes (e.g. authorization cards and strike support) are acceptable alternatives in appropriate circumstances. According to the Court, in the majority of the campaigns the employer will be aware of the union's solicitation attempts well in advance of the union obtaining a majority showing by cards. Also, any group pressures felt by employees are as likely to be felt inside the ballot booth as during card solicitations because elections arise most often with respect to small bargaining units where voter sentiments can be individually canvassed. Finally, the Court deemed Board processes sufficient to police misuse of union solicitation.

Having found that the Board was not precluded from considering card strength in issuing a bargaining order, the Court turned to the question of whether a bargaining order can be used to remedy employer unfair labor practices in the context of a representation campaign. The Court posited three categories of cases in which this issue might arise. The first consists of those cases where the employer's unfair labor practices have been "outrageous" and "pervasive," and where the union cannot show past majority status on the basis of cards or other circumstances. The Court noted, without explicitly approving, a Board policy of issuing bargaining orders in such cases to remedy substantial employer unfair labor practices. The second category of cases are marked by less pervasive employer unfair labor practices, a showing by the union of prior majority strength (usually through authorization cards), and a Board finding that on balance "the possibility of erasing the effects of past practices and of insuring a fair election (or a fair rerun) by the use of traditional remedies, is slight and that employee sentiment once expressed through cards would ... be better protected by a bargaining order...." In those cases, a bargaining order may issue. The final category is comprised of those cases where the employer unfair labor practices are not of sufficient gravity to sustain a bargaining order.

Where the employer does not commit substantial unfair labor practices, union authorization cards are important only for obtaining the showing of interest necessary to initiate the Board's election machinery. But where the union claims that the employer has prevented a fair election, or rerun election, through its preelection unfair labor practices, the union will want to prove its prior majority status through authorization cards, thus putting the case in category two rather than category one. In such a case, the employer will not only argue that the unfair labor practices were not sufficiently serious, or that it committed none, but also that the authorization cards were solicited in circumstances rendering them invalid. In that connection, it is important to note that in *Gissel* the Court approved of the Board's doctrine, announced in Cumberland Shoe Corp. (NLRB 1963), that if an authorization card is unambiguous (states that the signer authorizes the union to represent the employee in collective bargaining), then the card is not defective even though the solicitor of the card told the signer that the card probably would be used to obtain a Board election. The card is a defective indicator of majority status if the signer was told that a Board election was the card's *only* purpose.

Under current Board practice, approved by the Supreme Court in Linden Lumber Div. v. NLRB (U.S.1974), an employer can refuse a union's request for recognition even in the face of substantial evidence of majority employee support for the union, such as authorization card signatures or a strike by a majority of the employees. Authorization cards are somewhat suspect and "[f]ear may ... prevent some [employees] from crossing a picket line; or sympathy for strikers, not the desire to have a particular union in the saddle, may influence others." The Court approved the Board's abandonment of a good faith test for employer refusals to bargain in this context. The Court also rejected the contention that the failure of the employer to file a representation petition demonstrates the lack of a good faith doubt of the union's majority status. The Court hypothesized a controversy between an employer and a union over the appropriateness of proposed bargaining units. The employer should have the right to challenge the appropriateness of the union's requested unit, but if the employer files a petition for the bargaining unit that he deems appropriate, the petition will be dismissed unless it coincides with the unit sought by the union. Forcing the employer to file is thus no guarantee against delay. The Court ruled that where a union is refused recognition, the union has the burden of taking the next step by filing an election petition unless the employer is engaged in unfair labor practices warranting a *Gissel* remedy.

Is a bargaining order in a *Gissel*-type case justified because it is the only effective remedy for certain § 8(a)(1) and 8(a)(3) violations, or because the employer has been found to violate § 8(a)(5) by coupling its refusal to bargain with anti-union misconduct? This might make a practical difference if during the campaign or after the representation election the employer reduces wages (or other economic benefits) for purely economic reasons but without bargaining with the union. Such a unilateral change in economic benefits without bargaining with a lawfully designated union violates § 8(a)(5) and the union is likely to demand a backpay remedy for the economic reduction. If the bargaining obligation accrues only when the Board issues its *Gissel* order, then the unilateral reduction will not have been an unfair labor practice. Also, a § 8(a)(5) complaint permits a union to engage in recognitional picketing without violating § 8(b)(7)(C) even though the union files no election petition. In Steel–Fab, Inc. (NLRB 1974), the Board found a § 8(a)(1) violation after employer election misconduct but, by a three-to-two majority, refused to find a § 8(a)(5) violation. It held that unilateral changes made before the § 8(a)(1) bargaining violated the Act only if motivated by anti-union animus. This refusal to make *Gissel* bargaining orders retroactive to the time that the employer's serious unfair labor practices were committed was reversed in Trading Port, Inc., (NLRB

1975), where the Board grounded its order on § 8(a)(5).

Consider at what point in time the Board should determine whether the lasting effects of serious employer unfair labor practices prevent the holding of a fair rerun election. The Board could look at the election environment at the time the unfair labor practices are committed, at the time of the hearing on the refusal to bargain charge, or perhaps when the cease and desist order against the employer is enforced in the court of appeals. As the time of scrutiny moves away from when the unfair labor practices were committed, the chances become greater that employee turnover, changes in the employer's operations, etc., will make the imposition of a bargaining order without an election appear to be unfair to the employees. Yet to free the employer of the bargaining order for these reasons creates an incentive to delay the case in the administrative and enforcement stages.

A final issue is whether the Board has authority to issue a bargaining order where the employer has engaged in "outrageous" unfair labor practices but the union had not acquired majority status at any time. The current Board's position is that it lacks the authority to issue such an order. Gourmet Foods, Inc. (NLRB 1984). The Board does not believe that the Supreme Court meant to rule on this question of authority in *Gissel.*

CHAPTER IV

ORGANIZATIONAL PICKETING

A. Constitutional Protection of Picketing

Supreme Court treatment of the constitutional status of picketing as free speech has followed a twisted path. From the union view, the high point of protection came in Thornhill v. Alabama (U.S.1940), where the Court declared that, in general, peaceful picketing is within the constitutional guarantee of freedom of speech, and is protected against infringement by the First and Fourteenth Amendments. Thus a state statute cut too broadly when it was construed to ban all picketing without exceptions based on the number of persons engaged in the picketing, its peaceful character, the nature of the dispute, or the accurateness of the terminology used in notifying the public of the dispute. In American Federation of Labor v. Swing (U.S.1941), the Court held unconstitutional a state injunction against peaceful picketing based on the state's common law policy against such picketing when there was no immediate dispute between employer and employee—an attempt to ban picketing for the purpose of organizing.

The Court has retreated from these broad pronouncements, contending that even peaceful picketing involves more than communication and cannot be immune from all state regulation. An important and illustrative case is Giboney v. Empire Storage and Ice Co. (U.S.1949). There the union, attempting to organize independent peddlers, picketed a wholesaler dealer to coerce it to refrain from selling to non-union peddlers. The state court found the agreement a conspiracy in violation of state antitrust laws and enjoined the picketing. The Supreme Court affirmed the injunction, finding no Fourteenth Amendment violation. The Court upheld findings that the picketing of the wholesaler was part of an overall course of union conduct to compel the wholesaler to stop selling ice to non-union peddlers, a course of conduct in violation of the state's valid antitrust law. The union's members "were doing more than exercising a right of free speech or press ... they were exercising their economic power together with that of their allies to compel [the wholesaler] to abide by union rather than by state regulation of trade."

The history of Supreme Court treatment of the free speech implications of union picketing was described in Teamsters Local 695 v. Vogt (U.S.1957) and summarized as "[establishing] a broad field in which a state, in enforcing some public policy, whether of its criminal or its civil law, and whether announced by its legislature or its courts, could constitutionally enjoin peaceful picketing aimed at effectuation of that policy." State courts, and by necessary implication federal courts, may not issue blanket prohibitions against picketing, but can base an injunction on the rational implementation of a policy otherwise valid. On the facts of the *Vogt* case, the Supreme Court permitted the state to enjoin picketing by a union that sought to induce the employer's employees to join the union by publicizing that the job was not a union job. A consequence of the picketing was that several suppliers refused to deliver and haul goods to and from the employers plant, causing substantial damage.

While constitutional principles may not often contain state power over picketing, the doctrine of federal preemption continues to oust state courts of power to control many instances of union picketing.

B. An Overview of Section 8(b)(7)

There is no manageable distinction between organizational picketing and recognitional picketing. There is such a distinction in theory: "recognitional picketing" is picketing to induce or coerce an employer to recognize a union as the bargaining representative of his employees notwithstanding the employees' wishes; "organizational picketing" is picketing to persuade or coerce employees into supporting the union as their bargaining representative. No such distinction is easily made out in practice. The statute does not distinguish between the two but assimilates both into the prohibitions of § 8(b)(7).

On first appraisal, recognitional picketing appears proscribed by the broad terms of § 8(b)(1)(A), which cover interference with the right of employees to deny support to the union. But for several years after the passage of that section in 1947, the Board's General Counsel refused to go to complaint on such a theory. When a complaint was finally issued in the late 1950's, the Board took the position that coercion is an inherent ingredient of such picketing—the attempt to force an employer and its employees to accept an unwanted union. By the time the case reached the Supreme Court, the more detailed prohibitions of § 8(b)(7) had been enacted; so the Court in NLRB v. Drivers, Local Union No. 639 [Curtis Bros., Inc.] (U.S.1960) gave a narrow reading to the section: "[§ 8(b)(1)(A)] is a grant of power to the Board limited to authority to proceed against union tactics involving violence, intimidation and reprisal or threats thereof—conduct involving more than the general pressures upon persons employed by the affected employers implicit in economic strikes."

Section 8(b)(7) makes organizational picketing an unfair labor practice in three broad contexts: subsection (A), where the employer has lawfully recognized another union and a question of representation may not appropriately be raised under § 9(c) of the Act; (B), where within the preceding twelve months a valid election has been conducted; and (C), where organizational picketing has been conducted without an election petition being filed within a reasonable time that may not exceed thirty days from the commencement of such picketing. There are two exceptions to (C), and no exceptions to the first two subsections.

The statute nowhere provides a damage remedy for organizational picketing and the effect of § 8(b)(7) is only to make such picketing an unfair labor practice supporting a Board cease and desist order. However, § 10(*l*) provides for an injunction in federal district court on the regional director's petition after a complaint is issued.

A final prohibition should be noted. Section 8(b)(4)(C), enacted in 1947, prohibits a strike or other act of restraint or coercion to force an employer to recognize or bargain with a union as the representative of his employees if another union has been certified as their representative under the provisions of § 9. This is called "striking against the certification" and, unlike other prohibitions of recognitional picketing, will support a damage remedy under § 303 of the LMRA (Labor–Management Relations Act).

The workings of § 8(b)(7)(C) are complex and there is no alternative to working carefully through the varieties of issues that come up under that subsection. Section 8(b)(7) prohibits only picketing and threats to picket and it is not always clear whether particular activity should be deemed picketing or not. The Board has adopted the following test: "The important feature of picketing appears to be the posting by a labor organization or by strikers of individuals at the approach to a place of business to accomplish a purpose which advances the cause of the union, such as keeping employees away from work or keeping customers from the employer's business." Lumber and Saw Mill Workers Local 2797 (Stoltze Land and Lumber Co.) (NLRB 1976). A distinction between picketing and handbilling is very important for secondary boycott purposes, and any definition of picketing under § 8(b)(7) that fails to make a distinction between picketing and handbilling can pose problems. In *Stoltze*, handbilling was held to constitute picketing when it continued after unlawful placard picketing had stopped.

The Board has reasoned that a confrontation between union protestors and the targets of their appeal is necessary to constitute picketing and has held that a sign on a pole with union pickets watching from a nearby house may or may not constitute picketing depending on why the protestors are present. If they are there wholly to safeguard the sign, there is no picketing; but if they are intended to have the same effect as a patroller, then it is picketing. See NLRB v. United Furniture Workers (2d Cir.1964).

Picketing does not fall within § 8(b)(7) unless it is for the purpose of gaining recognition. The Board has held that union picketing to protest an employer unfair labor practice, such as a discriminatory discharge, is not recognitional picketing. It rejected the argument that a strike protesting a discriminatory discharge, having as its purpose to compel reinstatement of the employee, was tantamount to recognition. Hod Carriers Local 840 (Blinne Construction Co.) (NLRB 1962). Of course, picketing purportedly in protest of an unfair labor practice can mask a recognitional object. For that reason a protest strike coming upon the heels of an injunction against recognitional picketing, or when the General Counsel has refused to go to complaint over the employer's alleged unfair labor practice or has settled the charge against the employer, may be deemed recognitional picketing by the Board even though the union denies a recognitional purpose.

Recognitional picketing may continue under § 8(b)(7)(C) for a maximum of thirty days without being an unfair labor practice. However, if the picketing is having a substantial impact on the employer's ability to operate its business, the regional director is likely to hold that less than thirty days constitutes a reasonable period and the regional director will seek an earlier injunction against the picketing if a § 8(b)(7)(C) charge is filed. The union can avoid a § 8(b)(7)(C) complaint by filing an election petition within the reasonable time. A union that engages in recognitional picketing while filing an early election petition may continue to picket until the Board's election processes are completed. If the union wins the election, continued picketing will not constitute a § 8(b)(7)(B) violation.

If the union engages in recognitional picketing and files an election petition, the employer may

expedite the Board's election processes by filing a
§ 8(b)(7) charge. This signals the regional director
to order an expedited election pursuant to the
provisions of § 8(b)(7)(C). Another way in which
an expedited election will be ordered is if the union
engages in recognitional picketing and within the
first thirty days the employer files both an election
petition and a § 8(b)(7)(C) charge. An employer
can file an election petition only if a demand for
recognition has been made upon it, and the recognitional picketing will be deemed such a demand.
An employer might avoid filing an election petition
or a § 8(b)(7)(C) charge because it wants a full
hearing, rather than an expedited procedure, on
the issues raised by the union's recognition demand (e.g. bargaining unit issues). The union cannot obtain an expedited election without the employer's cooperation; only if the employer files the
§ 8(b)(7)(C) charge will an expedited election be
ordered.

An expedited election means that there is unlikely to be a preelection hearing on the appropriateness of proposed bargaining units, and if there
is a hearing it will be an abbreviated one with no
briefs filed. The regional director will designate
an election to be held in the smallest appropriate
unit that includes all the picketing employees.
Thus if the union is seeking a small unit and the
employer contends that only a large unit is appropriate, the regional director will have to make a
unit determination. If the employer prevails, the
election will be in the large unit even though the

union does not wish it so. Under the expedited procedure, the union does not have to demonstrate a showing of interest by employees, and the employer is not required to produce, for the union's benefit, a list of employee names and addresses. The Board does not engage in preelection review of the regional director's bargaining unit determinations and similar issues when an expedited election is at hand.

In the *Blinne* case, the union made several arguments that it should be free from the restraints of § 8(b)(7)(C). It claimed that it had the support of a majority of the employer's employees at the time it picketed for recognition and argued that majority unions were not intended to be covered by § 8(b)(7)(C). The Board rejected this, holding that only currently certified unions are free from the proscriptions of § 8(b)(7)(C).

The union had filed an election petition in that case but had done so outside the thirty-day period. The Board held that the petition would not prevent the § 8(b)(7)(C) remedy.

The major issue in the case was the effect of several unfair labor practice charges that the union had filed against the employer. The union filed § 8(a)(5), 8(a)(3) and 8(a)(1) charges against the employer and argued that these charges excused the union from filing its election petition. The Board held that if the regional director issued a complaint on the § 8(a)(5) refusal to bargain charge, such a complaint would be premised on the contention that the employer had a duty to bargain; the complaint would thus be inconsistent with the need for an election petition and the § 8(b)(7) charge would be dismissed even though no election petition had been filed. This accorded with the Board's longstanding practice of dismissing election petitions when § 8(a)(5) complaints were pending against the employer.

But in the instant case the regional director had not gone to complaint on the § 8(a)(5) charge, and the Board reached the question of whether § 8(a)(3) and 8(a)(1) complaints warrant dismissing a § 8(b)(7) charge even though no election petition has been filed. The Board held that these unfair labor practice complaints would not free the union from the constraints of § 8(b)(7)(C). However, the Board also noted its practice of holding an election petition in abeyance pending a satisfactory resolution of unfair labor practice charges against the employer. This is called the Board's "blocking charge" doctrine; in this context it means that if the union can persuade the regional director to go to complaint on § 8(a)(3) or 8(a)(1) charges, the union should also file an election petition and then ask that the election be stayed pending disposition of the unfair labor practice charges. The petition will prevent a § 8(b)(7)(C) complaint, allowing continued picketing, but no immediate election will be held.

A union's attempt to force an employer to bargain by filing a § 8(a)(5) charge against the employer, rather than seeking a Board election, is now subject to the standards developed by the Supreme Court in NLRB v. Gissel Packing Co. (U.S.1969). A bargaining order is appropriate only when pervasive unfair labor practices combine with a prior showing of majority status by the union to justify a Board conclusion that the majority showing is a better indication of employee sentiment than is the slim chance of a future fair election. Only on such a showing, then, would employer unfair labor practices support a § 8(a)(5) complaint, freeing the union from the constraints of § 8(b)(7)(C).

C. Publicity Picketing Under Section 8(b)(7)(C)

Section 8(b)(7)(C) prohibits recognitional picketing for more than a reasonable time (30 day maximum) without the filing of an election petition. A proviso, or exception, to that subsection says that the subsection is not to be construed to prohibit "any picketing" for "the purpose" of truthfully advising the public (including consumers) that an employer does not employ members of, or have a contract with, a labor organization. The union will lose the benefits of this exception, according to its terms, if the effect of such picketing is to induce any employee of any other employer not to pick up, deliver, or transport any goods, or to refuse to perform any services. In Smitley d/b/a Crown Cafeteria v. NLRB (9th Cir.1964), the union picketed for more than thirty days to secure recognition but did so by picketing to advise truthfully the public that the company employed nonunion employees and had no contract with the union. The picketing did not have the effect of inducing any stoppage of deliveries or services by the employees of another employer.

The company contended that the picketing violated section 8(b)(7)(C) because it had a purpose of immediate recognition. The employer argued that the proviso should be construed to encompass only those instances of picketing that had a long-term recognitional purpose but not a short-term recognitional purpose. The Board initially upheld the employer's argument but, following a change in its membership, reversed its position. The court of appeals agreed with the Board's second decision, that the union had not violated § 8(b)(7)(C). The court reasoned that the plain meaning of the section compelled this result and that the legislative history was inconclusive.

The Board has also ruled that where the union's picketing complies with the proviso, a single stopped delivery will not necessarily remove the union's protection. Interruptions of deliveries or other stoppages must have "disrupted, interfered with, or curtailed the employer's business" for the protection to be lost. Retail Clerks Local 324 (Barker Brothers) (NLRB 1962).

D. Area Standards Picketing

Where the picketing union does not expressly demand recognition by the employer but demands only that the employer pay union ("area standards") wages, should this be deemed recognitional picketing for § 8(b)(7) purposes? There are two arguments for concluding that this picketing has a recognitional purpose. First, since the union sets area standards, this is a form of recognition even though the employer does not actually bargain with the union. Second, since there are advantages to some employers in being unionized (some other employers will deal only with unionized concerns), an employer pressured to pay union wages and benefits will have a natural tendency to sign a bargaining agreement.

Furthermore, there is a difficulty with understanding precisely what is encompassed by "area standards." The union contends that it is merely trying to remove the competitive advantage that a nonunion employer has over the unionized employer. Many terms of a union's collective bargaining agreement have a significant economic impact—a few are wage rates, pensions, health and welfare benefits, travel pay, overtime and show-up guarantees, holiday and vacation pay and the like. If a union seeks compliance with all of these terms, it is difficult to see how this differs from requiring the nonunion employer to adopt the union's bargaining agreement, absent the recognition and grievance provisions. Yet were a union to picket the employer to secure all of these benefits for his employees, the Board would call that recognitional picketing.

In Houston Bldg. and Const. Trades Council (Claude Everett Const. Co.) (NLRB 1962), the Board held that picketing for area standards is not recognitional in purpose. Once the picketing was removed from the strictures of § 8(b)(7)(C), the fact that it substantially interfered with pick-ups and deliveries by employers doing business with the targeted company did not render the picketing unlawful. This continues to be Board law, but there are several rules to which the union must rigidly adhere in order to have its picketing deemed area standards. The timing of the announcement of the union's objective is important; area standards picketing following an earlier demand for recognition is likely to lead to a finding that the picketing is recognitional. If the employer is paying union scale, or if the union does not discover whether or not he is paying union scale, that will probably be fatal to the union. Finally, the union must be careful that its picket signs identify the employer as one that pays less than union scale, and that the signs cannot be construed as requesting recognition. The Board tends to apply strictly these requirements.

E. Recognitional Picketing in the Construction Industry

Section 8(f) of the NLRA permits a construction industry union and an employer in that industry to sign a collective bargaining agreement before the employer has hired its employees, and thus before the union has attained majority status. This enables the employer to use the union hiring hall; otherwise the short duration of many construction jobs would preclude unionization. The section is permissive; it does not authorize the union to coerce a firm into entering a prehire agreement.

In NLRB v. Iron Workers Local 103 (U.S.1978), the Court held that union picketing to enforce a prehire agreement violates § 8(b)(7)(C) if it extends beyond a reasonable time. Until the union has actually attained majority status, the employer may renounce the prehire agreement without violating its duty to bargain, and union picketing thereafter constitutes recognitional picketing.

CHAPTER V

EMPLOYER ECONOMIC RE- SPONSES TO CONCERTED EMPLOYEE ACTIVITY

A. The Meaning of "Concerted Activity"

Section 7 of the NLRA guarantees employees the right to engage in concerted activities for mutual aid or protection. In most cases involving § 7 rights, there is no dispute that the activity is concerted, nor that it is protected. Typical protected concerted activity involves union organizing, the discussion of unionization among employees, or the attempt by one employee to solicit union support from another employee. But concerted activity need not involve a union. Activities by groups of employees unaffiliated with a union to improve their lot at their work place are deemed protected concerted activities. A strike by a group of employees for greater benefits or an improvement in working conditions is protected concerted activity under § 7. For example, in NLRB v. Washington Aluminum Co. (U.S.1962) seven employees left work without permission to protest the cold temperature in their shop. The walkout was held to fall within § 7.

As we move away from familiar examples, the concept of protected concerted activity becomes more difficult to apply. One case is fairly well settled, however. If a single employee attempts to persuade others to support the union, or to engage in economic activity for mutual benefit, the employee is engaged in protected concerted activity even though she is ultimately unsuccessful in persuading other employees to join the effort. The protected status of such activity should not turn on whether another employee decides to join the activity. The question is how far this notion can be extended. In Interboro Contractors, Inc. (NLRB 1966), the Board held that an individual employee's attempt to enforce provisions of a bargaining agreement constituted concerted activity, even though the employee acted solely on his own behalf, because the effort was directed at a goal shared by other employees. In NLRB v. City Disposal Systems (U.S.1984), a truck driver was discharged when he refused to drive a truck that he honestly and reasonably believed was unsafe because it had faulty brakes. A provision in the collective bargaining agreement arguably protected the employee's refusal to drive the truck, but the union refused to prosecute a grievance on the employee's behalf.

The Board's General Counsel contended that the employee's refusal to drive the truck was concerted activity under § 7 and that the discharge thus violated § 8(a)(1). The ALJ agreed, reasoning that an attempt to enforce a collective bargaining agreement was in the interest of all employees covered by the agreement and was therefore concerted activity even though only one employee was involved in the particular incident. The Board adopted the findings and conclusions of the ALJ.

Describing the invocation of a collective bargaining agreement right as "an integral part of the process that gave rise to the agreement," the Supreme Court found the Board's rule to be a reasonable interpretation of the statute and upheld it.

In Meyers Industries (NLRB 1984) the Board held that where employees are not unionized, and there is no collective bargaining agreement, an employee's assertion of a right that can only be of presumed interest to other employees is not a concerted activity. The Board will find activity to be concerted only if it was engaged in with other employees or on the authority of other employees. Moreover, according to the Board, even if the activity is found to be concerted a discharge will not violate § 8(a)(1) unless the employer knew the activity was concerted. No authority was set out for the employer knowledge requirement, and that requirement appears to be inconsistent with other cases suggesting employer intent is not required in § 8(a)(1) cases.

An interesting feature of the *City Disposal Systems* and *Meyers Industries* cases is that in a situation where the employees have been able to gain the protection of a collective bargaining agreement, and so presumably could bargain for protection against discharge in these circumstances, protection against discharge is provided by application of § 7; but when there is no collective bargaining agreement, and thus the need for protection arguably is greater, no § 7 protection is afforded.

May an employee act "in concert" with strangers whom he has never met and with whom he shares no immediate common interests? The answer appears to be yes in the context of an employee's refusal to cross a picket line established by a union other than his own. The leading opinion is authored by Judge Learned Hand in NLRB v. Peter Cailler Kohler Swiss Chocolates Co. (2d Cir.1942), where the judge reasoned that honoring a stranger picket line is no different than going out on strike over the grievance of only one workman. Although the aggrieved workman is the only one with an immediate stake in the outcome, his fellow workers know that by supporting his cause they assure support for their own grievances should the occasion arise.

The Supreme Court approved a controversial Board development in this area in NLRB v. J. Weingarten, Inc. (U.S.1975). The Board held that an employee engages in § 7 activity when he requests that a union representative be present during an investigatory interview called by the employer. The Court upheld this application of § 7, but only after noting the limiting factors that had been stated by the Board. The right applies only when an employee specifically requests union representation, and then only when the employee "reasonably believes the investigation will result in disciplinary action." An employer has the option of refusing to continue with the interview if the employee insists on representation and, in any event, the employer has no duty to bargain with the union at such an investigatory interview.

The Court was persuaded on several grounds to uphold the Board. First, the employee's request was within the literal wording of § 7 even though only the employee involved had an immediate stake in the outcome. The Court quoted language from *Peter Cailler Kohler Swiss Chocolates Co.* The Board's holding in the instant case promotes equality of bargaining power, an important congressional goal in passing § 7. Finally, the presence of a union representative may facilitate communication with regard to the subject matter of the interview; otherwise the employee may be too fearful or inarticulate to relate relevant facts and circumstances accurately, or may not be personally aware of a variety of extenuating circumstances.

The Board has since extended the *Weingarten* doctrine to situations arguably not within the contemplation of the Supreme Court. In one case the Board held by a divided vote that an employer must permit union representation in an interview designed only to announce a disciplinary action to the employee. Certified Grocers of California (NLRB 1977). The case was soon overruled. Baton Rouge Water Works (NLRB 1979). There have been suggestions that the union could waive the employees' *Weingarten* rights in a collective bargaining agreement. If so, and since the union could bargain for *Weingarten* rights in the absence of any § 7 grant, the function of the *Weingarten* doctrine appears to be as a contractual gap-filler.

B. Loss of Protected Status

Not all concerted activity for mutual protection enjoys protected status. Acts and threats of violence are not likely to be protected, for obvious reasons. However, an employer's mistaken belief that employees are about to resort to sabotage of the plant in order to promote their organizational effort will not justify employer retaliation against those employees and discharge violates § 8(a)(1). NLRB v. Burnup & Sims, Inc. (U.S.1964). Also held to be unprotected are unannounced, quickie strikes and refusals to perform selected pieces of work. Pressure to force an employer to commit an unfair labor practice is unprotected.

A case less troubling on its facts than for its broad pronouncements is NLRB v. Local 1229, IBEW [Jefferson Standard Broadcasting Co.] (U.S.1953). Employees in that case did not strike but engaged in picketing, handbilling and other publicity to pressure the employer to grant the union's economic demands in collective bargaining. The employer operated a television station. During the union's publicity campaign, employees distributed handbills which attacked the quality of the station's broadcasting without mentioning the fact that there was a labor dispute. The employer discharged those engaged in disparaging its product. The Supreme Court upheld a Board decision that the discharged employees were not engaged in protected activity. The Court relied on § 10(c) of the NLRA which provides that "no order of the Board shall require the reinstatement of any individual as an employee who has been suspended or discharged, or the payment to him of any backpay, if such individual was suspended or discharged for cause." The Court construed this to mean that an employer can discharge an employee for insubordination, disobedience or disloyalty, although an employer may not use any of these grounds as an excuse to discharge where the real reason is to retaliate against an employee for engaging in protected, concerted activity.

While this rationale was broad, the Court emphasized the compelling facts of this particular case—that the handbills asked for no public support for the union and failed to disclose that there was a labor dispute. The Court approved the Board's analogy of the employees' conduct to acts of physical sabotage.

The problem with the Court's rationale is that it might permit the employer to discharge for virtually any concerted activity because such activity would presumably always transgress an explicit or implicit employer "rule," and thus constitute insubordination. That the broad language of *Jeffer-*

son Standard cannot survive was made clear in NLRB v. Washington Aluminum Co. (U.S.1962) where the employer discharged several employees for leaving work without permission in order to protest the cold temperatures in their shop. The Court held that the employer's interest in keeping the employees on the job was outweighed by the interference of the discharges with § 7 rights. Agreeing that an employer may discharge employees for "cause" under § 10(c), the opinion states that this cannot mean that the employer is free to punish an employee for engaging in concerted activity, and the plant rule in question was a plain interference with § 7 rights. *Jefferson Standard* was described as denying § 7 protection to activities characterized as "indefensible" because they showed a disloyalty to the employer deemed unnecessary to carry on legitimate economic activities.

In a well-known Board case, Patterson Sargent Co. (NLRB 1956), *Jefferson Standard* was relied on to deny § 7 protection to the distribution of handbills which warned that because of a strike, the employer's product was not being made by the employer's regular, well-trained employees; the handbills requested consumers not to purchase the product until the strike ended. The Board held that this was not protected activity, citing the disparagement of the product and the Board refused to treat as controlling the reference to the strike and the truthfulness of the handbill.

Some activities may lose their § 7 protection by being waived in a collective bargaining agreement.

Leslie, Labor Law 3d. NS—5

The most important example is the general rule that employees have no § 7 protection when they strike in breach of a no-strike clause in a collective bargaining agreement. This rule was qualified in Mastro Plastics Corp. v. NLRB (U.S.1956). Employees struck in protest of an employer's unlawful assistance to a union which was attempting to oust the incumbent union; when the strikers sought reinstatement to their jobs, the employer refused. The Supreme Court affirmed a Board order that the employees be reinstated. The Court assumed that the employees could have waived their § 7 right to strike against employer unfair labor practices, but refused to give that interpretation to the unqualified no-strike clause in this bargaining agreement. The typical no-strike clause, in the Court's view, assumes the continued existence of a lawfully designated bargaining representative and is meant to deal solely with the economic relationship between the employees and the employer during the term of agreement. Since the unfair labor practices sought to undermine that bargaining relationship, the no-strike clause was deemed not to apply.

The breadth of the *Mastro Plastics* rationale is open to question. A majority of the Board has held that only strikes against serious unfair labor practices are immune from the waiver of general no-strike clauses. A serious unfair labor practice has been defined as "destructive of the foundation on which collective bargaining must rest." Arlan's Department Stores, Inc. (NLRB 1961). While *Mas-*

tro Plastics' interpretation of the coverage of no-strike clauses apply in unfair labor practice cases (construing bargaining agreements for purposes of § 7 waiver), these interpretations are not necessarily binding in a suit for damages against the striking union, although in such a case the contract interpreter (court or arbitrator) might deem the interpretations persuasive.

The nature of the § 7 activity sought to be protected may prevent waiver in appropriate cases. In NLRB v. Magnavox Co. (U.S.1974), the union was not permitted to waive the solicitation and distribution rights of employees in a collective bargaining agreement. *Mastro Plastics* was distinguished on the grounds that the place of work is uniquely appropriate for the dissemination of news concerning the bargaining representative and bargaining issues, and that in light of the fact that those employees opposed to the union may not have their solicitation rights waived, employees supporting the union should have just as great a right.

C. Discharges and Refusals to Hire

The earliest form of retaliation against employees for joining or supporting a union was the black list—a known union supporter would not be hired by any employer. The Wagner Act outlawed this employer practice. The remedy imposed upon an employer who has refused to hire an employee because of her past or present union activity (or other concerted activity) is a cease and desist order and an order to offer the applicant employment with back pay and interest. From the back pay award is deducted monies earned elsewhere by the applicant in the interim period and a deduction is also made for monies the applicant failed to earn without excuse. These remedies are also imposed upon an employer who has discharged a present employee on account of her union status or concerted activity.

It is not clear that these remedies are adequate. They do no more for the employee or applicant than make her whole, in the narrowest sense. Although the General Counsel prosecutes these cases on behalf of discriminatees, gaining the remedy is not without expense and inconvenience to the discriminatee. There is also the risk that a discriminatory discharge will not be provable as such. Furthermore, the interest on the back pay award is well below market interest rates. The employer may conclude that the effects of such discrimination on union activities, such as organizing drives, are worth the cost.

The essence of § 7 protection is this: if an employer retaliates against an employee for protected concerted activity, the employer violates § 8(a)(1); if the employer retaliates against protected concerted activity that involves a union, the employer violates § 8(a)(3) and 8(a)(1). In many instances of discharge or other discipline the employer will contend that action was taken against an employee for reasons unrelated to her protected concerted activity. In such a case, the Board must determine the employer's true motivation. For example, an employee may have engaged in soliciting for a union but be discharged for striking a fellow employee. The burdens of proof in such cases were set out in NLRB v. Transportation Management Corp. (U.S.1983). The burden is on the General Counsel to show that the the employer fired the employee at least in part because of the employee's protected, concerted activity. The employer will then be found to have violated the Act unless the employer can show that the employee would have been discharged even had he not engaged in the protected, concerted activity (that striking the fellow employee, for instance would have occasioned the discharge without regard to the union activity). The Court stated that "[t]he employer is a wrongdoer; he has acted out of a motive that is declared illegitimate by the statute. It is fair that he bear the risk that the influence of legal and illegal motives cannot be separated, because he knowingly created the risk and because the risk was created not by innocent activity but by his own wrongdoing."

A strike is more than protected concerted activity; it is an economic weapon intended to pressure the employer into meeting employee demands, be they economic or organizational. While the employer is not permitted to retaliate against employees for engaging in protected concerted activities, the employer has the right to exercise its own economic weapons and to take actions necessary to promote his legitimate business interests. One of the most significant employer rights was recognized by the Supreme Court in NLRB v. Mackay Radio and Telegraph Co. (U.S.1938). The union in that case called an economic strike against the employer, and the employer brought in replacements for the striking employees. When some of the strikers asked to return to their jobs, the employer informed them that some of the replacements had been promised permanent positions. Eventually the company designated five union leaders as those who were deemed to have been permanently replaced. The narrow holding of the case is that an employer violates § 8(a)(3) and (1) when it discriminates on the basis of union activity or leadership in deciding which employees shall be reinstated. But in dictum that has never been successfully challenged, the Court declared that an employer whose employees are engaged in an economic strike can replace the strikers with new employees to carry on the business. Furthermore, once the strike is over, the employer need not discharge the replacements in order to make room for the striking employees. The Supreme Court has held that a state court suit by replacements discharged in breach of a promise that they would be permanent replacements is not preempted by federal law. Belknap, Inc. v. Hale (U.S.1983).

The *Mackay* dictum is troubling since the rationale was not necessary to the Court's decision and has a substantial effect on § 7 rights and the industrial balance of power. The Court failed to discuss, if it appreciated at all, the argument that an employer should not be permitted to hire permanent replacements unless it can show that temporary replacements are unavailable or inadequate.

In NLRB v. International Van Lines (U.S.1972), the Court adopted the widely understood meaning of the *Mackay* rule: that an economic striker may not be discharged but may be replaced. A striker's right to his job upon an unconditional offer to return depends on whether a permanent replacement has actually been secured. The Board has held that even if the striker's job has been filled by a replacement, some rights to employment remain. In Laidlaw Corp. (NLRB 1968), the Board held that economic strikers who unconditionally apply for reinstatement at a time when their jobs are filled by permanent replacements remain employees and are entitled to full reinstatement upon the departure of their replacements, unless the strikers have in the meantime acquired regular and substantially equivalent employment, or the employer can show that its failure to offer reinstatement was for legitimate and substantial business reasons. In a case decided under the Railway Labor Act, the Supreme Court held that an employer is not required to discharge strike replacements and workers who refused to join the strike in favor of replaced strikers with greater seniority. However, once a striker gains reinstatement, she also gains her prestrike seniority, which she can invoke in times of layoff if a collective bargaining agreement specifies layoffs by seniority. This rule presumably applies under the NLRA as well. Trans World Airlines v. Independent Federation of Flight Attendants (U.S.1989).

The right of an employer to replace strikers without violating the NLRA does not extend to a strike in protest of an employer unfair labor practice. In that situation, strikers have a right to their jobs upon an unconditional offer to return to work notwithstanding the fact that the employer may have replaced them. A strike that began as an economic strike may be converted to an unfair labor practice strike if the employer commits unfair labor practices during its duration that prolong the strike. Whether there has been such a conversion is a question of fact for the Board.

A case involving more than replacement of strikers was NLRB v. Erie Resistor Corp. (U.S.1963). During an economic strike by employees, the employer notified the union that it was giving strike replacements and strikers who had returned to work twenty years of additional seniority which could be used as credit against future layoffs, but could not be used for other employee benefits based on years of service. The union claimed this grant of super-seniority violated § 8(a)(3) and (1). The administrative law judge found that the employer had granted super-seniority without an intent to discriminate on account of the employees' concerted activity, but the Board held that specific evidence of a subjective intent to discriminate was not necessary and found an unfair labor practice.

The Supreme Court affirmed the finding of a violation, and in so doing made important comments about employer intent under § 8 of the NLRA. Citing the earlier case of Radio Officers v. NLRB (U.S.1954), the Court stated that some employer conduct may by its nature imply the required discriminatory intent because the natural foreseeable consequences of the conduct warrant the inference. First, "[w]hen specific evidence of a subjective intent to discriminate or to encourage or discourage union membership is shown, and found, many otherwise innocent or ambiguous actions which are normally incident to the conduct of a business may, without more, be converted into unfair labor practices.... Conduct which on its face appears to serve legitimate business ends in these cases is wholly impeached by the showing of an intent to encroach upon protected rights...." Second, where specific evidence of intent is not shown, the employer must still be held to have intended the consequences which foreseeably flow from its actions, consequences which, unless adequately explained away by a legitimate business justification, may make out an unfair labor practice. Even a business justification will not save the day for the employer in every case for "preferring one motive to another is in reality the far more delicate task ... of weighing the interest of employees in concerted activity against the interest of the employer in operating his business in a particular manner and of balancing in the light of the Act and its policy the intended consequences upon employee rights against the business ends to be served by the employer's conduct."

On the facts of *Erie Resistor* the employer's grant of super-seniority was deemed an unfair labor practice for several reasons. Super-seniority affects all strikers, unlike *Mackay* replacement which affects only those actually replaced. It affects those that participated in the strike as compared to non-strikers and those striking employees induced by the offer of benefits to abandon the strike. Super-seniority cripples a strike effort by setting those who have been accorded the super-seniority against the rest of the bargaining unit, and because of this conflict it renders future bargaining difficult, if not impossible. Thus the Board was entitled to treat the grant of super-seniority as an unfair labor practice notwithstanding the employer's contention that the grant was necessary in order to keep the business in operation.

In one context, the discharge-replacement distinction has been subjected to an embarrassing Supreme Court precedent. In NLRB v. Rockaway News Supply Co. (U.S.1953), the employer discharged an employee for refusing to cross a picket line at another employer's place of business, although the employer had not secured a replacement for the employee when he was "fired." The Supreme Court held that the discharge was not an unfair labor practice, apparently relying on the fact that protection against employer discharge for refusal to cross a picket line had been waived by the bargaining agreement's no-strike clause. Not content with this ground of decision, however, the Court also criticized the Board's application of the discharge-replacement distinction in this context. The distinction between discharge and replacement was deemed to be "unrealistic and unfounded in law" and not sanctioned by *MacKay*. "It is not based on any difference in effect upon the employee. And there is no finding that he was not replaced either by a new employee or by transfer of duties to some non-objecting employee, as would appear necessary if the respondent were to maintain the operation. Substantive rights and duties in the field of labor-management do not depend on verbal ritual reminiscent of medieval real property law."

The Court failed to explain why this case should be deemed different from *MacKay*. In later cases the Board has held that where the discharge of an employee honoring a picket line is to preserve efficient operation of the business, neither the terminology of the employment severance (discharge or replacement) nor the chronological order of severance and replacement will control. The critical factors are whether the employer had an economic justification because of the substantial adverse effect that the refusal to cross was having on his business, whether he could have conveniently assigned another employee to do this work, and whether he in fact hired a replacement. Overnight Transportation Co. (NLRB 1965); Redwing Carriers, Inc. (NLRB 1962); L.G. Everist, Inc., (NLRB 1963).

The Board has wavered on whether § 7 protection of a refusal to cross a picket line is waived by a general no-strike clause in a bargaining agreement.

D.   Economic Inducements

The Supreme Court has held that an employer violates § 8(a)(3) and (1) by granting or withholding economic benefits in order to interfere with an incumbent bargaining representative or an employee organizing effort.   In NLRB v. Exchange Parts, Inc. (U.S.1964), the Court held that threats to withdraw and promises to bestow benefits on employees are unlawful where the purpose is to undermine the incumbent or potential bargaining agent.   "The danger inherent in well-timed increases in benefits is a suggestion of a fist inside the velvet glove.   Employees are not likely to miss the inference that the source of benefits now conferred is also the source from which future benefits must flow and which may dry up if it is not obliged."   Such a grant of benefits is an unfair labor practice even though the benefits are conferred permanently and unconditionally.   Also see Medo Photo Supply Corp. v. NLRB (U.S.1944).

Where the employer reduces benefits in order to coerce employees, the remedy is a cease and desist order and a retroactive restoration of benefits.

Where the unlawful conduct is an increase in benefits, the Board will order the employer to cease and desist from similar future misconduct but will not require the economic benefits to be withdrawn.

The employer whose employees are engaged in an organizing campaign must walk a narrow path. It can grant benefits that are of a traditional sort, such as merit or percentage wage increases reflecting the start of a fiscal or calendar year, or reflecting an industry-wide wage increase. Where the wage increases are discretionary with the employer, managers must act very cautiously. Postponing benefits because of a pending election is also fraught with danger, because the Board may find the postponing of a regularly scheduled increase to be coercive and an unfair labor practice.

The solicitation of employee complaints during a union organizing campaign may be construed as an express or implied promise of benefit. Board case law purports to outlaw such solicitations only if the promise to remedy complaints is implied from the solicitation. Montgomery Ward and Co. (NLRB 1976); Uarco, Inc. (NLRB 1974).

A union does not have it within its power to grant or take away employment benefits; therefore, union promises of future benefits are treated differently from similar promises by the employer. A union does have the power to waive dues and initiation fees if employees will vote for it in the election. In NLRB v. Savair Mfg. Co. (U.S.1974), the Court held that the NLRB should have set aside an election victory where the union had promised that if it won, it would waive its initiation fees for all employees signing authorization cards before the election. According to the Court, the purchasing of cards in this manner creates an artificial showing of employee support likely to mislead other employees, and employees who sign might feel morally obligated to vote for the union. Employees who did not sign the cards might fear the wrath of the union if it won the election. The Court indicated, however, that a pre-election offer by the union to waive initiation fees for everyone if the union wins the election would not necessarily be objectionable.

E. Domination and Assistance

Two ways for employers to frustrate employee organizing efforts are to establish an employer-dominated bargaining representative as an alternative to the representative that would otherwise be selected by the employees, and to assist an independent employee bargaining representative with whom the employer feels comfortable in dealing.

Company-dominated unions were a widespread problem prior to the passage of the Wagner Act. Section 8(a)(2) is a legislative attempt to outlaw these company unions. In determining whether a bargaining representative is unlawfully dominated by the employer, the Board has looked to a variety of factors, which it tends to treat on a per se basis:

assistance or defrayal of the cost of a union election; interference or assistance in the drawing of the union's charter; arrangement for attorney services; direct financial support and indirect financial aid in the forms of meeting places, secretarial services, telephones and the like. Such cases are now uncommon.

An employer faced with an employee organizing effort may wish to substitute another union for the one that the employees might otherwise designate as their bargaining representative. To render assistance to either union in these circumstances violates the Act, as would according either union a grant of exclusive bargaining status. An employer violates § 8(a)(2) and (1) by a grant of recognition to a union not representing a majority of the employer's employees even if the employer acts in good faith. In ILGWU [Bernhard–Altmann Corp.] v. NLRB (U.S.1961), the Supreme Court held that the employer violated those sections by giving exclusive bargaining rights and signing a bargaining agreement with a union enjoying less than majority employee support, even though the employer had a good faith belief that the union had such support. The Court was aware that the remedy imposed no significant hardship on the employer. The union was ordered to stand a representative election and the employer was ordered to cease giving effect to the bargaining agreement.

Where an employer has an expired bargaining agreement with an incumbent union, a rival union may notify the employer during negotiations that it claims to represent a majority of the employees and that it has filed a representation petition with the Board. For many years the Board held that if the employer continues to negotiate after learning that "a real question of representation" exists, he violates § 8(a)(2). Shea Chemical Corp. (NLRB 1958). This was called the *Midwest Piping* doctrine. Midwest Piping and Supply Co. (NLRB 1945). It was overruled in RCA Del Caribe, Inc. (NLRB 1982). Under the new rule, the employer may negotiate and execute a bargaining agreement with the incumbent union; and the employer violates § 8(a)(5) if it withdraws from bargaining solely because of the filing of the petition. If the incumbent prevails in the representation election, any new contract executed between it and the employer will be binding. If the challenging union wins the election, the contract is not binding.

F. Management Restructuring

A few employers apparently would rather go out of business than deal with a union on behalf of their employees. In Textile Workers Union v. Darlington Mfg. Co. (U.S.1965), the question was whether an employer violated § 8(a)(3) or § 8(a)(1) by going out of business in order to avoid a union. No one contended that the employer must remain in business, the issue was whether the employer violated the Act by going out of business and must thus make its employees whole for any losses suffered as a result of the violation.

The Supreme Court held that complete shutdown by an employer who does not have a purpose of discouraging unionization elsewhere violates neither § 8(a)(3) nor § 8(a)(1). In so holding, the Court laid down important tests for violations of those sections.

According to the opinion, § 8(a)(1) is violated only when interference with employees § 7 rights outweighs the business justification for the employer's action. A violation of § 8(a)(1) presupposes an action by the employer which is unlawful even absent a discriminatory motive. Furthermore, "some employer decisions are so peculiarly matters of management prerogative that they would never constitute violations of § 8(a)(1), whether or not they involve sound business judgment, unless they also violated § 8(a)(3)." A decision to terminate completely a business was one of these prerogatives, the Court ruled.

The next issue was whether the shutdown violated § 8(a)(3). According to the Court, even if it is clear that the employer has closed the plant because of a desire to avoid the union, the closing violates § 8(a)(3) only if the liquidation of the business is intended to yield a future benefit to the employer. This future benefit can be found in cases of run-away shops—moving a plant from one location to another, or closing a plant in order to increase business at another location—or in cases where the employees could cause the plant to reopen by renouncing the union. But where no future benefit is involved, there is no violation of § 8(a)(3). The Court's reliance on the "future benefit" theory was unprecedented.

On the facts of *Darlington,* the Court remanded for consideration of the questions of whether this particular plant was a part of a larger single enterprise controlled by the owners of the plant, and of whether the closing was intended to chill unionization in those other plants. The Board was instructed that it must look to an actual showing of a motivation to chill unionization elsewhere; a finding that such a closing would necessarily have such an impact would not suffice.

It is not apparent why the Supreme Court established these standards for § 8(a)(1) and (3), other than an obvious antipathy to finding that a plant shutdown violates the statute. Had an order to continue plant operations been at stake, it would be easier to understand the deference to management prerogative. But it was surely beyond dispute that the employees had suffered injury by their decision to unionize, and that that injury was visited upon them by the employer. Why an employer who wishes to go out of business for discriminatory reasons should not be required to make the employees whole as a cost of going out of business is unclear. It is difficult to think of any business debt that can be so easily extinguished.

In any event, a *Darlington* shutdown has been distinguished from run-away shops and partial closings. If an employer moves its business in order to discourage union membership or to avoid collective bargaining, it violates § 8(a)(3); but if it moves for legitimate economic reasons, such as lower wage rates in the new geographic area, it does not violate the Act. This distinction, while reasonable in theory, often makes unfair labor practice liability dependent on verbalizations of the reasons for moving.

The Board is not prepared to order the employer to return to a previous location even where an unfair labor practice is made out. Prior employees can be given hiring preferences at the new location and can be made whole for any losses they have suffered. It is unclear whether the Board and the reviewing courts are prepared to adopt the remedy of ordering the employer to bargain with the union at the new location in the absence of a showing of majority employee support there. The bargaining remedy may be necessary to deter such conduct by taking away the unlawful gains from the employer, but the cost is sometimes forcing an unwanted union on the employees at the new location. See Local 57, ILGWU v. NLRB (D.C.Cir.1967).

Another way of avoiding union economic or organizing efforts is through a practice currently unique to the construction industry, the "double-breasted" operation. A unionized employer doing construction industry work, and wishing to bid on jobs where the general contractor or owner permits nonunion subcontractors to bid, forms a second company to work on nonunion jobs. Occasionally the company is a separate corporation, in other instances it is a wholly owned subsidiary. In either event, when a union-only job comes up for bids, the union corporation bids. There may or may not be an exchange of operating assets and supervisory personnel.

Unions have generally had difficulty in arguing that representation rights with respect to the unionized company carry over to the nonunion operation, or that the bargaining agreement reached with the union company is binding on the nonunion company. Two strands of NLRB doctrine are available to defeat the union's claim. First, the Board is likely to find that the two corporations are separate employers by looking at whether they have interrelated operations, common management, centralized control of labor relations and common ownership. Second, even if they are deemed the same employer, the Board may find that the two business entities are separate bargaining units. The Board was supported to some extent in South Prairie Const. Co. v. Operating Engineers, Local 627 (U.S.1976). Depending on your point of view, this can be seen as a rational reaction by employers to the economics of the market place, or as a rank form of discrimination against union employees.

G. Lockouts and the Last Word on Employer Intent

A lockout occurs when an employer attempts to bring economic pressure on a union by refusing to permit employees to work. The Supreme Court has decided three lockout cases and their holdings are simply stated. The cases are equally important, however, for their treatment of questions of employer intent under § 8(a)(3) and (1) and of the roles of the NLRB and the courts in assessment of bargaining weapons and relative economic strengths.

The first lockout case to reach the Court was NLRB v. Truck Drivers Union [Buffalo Linen] (U.S.1957). The employers engaged in multiemployer bargaining with the union. The union called a whipsaw strike, which means that the union struck one or more of the multiemployer group while continuing to work for the remainder. This tactic is designed to reduce the financial hardship of a strike on the union membership and to reduce the employers' economic strength by putting the struck employers at a competitive disadvantage. The employers in *Buffalo Linen* responded with a lockout of all the employees of the multiemployer bargaining group.

The Supreme Court upheld a Board finding that such a lockout did not violate § 8(a)(1) or § 8(a)(3) absent specific proof of an unlawful employer motivation. The Court characterized the problem as "the balancing of the conflicting legitimate interests" and approved the Board's balance.

The second case to reach the Court was NLRB v. Brown (U.S.1965) which, like *Buffalo Linen,* involved a multi-employer lockout in response to a union whipsaw strike. But in *Brown,* the struck employer continued to operate using temporary replacements and the other employers did the same, refusing jobs to their union employees while permitting replacements to fill the jobs temporarily. The Board disapproved of the lockout combined with the use of temporary replacements, holding that such conduct carried its own indicia of unlawful intent, making out an unfair labor practice without any further showing.

This time, the Supreme Court did not uphold the Board. The Court first cited with approval a test developed in previous Supreme Court precedent: that specific evidence of employer bad intent is not required "where the employer conduct is demonstrably destructive of employee rights and is not justified by the service of significant or important business ends." Cautioning the Board that it could not act as an "arbitrator ... of economic weapons," the Court disagreed with the application of this test to the facts of the case. The Court saw the use of temporary replacements as no more destructive of employee rights than was the lockout itself. Clearly the locking-out employers would be at a disadvantage if they were required to stay closed while the struck employer continued to operate.

Thus neither the lockout nor the use of temporaries were antiunion—they merely neutralized the economic effects of the union's whipsaw tactic.

After reviewing Court precedent bearing on the intent required to make out a § 8(a)(3) violation, and noting that by its terms § 8(a)(3) requires discrimination, a resulting discouragement of union membership, and unlawful intent, the Court found that the instant case would not support a § 8(a)(3) violation: "While the use of temporary non-union personnel in preference to the locked-out union members is discriminatory, we think that any resulting tendency to discourage union membership is comparatively remote, and that this use of temporary personnel constitutes a measure reasonably adapted to the effectuation of a legitimate business end." The fact that the replacements were temporary and that the union could end the dispute at any time by agreeing to the employer's bargaining demands were important to the majority opinion.

A difficulty with the Court's opinion in *Brown* is pointed out by the dissenting opinion of Justice White, who argues that if the struck employer can operate using temporary replacements, it is not clear that the non-struck employers have a substantial economic interest in locking out at all. The majority's response to this contention is cryptic at best. It characterizes Justice White's argument as saying that it is discriminatory for the nonstruck employers to offer jobs to temporary replacements while refusing the offer of regular employees to continue working. The majority then rejects the argument by construing the regular employees' willingness to work as merely a desire to further the objective of the whipsaw, and to break the employers' united front.

The lockout in response to a whipsaw strike was one variety of "defensive lockout" recognized as lawful by the NLRB. Other forms of lawful, defensive lockouts have been those designed to prevent seizure of a plant by a sitdown strike, avoid spoilage of materials that would result from a sudden work stoppage, prevent disruption of an integrated operation by quickie strikes, and the like.

The facts in the third Supreme Court lockout case, American Ship Building Co. v. NLRB (U.S.1965), suggested that the employer's lockout was defensive—to prevent a later strike when business activity would be at its peak—but the Board and the Supreme Court treated it as one in which a single employer with a long history of unionization had locked out his employees in order to pressure the union to reach a collective bargaining agreement favorable to him. The Board found this lockout to violate both § 8(a)(3) and 8(a)(1), and the Supreme Court reversed.

The Board's theory was that an offensive lockout (one to gain a bargaining advantage) violates § 8(a)(1) because it interferes with the employees' right to strike and with their right to bargain collectively, the latter interference occurring because they are being punished for presenting their views in collective bargaining. The Court, by contrast, emphasized that there was neither allegation nor proof that the employer was hostile to the collective bargaining process or that it intended to interfere with the union's capacity to represent the employees. The long history of vigorous representation of the employees by this union was cited in support. For the Court, the case turned to whether the offensive lockout was one of those acts "which are demonstrably so destructive of collective bargaining that the Board need not inquire into employer motivation...." The Court held that it was not; an employer's intent to promote its bargaining position must be distinguished from an intent grounded in anti-union animus. The Court was not persuaded that the offensive lockout is unlawful because it preempts the union's ability to call a strike. On these grounds the Court found that there was no violation of § 8(a)(1).

The Court then turned to the § 8(a)(3) issue. Violation of that section requires, according to the Court, discrimination, a resulting discouragement of union membership, and usually the showing of an antiunion motive on the employer's part. The Court emphasized that it had repeatedly construed § 8(a)(3) to render lawful some employer actions that serve legitimate business ends, even though those actions might also tend to discourage union membership. The Court admitted that "some practices [are] inherently so prejudicial to union interests and so devoid of significant economic justification that no specific evidence of intent to discourage union membership or other antiunion animus is required," but the Court disagreed with the Board that the instant case satisfied this test. The lockout had neither a tendency to severely discourage union membership nor was it devoid of significant employer economic interest. While the employees suffered an economic disadvantage from the lockout, their disadvantage was no greater than that often felt as a result of other legitimate employer economic actions.

The Court condemned in no uncertain terms the Board's assumption of a special competence to weigh the competing interests of employers and unions on an economic continuum. The Board had held that an offensive lockout would so substantially tip the scales in the employer's favor that it would violate the congressional policy underlying the Act. Said the Court, "We think that the Board construes its functions too expansively when it claims general authority to define national labor policy by balancing the competing interests of labor and management."

Several future lockout cases were left undecided by these Supreme Court cases. First, the offensive lockout in *American Ship Building* occurred only after a bargaining impasse had been reached between the employer and the union. In the absence of an impasse, would an offensive lockout violate the Act? Might it be strong evidence of an anti-union motivation since the processes of collective bargaining had not been exhausted in any meaningful sense? Second, could an employer engaged in an offensive lockout lawfully hire temporary or permanent replacements? And would the latter be any different than a discharge for organizing? Third, could an employer who locked-out in response to a whipsaw strike also hire permanent replacements, and would it be determinative that the struck employer had hired permanent replacements?

In the view of many, the lockout cases left the standards for determining violations of § 8(a)(3) and (1) in disarray. What was left, for example, of the Court's statement in NLRB v. Erie Resistor Corp. (U.S.1963) that the question of employer intent actually involves the task of weighing the interest of employees in concerted activity against the employer's interest in operating his business, and of balancing the consequences to employee rights against the business ends sought to be served? Also, are any of these tests capable of deciding concrete cases, or are they used by the Court as an excuse to overturn Board decisions on the merits of which the Court is in substantial disagreement with the Board?

A later Supreme Court case has the last word on the employer intent necessary to make out a § 8(a)(3) violation, but it is not clear that the case shines a great deal of light on the matter. In NLRB v. Great Dane Trailers, Inc. (U.S.1967), the employer was found to have violated § 8(a)(3) when it refused to pay striking employees vacation benefits accrued under a terminated bargaining agreement while it announced an intention to pay such benefits to striker replacements, returning strikers, and non-strikers who had been at work on a certain day during the strike. The Supreme Court had no trouble finding this to be discriminatory and capable of discouraging union membership by discouraging participation in concerted activity.

The Court had the following to say about the employer motivation requirement: "First, if it can reasonably be concluded that the employer's discriminatory conduct was 'inherently destructive' of important employee rights, no proof of an anti-union motivation is needed and the Board can find an unfair labor practice even if the conduct was motivated by business considerations. Second, if the adverse effect of the discriminatory conduct on employee rights is 'comparatively slight' an anti-union motivation must be proved to sustain the charge *if* the employer has come forward with evidence of legitimate and substantial business justifications for the conduct. Thus, in either situation, once it has been proved that the employer engaged in discriminatory conduct which could have adversely affected employee rights to *some* extent, the burden is upon the employer to establish that he was motivated by legitimate objectives since proof of motivation is most accessible to him." On the facts of the case, since the employer had offered no proof of legitimate and substantial business justification, the Court sustained the Board's finding of a violation.

CHAPTER VI

SECONDARY BOYCOTTS, HOT CARGO AGREEMENTS, UNION JURISDICTIONAL DISPUTES AND FEATHERBEDDING

A. Introduction

The secondary boycott provisions of the NLRA are perhaps the most complex in labor law. Several NLRA sections bear on secondary boycotts, although the two principal sections are §§ 8(b)(4)(B) and 8(e). Section 8(b)(4) begins by stating two unlawful means used by unions: (i) to engage in, induce or encourage a strike or other refusal to handle goods; and (ii) to threaten, coerce or restrain any person. These two unlawful means are followed by four instances of unlawful objects: (A) a strike to secure a bargaining agreement clause that violates § 8(e), or to force an employer or self-employed person to join a union; (B) in general terms, a secondary boycott—forcing or requiring one person to cease doing business or handling the products of another; (C) a demand that an employer recognize or bargain with one union when another union has been certified by the NLRB as the representative of the employer's employees; (D) jurisdictional disputes between unions.

Section 8(e) is an equally important part of the Act's secondary boycott prohibitions. It prohibits an employer and a union from entering into a contract or agreement in which the employer undertakes to engage in a secondary boycott of another employer. There are two exceptions ("provisos") to § 8(e). The first pertains to certain kinds of construction industry work that are to be done at the site of construction, and the second pertains to certain work done in the clothing and apparel industry.

Two remedial provisions are worth noting. Section 10(l) of the NLRA requires NLRB regional directors to seek an injunction in district court whenever they have reasonable cause to believe that § 8(b)(4) is being violated. Section 303 of the LMRA permits a private party injured by a violation of § 8(b)(4) to recover actual damages in federal district court, but does not permit a private party to secure injunctive relief.

Section 8(b)(4) nowhere uses the word "secondary," and "primary" appears only in a proviso to § 8(b)(4)(B). A literal interpretation of § 8(b)(4) would outlaw many strikes that, in common understanding, do not raise secondary boycott issues. For example, if a union calls out all the employer's rank and file employees and sets up a peaceful picket line around the employer's premises, the union intends that the employer will be unable to continue operations and will be forced to give in to the union's demands. The union has thus engaged in a strike where an object is forcing a person (the employer) to cease doing business with other persons (the employer's customers and suppliers). Section 8(b)(4)(B), literally read, has been violated although the strike would presumably be saved by the proviso to that section. Prior to the 1959 amendments to the NLRA there was no "primary strike" proviso and § 8(b)(4)(B) read essentially the same as it does now (although it was renumbered in 1959), yet no one would have thought that an ordinary economic strike was precluded by the secondary boycott provisions.

The term "secondary boycott" appears many times in the legislative history of the Taft–Hartley Act, and in NLRB v. International Rice Milling Co. (U.S.1951), the Court made a statement that most observers took to mean that § 8(b)(4) would be construed to cover only secondary activity. In *International Rice Milling* recognitional pickets appeared at the employer's place of business and caused a customer's truck not to cross the picket line to pick up goods. The prohibited means described by the statute in 1951 included encouraging a "concerted refusal" by employees to perform services and the Court's narrow holding was that the appeal to a single truck driver was not a concerted refusal within the meaning of the statute. But the Court also relied on § 13 of the NLRA to say that Congress did not intend by enacting § 8(b)(4)(B) to interfere with the ordinary strike. Section 13 says that, except as provided for in the Act, nothing in the Act is to be construed as to interfere with or diminish in any way the right to strike. In 1959, Congress amended § 8(b)(4) and in doing so reversed the holding of *International Rice Milling* by removing the word "concerted" from the definition of prohibited means. But by that time the case had come to be known for the proposition that § 8(b)(4) does not reach traditional, primary picketing at the employer's place of business.

B. Ally Doctrine

Consider the case of a unionized employer that manufactures lead pencils. Assume that the employees who paint the pencils are represented by the Painters' Union, and that employees performing other manufacturing functions are represented by other unions. The painters strike the employer for higher wages, which the employer refuses to pay. A picket line is established and the employer finds that he cannot secure replacement employees to paint his pencils, either because they are not available in this locality, or because potential replacements will not cross the union's picket line. The employer contracts with another employer for pencil painting during the Painters Union strike. Once the pencils are ready for paint, they are shipped to the second employer for finishing operations and distribution. The Painters Union, upon learning of this arrangement, places pickets around the second employer's place of business. Is this a secondary boycott?

The answer is no because the second employer is considered to be the ally of the first. Two issues worth considering are: what is the statutory source of the ally exception to secondary boycotts, and when will the exception apply?

The statutory argument for finding a secondary boycott in this situation is straightforward. The relevant section is § 8(b)(4)(B). Both "i" and "ii" appear to apply since the pickets are encouraging employees of the second employer either to refuse to do any work for the second employer, or at least to refuse to paint the pencils, and the pickets are also threatening or coercing the second employer under (ii). The object of the picketing is to force the second employer to cease doing business (pencil painting) with the manufacturer (the "primary employer").

There are, however, two technical readings that remove this strike from the prohibition of § 8(b)(4)(B). First, since (i) and (ii) both refer to "any person," a court or the Board might conclude that the primary and second employers in this hypothetical are not different persons within the meaning of that section. Or, a court or the Board might conclude that the cessation of business in this case is not the kind of cessation of business described in § 8(b)(4)(B).

There is some legislative history supporting this result. In the congressional debates of 1947 leading to the passage of § 8(b)(4), Senator Taft said that the secondary boycott "provision makes it unlawful to resort to a secondary boycott to injure the business of a third person who is wholly unconcerned in the disagreement between an employer and his employees." The argument supporting the ally doctrine is that the second employer in the hypothetical is not "wholly unconcerned" with the labor dispute between the primary employer and its employees. Greater support for the ally doctrine came from Senator Taft in 1949, two years after the passage of the Taft–Hartley Act, when he spoke approvingly of the doctrine. In 1954, President Eisenhower also approved of the doctrine in the context of making recommendations to Congress for revision of the NLRA. These statements are far less authoritative than contemporaneous legislative history, but they have been relied on by courts.

Three facts in the pencil painting hypothetical support an exception to the secondary boycott prohibition. First, the second (secondary) employer's employees are doing "struck work"—work which otherwise would have been done by the striking employees of the primary employer. Second, there is an arrangement between the primary employer and the secondary employer by which this work is done. Third, the primary and secondary employers both receive an economic benefit from the arrangement—the secondary employer is doing work it would not have done but for the strike, and the primary employer is able to avoid the full effect of the strike (the inability to produce painted pencils). It is important to consider which of these factors must be present for the ally doctrine to apply.

A leading case is NLRB v. Business Machines and Office Appliances Mechanics Conference Bd., Local 459 [Royal Typewriter Co.] (2d Cir.1955). Royal had service contracts to repair typewriters, and also was obligated to repair typewriters on warranty. When Royal's service personnel went out on strike, Royal instructed its office personnel to tell contract customers to select an independent repair shop from the telephone directory, have the repair made by that shop, and send a receipted invoice to Royal for reimbursement. Many of the customers sent repair bills directly to Royal for payment. The union picketed the independent typewriter repair shops.

The Second Circuit reversed a Board finding that picketing of the independents constituted a secondary boycott. The court acknowledged that there was little or no evidence of direct contact between Royal and the independents, and that a finding of an "arrangement" was difficult to make; but the court noted that the economic effect on both Royal and the independents was precisely the same as if the independents had been hired by Royal as strikebreakers. The independents were doing struck work that rendered an economic benefit to Royal (it permitted Royal to continue good customer relations and allowed Royal to avoid breaching its warranty and service contracts). Moreover, the independents could tell they were doing struck work, by the fact of the picketing if nothing else.

While various fact situations have created problems under the ally doctrine, two kinds of cases are worthy of special note. Suppose, for example, that the business of the primary employer is mixing cement and delivering it to construction jobsites for use there by jobsite employees. The cement company's drivers engage in an economic strike and the cement company is unable to deliver. If a construction company hires an independent trucking company to pick up the cement at the primary employer's premises and deliver it to the construction jobsite, is the independent trucking company an ally of the primary employer? The independent trucking company is doing struck work—work that but for the strike would have been done by primary employees. And both the trucking company and the primary employer are gaining an economic benefit from the trucker's handling of the goods. The trucker is getting work that he would not have had but for the strike. And while the cement company may be losing whatever profit it makes from this delivery service, it is able to deliver the cement and thus can continue to operate the cement plant.

One could argue that an arrangement is required and that there is no arrangement between the primary employer and the independent trucker in this case. But the requirement of an arrangement only encourages an under-the-table suggestion by the primary employer that its customer should contact the independent trucker. How much sympathy should we have for the customer? Will we say that its need to engage in self-help in securing the product necessary to build its building overrides ally doctrine policy in this circumstance? For example, there may be no other available cement supplier in this locality. Refusing to deem picketing of the independent trucker a secondary boycott (i.e., allowing the picketing) will spread the effect of the strike at the cement company to all local employers that use cement. But absent alternative suppliers, a completely successful strike of the cement company would also do precisely that. We might conclude that the ally doctrine in this context spreads the impact of the strike no further than it would be spread by a completely successful strike against the cement company.

One other point is worth noting. If the customer can find an alternative supplier of cement, the alternative supplier cannot be picketed on an ally doctrine rationale because there will be no economic benefit to the primary employer.

A second troublesome case is where, as the result of a strike, a company ceases to manufacture a component of its product and instead orders that component from a national supplier. It would be unusual for the pickets to show up at the doorstep of a national supplier a thousand miles away, but the ally doctrine might permit this picketing. Although the national supplier may not be aware of it, its employees are now producing a component that would otherwise have been produced by striking primary employees. It is thus engaged in struck work. Both the primary employer and the national supplier gain an economic benefit. In response to the argument that the national supplier is not knowingly performing struck work, the union can cite *Royal Typewriter* for the proposition that the national supplier gains knowledge when the pickets show up at its place of manufacture. We might want to say that this is not sufficient, especially if we see a policy in isolating national suppliers from the fallout of labor disputes.

If an employer is an ally, the union can picket, asking all his employees to stop all work: the pickets need not restrict their appeal to those employees that are doing struck work by asking them to discontinue the struck work. Shopmen's Local 501, Ironworkers (Oliver Whyte Co.) (NLRB 1958). Several reasons support this result. On a technical reading of the statute, the union can appeal to the second employer's employees either because the employer is not "doing business" with the primary under § 8(b)(4) or because it is not another "person" under that section—but no reading would seem to permit that employer to be an ally for part of its work and not for the remainder. It is also arguable that an employee who refused to do the struck work while agreeing to do all other work for his employer would be deemed to be engaging in a partial work stoppage and would lose his § 7 protection, subjecting him to discharge. Finally, if appeal could only be made to those doing struck work, there would be some incentive for the picketed employer to mingle the struck work with nonstruck work in order to make it impossible to know which of its employees were doing struck work.

Another ally doctrine allows picketing that would otherwise seem to be secondary. Recall the hypothetical manufacturer of lead pencils. Suppose that at a time when there is no strike or other labor problems, the manufacturer splits its operations into two separate corporations. The first corporation produces the entire lead pencil except for painting, packaging, and distribution. These operations are done by the second corporation. All the operations continue to be housed at the same location. If the painters go on strike, will they be permitted to appeal to the employees of both corporations for a work stoppage? Had the business remained unitary, the union could have appealed to every employee. One possibility is that the two corporations will be deemed alter egos of one another for labor purposes. That would probably be the result if their separate identities were essentially a fiction, maintained primarily for labor relations purposes. But assuming each corporation has a separate identity, might we still want to hold them allies of one another? The case law suggests that if this is an "integrated enterprise," the two operations will be held to be allies. The easiest case is one where there is common ownership, common control of operations, especially labor relations, and a straight-line operation at the same location. The result is not clear when any of these factors is missing, but common control of labor relations seems to be most important.

Where a single corporation operates two businesses as subsidiaries of the corporation, the NLRB is prepared to hold that the subsidiary businesses are not allies so long as they exercise independent control over their operations. Thus when a union striking a newspaper in one state attempted to picket a newspaper in another state owned by the same corporation, the Board held that the two newspapers were not allies and that the picketing was a secondary boycott. Los Angeles Newspaper Guild (Hearst Corp.) (NLRB 1970). It should be emphasized, however, that if a single employer at one location is composed of several separate bargaining units, all its employees at that location are primary and strikers from one bargaining unit can appeal to employees from other bargaining units without running into § 8(b)(4) problems.

One application of the "integrated enterprise" ally doctrine was rejected by the Supreme Court in a case that exerts considerable influence in construction industry secondary boycott law. In NLRB v. Denver Bldg. and Const. Trades Council (U.S.1951), unions struck a general contractor that had awarded a subcontract for electrical work to a company employing nonunion workmen. The strike and picketing had the effect of shutting down the entire construction project. The Supreme Court upheld the Board's conclusion that picketing aimed at the general contractor and its employees violated § 8(b)(4)(B). The unions' claim was that their dispute was only with the general contractor, and that the strike and picketing were to force it to have an all-union job. The Court, however, agreed with the Board that an object of the unions' unhappiness was the nonunion status of the subcontractor. If all the employees had been employed by the general contractor, a strike to replace his nonunion employees with union members would not have implicated § 8(b)(4), but the strike in this case required the general contractor to terminate his dealing with a second employer, the nonunion subcontractor. Even assuming that one object of the unions was to influence the general contractor to let out his work only to union subcontractors, another object of the strike and picketing was clearly to force the nonunion subcontractor off the job. The Court held that so long as *an* object was to force a cessation of business, the strike and picketing violated § 8(b)(4)(B).

The union's second line of defense was that the general contractor and subcontractor on this construction project were allies in the integrated enterprise sense. Presumably the union would have described these employers as working very closely together on the same premises, as having a need to coordinate day-to-day activities, as being under the ultimate supervision of a single construction supervisor, and as having the common purpose of producing a single product (a finished building). The

Court rejected this argument virtually without discussion, saying only that "the business relationship between independent contractors is too well established in the law to be overridden without clear language doing so." Thus the integrated enterprise ally doctrine does not apply in the construction industry.

C. Appeals to Secondary Employees

Assume that a union representing employees of a company calls the employees out on strike over an economic matter such as higher wages. If the strike is successful in withdrawing all the employees, and if the employer cannot operate through supervisors or replacements, there is presumably no cause to picket a closed business. But if the company is able to continue to operate notwithstanding the strike, the union is likely to put pickets around the workplace and hope to persuade employees of other companies who approach the jobsite to honor the picket line. The employer with whom the union has its dispute is called the primary employer; employers doing business with the primary employer are called secondary employers, and their employees are called secondary employees. Such appeals might ask secondary employees to refuse to do any work that brings them into contact with the primary employer, or they might be asked to stop all work for their own employer in order to force it to cease doing business with the primary employer until the primary strike is settled.

The Board's original approach to union appeals to secondary employees was geographic. Congress had not intended, in the Board's view, to prohibit primary strikes or primary picket lines, but since one object of all primary picketing is to persuade third persons not to do business at the primary employer's premises, forbidding this object would have the undesired effect of banning all picketing at the primary employer's premises. So in the early 1950s, the Board held that a union could ask secondary employees not to do any work at the primary premises. In addition to picket line appeals, solicitations at the homes of secondary employees, "unfair" lists, and similar kinds of communications were permitted so long as the appeals were limited to asking secondary employees not to work at the premises of the primary employer.

Occasionally primary employees leave the primary premises during work: a common example is when a truck driver for the primary employer makes deliveries at secondary premises. Under the geographic approach, the Board held that the primary employees could follow the truck and continue to picket around it even when it was stationed at the secondary employer's premises. The truck itself was deemed part of the primary situs and it was thus appropriate for the pickets to follow it so long as the picketing was strictly limited to the area around the truck while it sat at the secondary premises.

The significant case of Sailors' Union of the Pacific and Moore Drydock (NLRB 1950), was decided at a time when the Board adhered to these geographic rules. The primary employer in that case was a shipowner with whom the union had a representational dispute respecting one of its ships. This ship was sent for repair to a drydock owned by an independent company. While the ship was in drydock being outfitted for a new voyage, the ship's sailors engaged in training exercises. The union asked to picket adjacent to the ship but was refused and took up picketing around the entire drydock, at which were lodged ships belonging to several other companies.

The problem for the Board was not in insulating the secondary employees (drydock workers) from all picket line appeals; to the extent that the pickets only asked secondary employees not to work on the primary ship, the appeals were not considered to be a call for a secondary boycott. But if the pickets asked the secondary employees to stop work on all ships at the drydock, it would be prohibited secondary activity. The Board laid down a four-part test for determining whether the pickets had, as far as possible, confined their appeal within permissible bounds. The factors are: (1) the picketing is limited to times when the situs of the dispute (the Board analogized this to a roving situs case, like a truck) is located on the secondary employer's premises; (2) at the time of the picketing the primary employer is engaged in its normal business at the situs; (3) the picketing is limited to places reasonably close to the location of the situs; and (4) the picketing discloses clearly that the dispute is with the primary employer. Since these four conditions were met in the instant case, the picketing was held lawful.

It was important to the Board that the ship was being prepared for a voyage and that primary employees (the sailors) were engaged in training activities on the ship while it was in drydock. This made the ship a roving situs and distinguished the case from one where a primary employer sends out a part of his assembly line or the like, for repairs or servicing.

In the middle 1950s, with changes in Board membership, the Board shifted from a geographic approach to a literal approach to secondary boycotts. The new theory was that the statute demanded that a union entirely avoid appeals to secondary employees, at least as far as possible. Rules were established to permit appeals to primary employees while prohibiting appeals to secondary employees except insofar as they were "incidental" effects of a primary picket line. For example, if the union were to picket the primary premises at a time when no primary employees were present, then the object must be an appeal to secondary employees and the picketing was unlawful. When secondary employees were working at the primary employer's premises over an extended period of time, the union had to take all possible steps to insulate secondary employees from the dispute. The standard for whether the union had taken the required steps was the four-part *Moore*

Drydock test. Also, when primary employees went to a secondary employer's premises to work, the union had to comply with *Moore Drydock* in order to avoid unlawful appeals to secondary employees. In the latter situation, the Board ruled that when the union had an adequate opportunity to appeal to primary employees at primary premises, any picketing of secondary premises would violate § 8(b)(4), notwithstanding compliance with *Moore Drydock* tests.

The Supreme Court put its mark on this line of cases in Local 761, International Union of Electrical Workers v. NLRB [General Electric Co.] (U.S.1961). General Electric was the primary employer, operating a manufacturing facility which was struck and picketed by its production and maintenance workers over an economic dispute. General Electric had established separate entrances (gates) for secondary employees working at General Electric's premises. These secondary employees performed a variety of tasks: installation and repair of equipment, retooling and rearranging operations necessary to the manufacture of new models of General Electric products, and general maintenance work. The union picketed the gates established for these secondary employees, raising directly the question whether such an appeal violates § 8(b)(4)(B).

Several theories were argued in the case. The union essentially argued the geographic approach and contended that at the primary situs a picketing union can appeal directly to all secondary employees except those employees who perform no service whatsoever for the primary employer. The company advocated the literal approach, arguing that a direct appeal to any secondary employee violates § 8(b)(4). NLRB counsel claimed that the union should be permitted to appeal to secondary employees who made only occasional pick-ups, deliveries, and the like, to General Electric but that the union should not be able to appeal to secondary employees who worked on the primary premises "in a substantial and continuous manner as a regular work place."

The Court first noted that the object of all picketing is to appeal to secondary employees but that that object standing alone does not render such picketing unlawful. (While *Denver Building Trades* was not mentioned, this language seems incompatible with the theory that picketing is unlawful if it has as "an" object something prohibited under § 8(b)(4).) The *General Electric* Court then undertook a lengthy review of NLRB precedents. The test ultimately set out by the Court, however, was one of its own making. Pickets at the primary employer's premises may directly appeal to secondary employees if, but only if, the work of those secondary employees is related to the work done by the struck primary employer.

While it is not entirely clear what "related work" was intended to mean, at one point in the opinion it is described as "work unconnected to the normal operations of the struck employer." Also included in the definition of related work is "work ... of a kind that would ..., if done when the plant were engaged in its regular operations, necessitate curtailing those operations."

Thus if secondary employees are doing related work they cannot be insulated from picket line appeals. If they are doing unrelated work, then to avoid committing a secondary boycott the union must take steps to avoid direct appeals to them, and the test of whether the union has made a sufficient effort is the four-part *Moore Drydock* test. Where a separate gate is used both by secondary employees doing related work and by secondary employees doing unrelated work, the gate will be deemed "mingled" and the union can station pickets there without violating the *Moore Drydock* standards, unless the use by employees doing related work is de minimis.

The question of first significance after *General Electric* is how to define "related work." The *General Electric* opinion tells us that secondary employees delivering goods to or from the primary employer, and secondary employees doing maintenance work necessary for the operation of the plant, are engaged in related work. One theory of related work looks at the effect on secondary employers of an entirely successful strike against the primary. Certain secondary employees, such as those building a new building for the primary employer, would not be affected even by a successful strike against the primary. Such is not the case, however, for delivery employees of a secondary employer. If the strike against the primary is successful, the plant is not in operation and there is no occasion for delivery persons to make deliveries. This theory says that an appeal is to employees doing related work if the effect of the appeal would be no greater than would be occasioned by a completely successful shut-down of the primary employer.

A second, and connected issue, is whether the related work doctrine is meant to apply when primary employees go to secondary premises. Although the picketing in *General Electric* was at the primary premises, nothing in the opinion suggests that its standard should not apply at secondary premises as well. A later Supreme Court case, United Steelworkers of America v. NLRB [Carrier Corp.] (U.S.1964), says that "location of the picketing is an important but not decisive factor," and proceeds to apply the related work doctrine even though the picketing occurred on secondary premises. But the facts of that case were unusual in that the secondary employer's property (a railroad right-of-way) was located immediately adjacent to the primary employer's property and both were surrounded by a common locked gate.

If *General Electric* applies at secondary premises, it means that a picket may appeal to secondary employees to cease doing work at the secondary premises that is related to the work of primary employees. Under any test, a distinction must be drawn between the *work* of primary employees and the *product* of the primary employer, for it is clear that Congress intended to make following the primary employer's product through the stream of commerce a secondary boycott (see section E, "Hot Cargo" Agreements). Once the primary employer's product reaches a retailer's shelves, it would be a clear violation of § 8(b)(4)(B) for pickets to ask the retailer's clerks to refuse to handle the product inside the store. It would be the equivalent of declaring the product to be "hot" and asking others not to handle it, which is a prohibited call for a secondary boycott. If *General Electric* is applied at secondary premises its effect must turn on a factor appearing artificial: a difference in result between work related to the primary employer's product and work related to the work of the primary employees.

If *General Electric* does not apply at secondary premises at all, then pickets will be able to follow the primary employer's employees on a roving situs theory but will have to comply with *Moore Drydock* standards. In the typical case, application of the related work test and the *Moore Drydock* test will yield the same results at secondary premises.

The Board has adopted what can only be called a special rule for picketing in the construction industry. In Building and Const. Trades Council of New Orleans (Markwell and Hartz, Inc.) (NLRB 1965), the union had an economic dispute with a construction industry general contractor. When separate gates for subcontractors were established at the construction jobsite the union picketed those gates and contended that *General Electric*'s related work doctrine protected their picketing. The Board rejected the contention in a 3–2 decision. The primary employer, the general contractor, was described as "but one of several employers operating on premises owned and operated by a third party ...," a circumstance the Board called a "common situs." *General Electric* was held not to apply to a common situs for several reasons. First, Congress showed an intent in 1959 that the Board was to continue to adhere to *Moore Drydock* in construction industry cases. Second, approval of *Moore Drydock* standards by the Supreme Court in *General Electric* showed a similar intent. Finally, to apply the related work doctrine in the construction industry would be inconsistent with NLRB v. Denver Building and Construction Trades Council (U.S.1951).

One may agree with the result, but the reasons fail to persuade. It is clear that Congress was not trying to preserve *Moore Drydock* in 1959 but rather was trying to avoid legislating with respect to this construction industry problem because to do otherwise might have deadlocked Congress on any labor legislation. Nor is the interpretation of *General Electric*'s treatment of *Moore Drydock* correct. The Court there was describing the evolution of Board standards, and to the extent that it departed from traditional Board doctrine, it was clearly framing a new test. If the *General Electric* opinion speaks to this issue at all, it seems to describe the facts before it as raising a common situs issue. Finally, *Denver Building Trades* only rejected the integrated-enterprise ally doctrine: it could hardly have rejected a related work doctrine that had not yet been born.

The dissenters in *Markwell and Hartz* would apply the related work doctrine in the construction industry, but only when the strike is against the general contractor and the issue is whether subcontractors are engaged in related work. They would not apply the related work doctrine when a subcontractor is the primary, nor on the facts of *General Electric* if one of the subcontractors working at General Electric's property were the primary employer.

The majority in *Markwell and Hartz* seemed to argue that the case was distinguishable from *General Electric* because the general contractor and the subcontractors were working on property owned by a third party. A distinction turning on ownership of the property bears no relation to secondary boycott or other labor policy and cannot support a difference in results. The Board itself abandoned this rationale in Carpenters Local 470 (Mueller–Anderson, Inc.) (NLRB 1976), refusing to apply the related work test to construction industry picketing where the general contractor, the primary, owned the land and was building an apartment complex for himself.

Application of the related work doctrine to construction industry picketing would increase the economic power of construction industry unions and might be objectionable on that ground. Both union and management interests have had sufficient power in the Congress to block both legislative approval and legislative reversal of *Markwell and Hartz*.

D. Appeals to Consumers

When a union is unable to shut down a primary employer by striking and picketing, the union would like to appeal to consumers of the primary's product or services not to use those products or services for the duration of the union's economic dispute. One class of consumer is another employer in the manufacture-to-retail sale chain. It does not violate § 8(b)(4)(B) for a union to request a secondary employer to stop handling goods produced by the primary employer so long as that request does not threaten or coerce. In such a circumstance, "(i)" is not violated because the appeal to the secondary employer's manager is a request that she use management discretion to cease doing business with the primary, and is not a request to engage in a work stoppage. The appeal will violate "(ii)" if it implies a threat or coercion. A peaceful request accompanied by a threat to engage in lawful conduct against the secondary employer also falls outside the prohibition. NLRB v. Servette, Inc. (U.S.1964). In that case a peaceful request to the secondary employer was accompanied by a threat to engage in handbilling that was itself protected by a proviso to § 8(b)(4)(B). Since the threat was that the union would engage in lawful conduct it did not fall under "(ii)."

If the primary employer sells goods or services directly to the public, then the secondary boycott provisions will not be implicated when the union appeals to the public not to purchase those goods or services during the union's dispute. But the union would like to make the same appeal to the consuming public when the primary's goods or services are sold to the public by an independent, and thus secondary, employer. A secondary employer will argue, of course, that an appeal by the union to his customers has the effect of putting pressure on him to cease dealing in the products or services of the primary employer, and is thus condemned by § 8(b)(4)(B). One could reasonably conclude that Congress has balanced the competing interests in this situation by enacting the proviso to § 8(b)(4), which says that nothing in that section shall be "construed to prohibit publicity, other than picketing, for the purpose of truthfully advising the public, including consumers and members of a labor organization, that a product produced by the primary employer is distributed by the secondary employer, so long as such publicity does not cause any secondary employee to refuse to pick up, deliver, or transport any goods or not to perform any services, at the secondary employer's premises."

This proviso would permit, for instance, union handbilling at the premises of a secondary employer asking the public to cease buying all goods or services from the secondary employer as he continues to sell goods or services produced by the primary employer. But the Supreme Court held in NLRB v. Fruit and Vegetable Packers and Warehousemen, Local 760 [Tree Fruits] (U.S.1964), that the union is not limited to the actions permitted by the proviso. The primary employers in that case were companies packing and warehousing fruits in the state of Washington. The union picketed retail grocery stores that sold the fruit packed and warehoused by the primary employer. The pickets' placards were carefully drawn so as to ask the public only to cease purchasing this fruit and to inform the public that the picketing was not directed at the store generally. The picketing did not cause any of the retail store's employees to stop work.

Because of the potential First Amendment implications of a broad ban, the Court was not prepared to view § 8(b)(4)(B) as prohibiting peaceful consumer picketing absent a clear congressional intent to do so. It found no such intent in § 8(b)(4)(B) and the proviso and instead drew a distinction between kinds of consumer picketing. Proscribed is consumer picketing at a secondary site to persuade consumers to cease all purchases from the secondary employer in order to force the secondary to cease doing business with the primary employer and thus to influence the primary to settle his union dispute upon terms favorable to the union. Permitted is peaceful picketing at a secondary site that merely asks the public to withhold its patronage of the primary's products from the secondary employer. Although congressional opponents to the stiffening of the secondary boycott provisions in 1959 had expressed fear that the soon to be enacted amendments would prohibit consumer picketing directed at the primary employer's product, proponents of those amendments failed to respond to that criticism. It was the silence of the proponents that persuaded the Court.

The enactment of the proviso in 1959, according to the Court, did not evidence a different intent by Congress, for the proviso permits an appeal both broader and narrower than that involved in *Tree Fruits*—an appeal to consumers to cease all trade with a secondary employer who retails the primary employer's goods, but only through non-picketing appeals.

The employer in *Tree Fruits* argued that customers would fail to heed the limited appeal on the union's picket signs and would instead turn away from his store completely. Even assuming that to be true, the Court was not prepared to say the picketing was unlawful. The Court reasoned that the distinction between consumer product picketing and a broader request that all trade with the secondary be stopped has an economic basis because although there is a cessation of business between the primary and secondary employers in each case, in the former it occurs only because consumer demand has diminished, whereas in the latter the cessation of business is caused by an infliction of general business injury on the secondary employer by the union's picketing.

The Court substantially qualified the *Tree Fruits* doctrine in NLRB v. Retail Store Employees Union, Local 1001 [Safeco] (U.S.1980). The union's dispute was with a title insurance company, but they picketed local title insurance companies who sold the primary company's policies. The picketing was confined to appeals to consumers not to buy those policies. The Court held that *Tree Fruits* did not immunize the picketing and it enforced the Board's order that the picketing violated § 8(b)(4)(B).

The majority opinion in *Safeco* reasoned that the picketing in *Tree Fruits* was aimed at a single product that was but one of many sold by the secondary employer, and a successful appeal to the public would only induce the secondary to drop the product as a poor seller or to reduce its orders for the product. The neutral employer has little incentive to become involved in the primary dispute. In this case, by contrast, the policies accounted for substantially all the secondaries' sales and successful picketing would curtail all retail sales by the secondary. According to the Court, "[i]f the appeal succeeds, each company 'stops buying the struck product, not because of a falling demand, but in response to pressure designed to inflict injury on [its] business generally.' Thus, 'the union does more than merely follow the struck product, it creates a separate dispute with the struck employer.' (quoting *Tree Fruits*) Such an expansion of labor discord was one of the evils that Congress intended § 8(b)(4)(B) to prevent." The majority did not discuss the fact that the union had confined its appeal to the struck product and that no appeal to consumers by picketing was otherwise possible.

The union claimed that its picketing was protected by the First Amendment. The argument was based on several uncontroversial facts. First, the picketing, qua picketing, was lawful; no time or place restrictions were claimed. Second, the picketing appealed to no one to do an unlawful act. Thus newspaper or radio advertisements calling for a boycott of the secondary employer would have concededly been lawful. Justice Powell, speaking for himself and two other Justices, rejected the argument virtually without discussion. Two concurring Justices found Justice Powell's easy rejection of the constitutional argument unsatisfactory, but themselves rejected the constitutional argument, although not on the same ground. Three Justices dissented, on the constitutional issue as well as on the statutory issue.

While not directly at issue in *Safeco,* the holding in that case will surely foreclose consumer picketing where the product produced by the primary is merged into the product of the secondary. An example would be the selling by restaurant of a hamburger where the bun is from a bakery that has a dispute with a union.

In Edward J. DeBartolo Corp. v. Florida Gulf Coast Bldg. & Const. Trades Council (U.S.1988), the Court distinguished calling for a boycott through picketing and calling for a similar boycott through handbilling. The Court held that peaceful handbilling calling for a consumer boycott of a secondary employer is not "coercive" under § 8(b)(4)(B). The Court was of the view that to proscribe peaceful handbilling in this circumstance would raise serious First Amendment issues. The Justices reasoned that the success of handbilling depends on the persuasiveness of the message carried while picketing adds a distinguishing confrontational element.

E. "Hot Cargo" Agreements

Since a union can make a peaceful noncoercive request that a secondary employer stop dealing in the goods or the services of a primary employer without violating § 8(b)(4)(B), NLRB v. Servette, Inc. (U.S.1964), should not the union be able to secure a binding commitment in advance from such a secondary employer? This issue first came before the Supreme Court in United Bhd. of Carpenters and Joiners, Local 1976 v. NLRB [Sand Door] (U.S.1958). Three cases were decided under this caption and their facts illustrate the types of commitments that a union might seek from secondary employers. In one case, the Carpenter's Union negotiated a bargaining agreement clause with a construction contractor providing that the contractor's workmen would not be required to handle nonunion material. When the contractor reneged by bringing nonunion doors onto the jobsite, the union carpenters refused to install them, relying on the clause. In the other two cases, the Teamster's Union ordered its members working for carriers not to handle freight produced by a manufacturing company with whom the Teamsters had a dispute. The union relied on a provision in its bargaining agreement with the carriers providing that no union member would be allowed to handle or haul freight to or from an "unfair" company. The unions argued that a strike or a concerted refusal by their members to handle the goods of the primary employer did not violate § 8(b)(4)(B) (it was then numbered § 8(b)(4)(A)) if the strike or refusal enforced a collective bargaining agreement clause. An employer who has agreed to such a clause is no longer a neutral party, the union claimed; the union has a dispute with it over its violation of the clause.

The Supreme Court disagreed, holding that while an employer had the right voluntarily to boycott the primary employer, the secondary boycott provisions contemplated that the secondary employer would have the choice of whether or not to boycott at the time the question arose. Thus the bargaining agreement clause was not a defense to a strike for a secondary boycott. The Court went on to observe that neither the execution nor the voluntary observance of such a clause violated the statute, although the NLRB was permitted to presume conclusively that an employer's observance was non-voluntary when the union ordered its members not to handle the offending goods. The Court seemed to suggest that such contract clauses might be peacefully enforced through arbitration or court action for damages. In labor parlance, these clauses are called "hot cargo" clauses.

Congressional reaction was swift. In the 1959 Landrum–Griffin amendments to the NLRA, Congress passed § 8(e) and the new § 8(b)(4)(A), which substantially altered the law of hot cargo clauses. Congress apparently felt that such clauses were seldom the product of true voluntary agreement, and thus Congress outlawed hot cargo clauses in § 8(e).

Exceptions to the § 8(e) prohibition were made for the construction industry and the apparel and clothing industry. Unions in the clothing and apparel industry are permitted by a proviso to § 8(e) to strike for and enter into hot cargo agreements without violating § 8(e) or § 8(b)(4)(A), and are permitted to strike to enforce such agreements without violating § 8(b)(4)(B).

The construction industry exception is narrower in scope. It relates only to "contracting or subcontracting of work to be done at the site of construction," and in National Woodwork Manufacturers Ass'n v. NLRB (U.S.1967), it was held that this exemption affords no protection to a clause which covers work that will be performed at a factory and brought to the construction jobsite. Current authority is that a construction industry union can strike to obtain one of the permitted clauses without violating § 8(b)(4)(A), a section which otherwise prohibits striking to secure a clause that is itself prohibited by § 8(e). Building and Construction Trades Council Centlivre Village Apartments (NLRB 1964).

Nothing excludes construction industry clauses from the constraints of § 8(b)(4)(B) and current authority holds that strikes to enforce clauses permitted by the construction industry proviso violate § 8(b)(4)(B). Peaceful enforcement of these clauses through arbitration or court action is lawful: otherwise the clauses would be completely unenforceable and the construction industry proviso would be a practical nullity. California Dumptruck Owners Assn. (NLRB 1976); Hughes Markets, Inc. (NLRB 1975).

The Supreme Court narrowly interpreted the construction industry proviso in Connell Const. Co. v. Plumbers Local 100 (U.S.1975). The union sought to organize construction industry subcontractors by picketing a general contractor for an agreement that he would subcontract jobsite work only to companies having a bargaining agreement with the union. Defending itself from an alleged violation of the antitrust laws, the union argued that the clause fell with § 8(e)'s construction industry proviso. Without the benefit of an NLRB decision on the issue, the Supreme Court found that Congress' intent in enacting this proviso was to allow unions to protect their members from having to work alongside of nonunion workmen on construction jobsites. The union in the instant case represented none of the general contractor's employees. Since the scope of the agreement was not limited to jobsites where the union's members would necessarily be working, and since the clause did not prevent the use of other nonunion subcontractors in other crafts working on the jobsites, the Court held that the clause was not within the construction industry proviso. Unwilling to assume that Congress intended to sanction this sort of topdown organizing, the Court held that the construction industry exemption "extends only to agreements in the context of collective-bargaining relationships and ... possibly to common situs relationships on particular jobsites as well." In Woelke & Romero Framing, Inc. v. NLRB (U.S.1982), the Court held that so long as a clause barring construction jobsite work to union subcontractors is negotiated in the context of a bargaining relationship, it is not necessary that it be limited to particular jobsites at which union and nonunion workers are employed.

Hot cargo clauses come in several varieties and the influential case of Truck Drivers, Local 413 v. NLRB (D.C.Cir.1964) dealt with three typical kinds of clauses raising hot cargo issues. The first is a picket line clause. An employer does not violate § 8(a)(3) or (1) when it replaces an employee who honors a picket line. The union, in turn, would like to negotiate a clause in which the employer agrees that it will not discipline or replace an employee who honors a picket line. The circuit court held that where a clause protects an employee who honors a picket line in connection with a primary dispute at the contracting employer's own premises, there is no § 8(e) problem. However, if such a clause were to sanction the honoring of a picket line at the contracting employer's own premises when the picketing itself promoted a secondary strike or boycott, the clause would then sanction a secondary boycott by the contracting employer's employees and would be unlawful under § 8(e).

A proviso to § 8(b)(4) permits a clause to protect employees who honor a picket line at secondary premises if that picket line is established by employees of the secondary employer and is ratified or approved by a union that the secondary employer is bound to recognize. But the *Truck Drivers* court held that the protection can be broader: the clause can protect employees who honor any primary picket line at a secondary premises.

A second kind of clause is a struck goods clause. An employer's agreement not to handle the goods produced by another employer, with whom the union has a dispute, is a classic, and unlawful, hot cargo clause. A variant of this clause is one in which the employer merely agrees not to discipline or discharge an employee who decides that he will not work on hot goods. This has also been held to violate § 8(e). The only kind of struck goods clause that has been permitted is one in which the employer agrees not to force employees to work on goods sent to the contracting employer by another employer deemed an ally under the doctrine described in NLRB v. Business Machine & Office Appliance Mechanics Conference Bd., Local 459 [Royal Typewriter Co.] (2d Cir.1955).

A third variety of hot cargo clause is a subcontracting clause. A union in a dispute with an employer might like to bring pressure on that employer by seeing to it that it receives no business subcontracted out from other firms. The union might therefore seek a commitment in advance from employers not to subcontract work to any employer that has a dispute with the union. Such a clause would be forbidden by § 8(e). But the union is thought to have a legitimate interest in preserving its members' work with a particular employer, and it might wish to prohibit all subcontracting in an effort to preserve that work. Arguably then, a clause completely prohibiting subcontracting would not be a secondary boycott even though its enforcement would mean that the primary employer would not do business with a potential subcontractor. The employer, in turn, might resist agreeing to such a clause by arguing to the union that while it is willing to agree not to avoid the union's wage and benefit scale by subcontracting, other economic conditions might make it profitable for the firm to subcontract. Some unions have agreed to a clause whereby the employer commits himself not to subcontract to any subcontractor paying less than union wages, hours and working conditions (a "union standards" clause).

The *Truck Drivers* court held that such a clause is lawful under § 8(e) and that it is distinguishable from a clause by which an employer agrees not to subcontract to any employer that does not have a bargaining agreement with the union. The effect of the latter clause (a "union signatory" clause) is that it requires the primary employer to look to the union or nonunion status of a potential subcontractor before deciding whether the primary can subcontract to that employer. The key relationship under a union signatory clause is between the union and the potential subcontractor; thus the potential subcontractor is the primary employer, and the union signatory clause is void under § 8(e).

F. Work Preservation

A product boycott is a classic form of secondary boycott. When an employer with an ongoing dispute with the union sends its product into the stream of commerce, the union would like to notify union supporters in the stream of commerce not to handle the employer's product. This is a product boycott. The union's request that other workers refuse to handle the goods violates § 8(b)(4)(B), as would another union's direction to its members not to handle the goods in support of the first union. If a second union agreed with a secondary employer not to handle the offending goods, the agreement would violate § 8(e).

In National Woodwork Manufacturers Ass'n v. NLRB (U.S.1967), the Supreme Court held that a work preservation agreement does not violate § 8(b)(4)(B). A construction industry general contractor had agreed with the Carpenters' Union that no union carpenter "will handle ... any doors ... which have been fitted prior to being furnished on the job...." This was an attempt by the union to ensure that doors would be fabricated by its members on jobsite and would not be purchased prefabricated from a factory. When the contractor brought factory prefabricated doors onto the jobsite, the union refused to install them. The contractor argued that the clause in the agreement violated § 8(e) and that the refusal to handle the doors violated § 8(b)(4)(B). A bare majority of the Supreme Court disagreed.

The Court examined Allen Bradley Co. v. Local 3, IBEW (U.S.1945), a celebrated labor antitrust case involving an extensive network of product boycotts designed to monopolize electrical contracting and manufacturing for unionized New York City employers. This antitrust case was decided before the NLRA's secondary boycott provisions were enacted and it played a major role in the 1947 debates leading up to the passage of § 8(b)(4). The

National Woodwork Court proceeded to distinguish *Allen Bradley:* "The boycott in *Allen Bradley* was carried on, not as a shield to preserve the jobs of [the union's] members, traditionally a primary labor activity, but as a sword, to reach out and monopolize all the manufacturing job tasks for [the union's] members." According to the Court, a union violates neither § 8(b)(4)(B) nor § 8(e) when it bargains or strikes to retain work traditionally performed by its members for the employer.

This is "work preservation," and although it prevents the primary employer from doing business with potential providers of prefabricated goods or other services, it does not have the secondary intent necessary to make out a violation of § 8(b)(4)(B) or § 8(e). Whether employees will continue to perform the work they have traditionally done is a matter of considerable economic significance to the union members, as it is for the employer. The Court was not prepared to believe that Congress intended to call union efforts in these matters "secondary" without a more explicit showing of congressional effort.

The test for § 8(b)(4)(B) and § 8(e) liability announced in *National Woodwork* was "whether, under all the surrounding circumstances, the union's objective was preservation of work for [the contractor's] employees, or whether the agreements and boycott were tactically calculated to satisfy union objectives elsewhere." As cases arise the Board and the courts are to determine factually whether the union's interest is in the labor relations of the factory or other supplier, or in the labor relations of the employer with whom it has an agreement or for whom it is refusing to handle goods. Four members of the Court dissented.

In a companion case, Houston Insulation Contractors Ass'n v. NLRB (U.S.1967), the Court held that there was no § 8(b)(4)(B) violation where employees represented by one local union refused to handle goods in order to preserve traditional work for other employees of the same employer and represented by a sister local union. The fact that all the workers were employed by the primary employer rendered the work preservation attempt primary.

Most cases after *National Woodwork* have held that a union's attempt to acquire work for employees whom it represents, but which they have not previously performed, is unlawful on the "sword and shield" analogy. However, in Meat Drivers Local 710 v. NLRB (D.C.Cir.1964), the circuit court held that a union could seek to "recapture" work it had lost some time before as long as the work fell within the bargaining unit and was "fairly claimable." Satisfying that standard showed the effort was primary and not secondary. This view of work preservation, however, appears to have been undercut by Supreme Court dictum in NLRB v. Enterprise Ass'n of Pipefitters (U.S.1977), where a majority of the Court suggested that work preservation would not be a defense where the union's object was "not to preserve, but to aggrandize, its own position and that of its members. Such activity is squarely within the statute." Why this should be true is not apparent. The effect on the secondary employer is likely to be the same whether the union's effort to exclude its products is a part of a work preservation effort or a part of a work acquisition effort. The effect on the primary employer is also the same. One would, therefore, suppose that secondary boycott liability turns on the question of the union's tactical objective. A work preservation effort is primary because the union's objective is to improve the economic well-being of its members with respect to their work for the primary employer. Why should the union's efforts go from primary to secondary just because it seeks to expand its work for the primary employer rather than holding on to the work it has?

Defining the work in controversy was at issue in NLRB v. International Longshoremen's Assn. (U.S.1980). The union had loaded and unloaded cargo for ocean vessels on a piece-by-piece basis for many years. The union agreed to permit shipping companies to ship containers of cargo (some as large as $8 \times 8 \times 40$ feet). The companies agreed, in turn, that if the containers were themselves loaded or unloaded (stuffed or stripped) within fifty miles of port by anyone other than the beneficial owner of the cargo, only the union's members would do the work. Independent companies, who sought to stuff and strip containers with their own employees, challenged the agreement between the union and the shipping companies as a violation of § 8(e). The independents argued that the union was not preserving traditional bargaining unit work, but was seeking to do work that was now being done by independents. The Board agreed; but the Supreme Court reversed the Board, holding that this description of the work was incorrect as a matter of law. The Board "must focus on the work of the bargaining unit employees, not on the work of other employees who may be doing the same or similar work...." Had the ruling been otherwise, the Court reasoned, *National Woodwork* would have been incorrectly decided because the Carpenters Union would have been acquiring work: the factory prefabrication of doors away from the construction site.

Work preservation efforts in the construction industry were dealt a substantial blow in *Enterprise Ass'n*. In that case a construction industry subcontractor had signed a bargaining agreement with the union representing its employees that promised, in effect, that the company would not bid on any construction industry contract if its specifications would require company employees to install prefabricated air conditioning components. After signing the bargaining agreement, the subcontractor bid on a job that specified that its employees would install factory prefabricated air-conditioning units. When the units arrived at the jobsite, the subcontractor's employees refused to install them. The subcontractor filed an unfair labor practice charge that the refusal violated

§ 8(b)(4)(B). The bargaining agreement clause itself was apparently not challenged and the NLRB decision referred to it as a valid provision, probably because the union had fabricated these air-conditioning units on area jobsites in the past and the clause itself was seen as an attempt to preserve bargaining unit work.

The NLRB adhered to a longstanding position that a strike in these circumstances violates § 8(b)(4)(B) because control over whether factory units would be brought for jobsite installation is vested in the general contractor (who drew up the specifications), and not in the subcontractor. This "right to control" is enough, in the NLRB's view, to render secondary a union's strike, or refusal to handle, directed at the subcontractor. The Court of Appeals reversed, taking the view that the refusal to handle the prefabricated units was not a violation of § 8(b)(4)(B), but was an attempt by the union to require the subcontractor to comply with a valid work preservation agreement.

The Supreme Court upheld the Board 5 to 4. The Court held that the circuit court's theory was inconsistent with United Bhd. of Carpenters, Local 1976 v. NLRB [Sand Door] (U.S.1958), which held that a bargaining agreement clause was no defense to a § 8(b)(4)(B) charge against self-help enforcement by the union.

The dissenting Justices viewed the subcontractor as the primary employer in this dispute and relied on several facts supporting this conclusion. The benefits sought to be achieved by the refusal to handle would go to the subcontractor's employees. The economic pressure brought by the union was directed at the subcontractor and the collective bargaining agreement clause was with the subcontractor. Furthermore, the subcontractor had breached that bargaining agreement clause.

The majority opinion found that the subcontractor was a secondary employer because the union's tactical objective had to be the general contractor: the benefits to bargaining unit employees could be secured only through the action of the general contractor because it alone had the right to control the decision to import prefabricated goods. The majority described the effect on a secondary employer in a true work preservation case as "incidental" to the primary, work preservation effort. In this case, however, the majority appeared to construe the union's effort as work acquisition, not work preservation: "Here ... the union sought to acquire work that it never had and that its employer had not power to give it, namely, the piping work on units specified by any contractor or developer who prefers and uses prepiped units.... [The] union's tactical objects necessarily included influencing [the general contractor]...."

The majority opinion relied on NLRB v. Denver Bldg. and Const. Trades Council (U.S.1951), for the proposition that the union's action is secondary so long as one of the union's objective was to influence a secondary employer, a proposition most thought overruled *sub silentio* by the Court's decision in Local 761, International Union of Electrical Workers v. NLRB [General Electric Co.] (U.S.1961).

National Woodwork's work preservation defense may no longer be of great relevance in the construction industry because if either the owners of buildings or their architects specify cost-cutting prefabricated materials a union cannot strike for its work preservation objective. This result is troubling. It is not clear that there is any primary employer in a "right to control" situation. The Supreme Court has ruled that the subcontractor is secondary and it seems unlikely that the Court would be willing to say that the general contractor, or the owner, neither of whom will employ the union's members in a typical case, is a primary employer and therefore a lawful target of union pressure. To picket one employer with an object of securing benefits for the employees of a second employer would seem to be secondary activity. This means that because of the splitting of ownership in the construction industry, first held dispositive in NLRB v. Denver Bldg. and Const. Trades Council (U.S.1951), the union is now foreclosed from picketing anyone to maintain its bargaining unit work.

One possibility remains open, however. The union might secure a clause from a subcontractor such as that negotiated in *Enterprise Ass'n* but then attempt to enforce it in a "right to control" situation by a damage action, rather than a refusal to handle goods. Court (or arbitration) enforcement of a valid clause in secondary circumstances points up a difficult technical issue with respect to the relationship of § 8(b)(4)(B) and § 8(e). The Court in *National Woodwork* said that a collective bargaining agreement clause is to be examined for § 8(e) validity at the time the clause is entered into. This is consistent with the language of § 8(e), which makes it an unfair labor practice "to enter into any contract or agreement" which is prohibited by the section.

But a contract provision can be valid in the sense that it has as its purpose work preservation, yet be applied in circumstances where coercive pressure would be secondary. Examples are a work preservation clause enforced in a "right to control" circumstance, a work preservation clause enforced selectively to permit prefabricated goods carrying a union's label to come on jobsites but keeping out nonunion goods, and a "union standards" subcontracting clause selectively enforced so as to convert it into a "union signatory" subcontracting clause.

One might consider seeking damages to be "coercion" within the meaning of § 8(b)(4)(B), thus enabling a court or the Board to consider the context in which the clause is enforced. But up until now the Board and the courts have held that court enforcement of a bargaining agreement is not "coercion" under that section. California Dump

Truck Owners Ass'n (NLRB 1976); Hughes Markets, Inc. (NLRB 1975); Local 49, Sheet Metal Workers (Los Alamos Constructors, Inc.) (NLRB 1975) (liquidated damages). As we have seen, a damage suit to enforce a "hot cargo" clause permitted under the construction industry proviso to § 8(e) does not violate § 8(b)(4)(B), even though striking or picketing to enforce the clause would. Court enforcement cannot violate § 8(b)(4)(B) or the construction industry proviso would be rendered a nullity. The only technical reading of the Act that permits a construction industry clause to be judicially enforced is that such enforcement of a bargaining agreement is not "coercion." It seems too great a gloss on the language of § 8(b)(4)(B) to define "coercion" to include court damage actions when a non-construction industry clause is enforced in secondary circumstances, but not to include court damage actions if the clause is excepted from § 8(e).

An alternative is to dismiss *National Woodwork*'s dictum that a clause may only be scrutinized on its face and when it is entered into, and instead, to test the validity of a clause both on its face and as applied. A clause valid on its face but not as applied could still be preserved for all other applications of the clause. That is, a clause found to be secondary in a particular operation would still remain part of the contract for nonsecondary contexts.

G. Jurisdictional Disputes Between Unions

A jurisdictional dispute is a controversy between two unions (or two groups of employees, either or both of whom may be unrepresented) over which union's members shall do certain job tasks for an employer. (In a representational dispute, it is known which employees will do the work, but it is disputed which union will represent the employees.) In 1947, Congress enacted § 8(b)(4)(D) to prevent strikes over these disputes. While a jurisdictional strike may be more or less disruptive than any other strike, one aspect of a jurisdictional strike makes it virtually intolerable. An employer subject to a jurisdictional strike may have no way of extricating itself. Giving the work to either of the two contending groups of employees will simply precipitate a strike by the other group. Congress thought that jurisdictional strikes should be controlled but also felt that a simple ban against these strikes would leave disputes festering and so it made special provisions in the statute for the resolution of jurisdictional disputes.

Section 8(b)(4)(D) makes it an unfair labor practice for a union to induce a strike or a concerted refusal to handle goods in order to compel an employer to assign particular work to employees represented by one union rather than to employees represented by another union. (In this, as in the rest of the discussion of jurisdictional disputes, one or both of the disputing groups of employees may be unrepresented.)

The procedure for NLRB handling of a jurisdictional dispute is as follows. Either an employer or a competing union files an unfair labor practice charge with the NLRB's regional director if a union strikes or threatens to strike to secure work. This is the § 8(b)(4)(D) allegation. The regional director will then issue a complaint and immediately seek a federal district court injunction against the strike pursuant to § 10(l) of the NLRA. Just as with secondary boycotts, the test for an injunction will be whether the regional director has reasonable cause to believe that a violation has occurred—a very low standard. A field examiner from the NLRB's regional office will then preside over a hearing provided for in § 10(k) of the NLRA. This is a special hearing for § 8(b)(4)(D) cases. The field examiner is an employee of the regional office and is empowered only to collect evidence with respect to the jurisdictional dispute. She does not render a recommended decision and she makes no factual or credibility determinations. The purpose of this hearing is to determine which of the two contending employee groups has the better claim to the work. The striking union can contend on the merits of the work assignment or it may argue that the dispute is not truly a jurisdictional dispute at all. At the end of the hearing, the field examiner sends the record to the NLRB in Washington.

Once the record of the § 10(k) hearing reaches Washington, the Board will render a § 10(k) opinion. The Board will decide whether there is reasonable cause to believe that the dispute in this case is a jurisdictional dispute. If it finds there is not, it will dismiss the charge. If the Board finds reasonable cause to believe the dispute is jurisdictional, it will then write an opinion considering the various factors supporting an assignment of the work to one union or to the other and issue an award declaring which union has the greater entitlement to the work.

After the Board issues the § 10(k) award, the regional office will contact the losing union and ask for a commitment that it will not continue to seek the work by prohibited means. If the union agrees, the case is ended. But if the union refuses to accede to the Board's award, the § 8(b)(4)(D) complaint will be further processed. Since the evidence on whether the dispute is jurisdictional has already been collected in the § 10(k) hearing, any § 8(b)(4)(D) hearing before an administrative law judge is likely to be a summary affair and the Board may issue a summary judgment at this point. When the case returns to the Board after the § 8(b)(4)(D) hearing, the Board will not relitigate the merits of the § 10(k) award, and is likely to defer to its original finding that the dispute was jurisdictional. A cease and desist order will then issue against the losing union ordering that union not to engage in prohibited conduct to gain the disputed work.

The employer is not bound to follow a § 10(k) award. The award does not declare that the union

the Board has found to have the greater entitlement to the work will actually be assigned the
work; its only effect is that the losing union will
not be able to strike for the work without violating
§ 8(b)(4)(D). If the employer refuses to assign the
work to the union the Board has favored by the
§ 10(k) award, that union will then be able to
strike or take other coercive action without violating § 8(b)(4)(D).

The Board has always been reluctant to make
§ 10(k) awards on the merits. For many years
after the passage of this section the Board awarded
the work in a § 10(k) hearing to the striking union
(the union without the employer's assignment of
the work) only if that union was deemed to have a
right to the work under an outstanding Board
order or certification, or in a collective bargaining
agreement with the employer. In NLRB v. Radio
& Television Broadcast Engineers, Local 1212
[CBS] (U.S.1961), the Court held that the Board
had viewed its role too narrowly and that it had
the statutory duty to decide in § 10(k) proceedings
which union had the better claim to the work.
The Court rejected arguments that the Board
lacked the expertise to make such economic determinations and that a § 10(k) award on the merits
would cause an employer to discriminate against
members of the losing union in violation of
§ 8(a)(3) and § 8(b)(2) of the NLRA. The Court
finessed the second argument by simply stating
that it felt "entirely confident that the Board, with
its many years of experience ..., would devise

means of discharging its duties under § 10(k) in a manner entirely harmonious with those sections."

It is not clear that the Board has heeded the order to decide § 10(k) awards on the merits. In the decade after the CBS decision, the Board affirmed the employer's preference for awarding the work in 95.1 percent of all § 10(k) cases and in 96.5 percent of the awards involving the construction industry. So, although the Board purports to consider many factors in reaching its § 10(k) awards, the employer's preference is almost always determinative. This can be explained either on the ground that an employer operating in its own economic self-interest will consider the same factors as the Board does in its § 10(k) awards, or on the ground that the number of jurisdictional strikes will be reduced if the unions to which the employer are adverse are precluded from striking. Of course, the latter ground is not consistent with *CBS* or with any explicit statutory policy.

Although defining "jurisdictional dispute" has not been a particularly difficult problem for the Board and the courts, the content of the term is not intuitively obvious. Consider the facts in National Woodwork Manufacturers Ass'n v. NLRB (U.S.1967). There the Carpenters Union struck in order to preserve its jobsite work of manufacturing wooden doors, and refused to handle wooden doors that had been prefabricated by the factory. Why was this not a jurisdictional dispute between jobsite carpenters and factory employees many miles away? The answer is not clear, although it is certain that the Board would not consider this a jurisdictional dispute. It might be that the intent of the union controls. Thus in *National Woodwork* the Carpenters Union was not looking outward, so to speak, to see whether its historical claim for the work was better than the historical claim of factory workers. Its claim was grounded in its jobsite economic interest in doing the work it had always done.

On only a few occasions the Board has held that work preservation is a defense to a jurisdictional dispute charge. In Local 8, ILWU (Waterway Terminal Co.) (NLRB 1970), the employer terminated a subcontract and assigned previously subcontracted work to its own employees. The union representing the subcontractor's employees picketed the employer that controlled the work and that employer filed a jurisdictional dispute charge. The Board held that this was not a jurisdictional dispute between the two sets of employees but was rather a protest of a loss of work by the subcontractor's employees. The controlling issue, in the Board's view, was the union's intent in picketing; since the impetus for the union's demand was restoration of the "job rights of terminated employees," the strike was not to be considered a jurisdictional dispute even though the Board conceded that another union was actively competing for the work. On appeal, the circuit court reversed, holding that a jurisdictional dispute was present (9th Cir.1972).

The Board never finds work preservation to be a defense to a jurisdictional dispute charge between two unions on a construction industry jobsite. Suppose that carpenters have always done a certain kind of work on local construction sites but that the general contractor on a particular site has subcontracted this work to a subcontractor regularly using members of the Sheet Metal Workers Union. Certainly a strike by the Carpenters Union to get the work would raise secondary boycott/right to control problems. But leaving that aside, the Carpenters Union would like to argue that its strike is not a jurisdictional dispute because it has no concern with conflicting historical demands of the two unions, it is only trying to preserve traditional work. The NLRB would find a jurisdictional dispute. Another peculiarity about this situation is that it is as much a dispute between subcontractors as between their workers: both the employer hiring carpenters and the employer hiring sheet metal workers would like to have this work.

Even more important, the decision of which of the three employers (the two subcontractors and the general contractor) will be deemed the "assigning employer" for § 10(k) purposes will determine the § 10(k) award. If the sheet metal workers' employer is deemed the assigning employer, then virtually all of the Board's traditional factors will stack up in favor of members of the Sheet Metal Workers Union. Its job assignments will traditionally have gone to them and a collective bargaining agreement with that union is likely to guarantee them the work. Moreover, if under pressure the firm gave the job task at issue to the carpenters, it would have to hire a carpenter for what might be only a very small portion of the firm's jobsite work, causing inefficiency. If the carpentry subcontractor were the assigning employer, the factors would line up just as solidly in favor of members of the Carpenters Union. If the Board were to regard the general contractor as the assigning employer, it would allow a more economically realistic appraisal of the factors. The general contractor actually controls which subcontractor will do the work on this jobsite. Yet once the subcontract is let, the NLRB invariably holds that the subcontractor who has received the work from the general contractor becomes the assigning employer for § 10(k) purposes.

Sections 8(b)(4)(D) and 10(k) provide that if the jurisdictional dispute can be privately resolved by the parties, then the NLRB should stay its hand. With this in mind, the AFL–CIO established a private arbitration panel to resolve jurisdictional disputes between affiliated unions. Suppose two unions to a jurisdictional dispute reach a voluntary resolution and inform the employer which one of them should get the work. Is the jurisdictional dispute settled or does the fact that the employer did not participate in this "voluntary adjustment" make it less than an adjustment under § 10(k)? In NLRB v. Plasterers' Local 79 (U.S.1971), the Supreme Court held that the employer is one of the "parties to the dispute" under § 10(k) and that the employer's stipulation to the union's settlement mechanism is a prerequisite for Board deferral. There is no doubt that the employer has a substantial economic interest in which employee group will ultimately do the work in question. Yet it is not clear that § 8(b)(4)(D) and § 10(k) were enacted with this economic interest in mind. Arguably Congress was only interested in removing the employer from the dilemma of being caught between two disputing factions, each of whom will strike if the employer gives the work to the other. There is no indication in the statute or in its procedures that Congress also had in mind protecting the employer's economic interest in who should get the work. Nor does a voluntary adjustment necessarily preclude the employer from protecting his economic interest: he is not required to assign the work to the union that prevailed in the voluntary adjustment. The Supreme Court ignored these considerations in *Plasterers' Local 79.*

If one of the unions in a jurisdictional dispute effectively disclaims a desire for the work, the Board stops the § 10(k) and § 8(b)(4)(D) proceedings because the only remaining dispute is between the employer and the claiming union. *Local 107 Highway Truck Drivers (Safeway Stores, Inc.)* (NLRB 1964). Exceptions to the doctrine have all but destroyed it. For example, where the union disclaims the work but the employees it represents do the work at the employer's request (perhaps as required by a collective bargaining agreement), the

Board will entertain § 8(b)(4)(D) charges and proceed to a § 10(k) hearing. In one case the members of one of the two unions disclaimed the work and refused an employer's order to perform it. The Board found that the disclaimer was not controlling because the disclaiming employees were compensated on a monthly salary basis and would suffer no pay loss by disclaiming this work. Nor was their refusal to do the work when ordered to by their employer significant, for the Board found that "they cannot lawfully refuse because to do so would involve a breach of their collective bargaining contract and possibly infringement of applicable maritime law." Local 1291, ILA (Pocahontas Steamship Co.) (NLRB 1965). The case is best seen as an example of the Board reaching out to declare a strike to be a jurisdictional dispute in order to enjoin it and restore "industrial peace."

In a later case, the Board breathed some life back into the disclaimer doctrine. In Teamsters Local 85 (United California Express & Storage Co.) (NLRB 1978), a divided Board held that a union's disclaimer was not invalidated by its members' continued claim to the work. Prior cases were distinguished on the ground that union officers had condoned or given affirmative support to the members' claim even while officially disclaiming the work on the union's behalf.

Assume that a union has been guaranteed certain job tasks in a collective bargaining agreement and that the employer breaches the agreement by assigning those tasks to members of another union in a different bargaining unit. The Board will find a jurisdictional dispute if the union strikes for the work, so the union might instead sue the employer for breach of contract damages. The Board has held that if the union seeks damages, while refraining from self-help, there has been no prohibited conduct. Local 49, Sheet Metal Workers (Los Alamos Constructors, Inc.) (NLRB 1973); but see Associated General Contractors of California, Inc. v. NLRB (9th Cir.1975). However, in this situation the union receiving the employer's work assignment may threaten to strike if the work is taken away from its members. The Board then pulls both unions into a § 10(k) hearing and is likely to affirm the employer's preference, thus creating an incentive for the employer and the preferred union to manufacture a convenient strike threat. Should this now preclude the losing union's breach of bargaining agreement claim?

In Carey v. Westinghouse Electric Corp. (U.S.1964), the union and the employer had agreed to arbitrate all breach of contract disputes. The Court held that the agreement to arbitrate should be enforced even though the breach of contract issue raised by the union arguably involved either a jurisdictional or a representational dispute with another union subject to NLRB procedures. In stating its reasons why the breach of contract claim could go forward, the Court said: "should the Board disagree with the arbiter, by ruling, for example, that the employees involved in the controversy are members of one bargaining unit or another, the Board's ruling would, of course, take precedence; and if the employer's action had been in accord with that ruling, it would not be liable for damages. . . ."

Lower courts have construed the dictum in *Carey* to require that a collective bargaining agreement arbitration award cannot be enforced where the Board has ruled contrary to the arbitration award in a § 10(k) hearing. Is this the better result? It is likely that the bargaining agreement assignment of the work to the union was the product of trading and that the employer gained some economic benefit in return for this guarantee. Even though the union is now foreclosed from actually receiving the work, it is not clear that the union should also be foreclosed from compensation for the loss of the economic benefit. Restitution, as well as expectation, might support a damage award. The contrary argument is that the possibility of damages will cause the employer to give the union the work rather than responding in damages and will thus exacerbate the jurisdictional dispute.

H. Damages for § 8(b)(4) Violations

Section 303 of the LMRA provides a damage remedy in federal district court for violations of § 8(b)(4). Either a primary or secondary employer may sue. Neither punitive damages nor an injunction are obtainable in a § 303 suit. State remedies for secondary boycotts are preempted by § 303, although state claims for violence remain and a federal court may take pendent jurisdiction over such a claim. Teamsters Local 20 v. Morton (U.S.1964).

Section 303 suits and § 8(b)(4) proceedings are deemed independent. Thus a § 303 suit may be brought before, during or after Board unfair labor practice proceedings. Where the NLRB rules on a § 8(b)(4) complaint before a § 303 judgment is entered, the majority of cases have held that the Board decision is res judicata in the § 303 action, but a § 303 judgment is not binding on the NLRB. Arguably, if a § 10(*l*) injunction effectively moots a dispute giving rise to a § 8(b)(4) complaint, the Board should not decide the merits of the § 8(b)(4) complaint unless the dispute is likely to recur. Since the Board, by hypothesis, is not deciding a current dispute between the parties, its only effect will be to bind the later district court. The employer, who will have expended no funds in having the unfair labor practice complaint litigated before the Board, will have no interest in having the case come to an end, but the union will have to litigate it fully for fear of later preclusive effect in the § 303 action.

I. Featherbedding

Section 8(b)(6) of the NLRA makes it an unfair labor practice for a union "to cause or attempt to cause an employer to pay or deliver or agree to pay or deliver any money or other thing of value, in the nature of an extraction, for services which are not performed or are not to be performed." This section does not forbid a union's demand that the employer pay for work that the employer does not want, it only forbids a demand that the employer pay for work not actually performed. A broader statutory prohibition would preclude unions from bargaining over work preservation and job manning.

In American Newspaper Publishers Ass'n v. NLRB (U.S.1953), the Court held that § 8(b)(6) was not violated when a union demanded pay for employees setting "bogus" printing type—type that was to be set and then discarded because new production methods had obviated the need for it. In NLRB v. Gamble Enterprises (U.S.1953), no violation was found when the musicians' union would not permit its members to play in traveling bands for an employer who refused also to hire a local band to play during intermissions, although the employer wanted no band to play during intermissions.

CHAPTER VII

THE DUTY TO BARGAIN

A. Good Faith Bargaining

Sections 8(a)(5) and 8(b)(3) of the NLRA require bargaining in good faith by every employer and union party to a representation relationship. The contours of the duty are described in § 8(d) of the NLRA. The concept of good faith bargaining has been controversial. Some have argued that the term is meaningless or, at least, is unenforceable because, stripped to its essentials, it is a legislative requirement that parties subject to the duty maintain a certain frame of mind. Others have construed the duty to mean that it sends union and employer negotiators into the bargaining room and closes the door, but it does not examine what happens inside the room.

The option apparently adopted in the NLRA construes good faith bargaining as the obligation to meet and discuss terms with an open mind but without being required to come to an agreement. The difficulty of giving meaning to the concept is compounded because negotiations seldom take place in a vacuum. Economic weapons may be used before, during, or after good faith bargaining, or they may be used to frustrate bargaining. Deciding whether an action by an employer or a union is a lawful use of an economic weapon or an unlawful refusal to bargain in good faith is a recurring problem.

The Supreme Court has interpreted the duty to bargain in a series of cases, rather than in a single landmark decision. An early case was NLRB v. American Nat. Ins. Co. (U.S.1952) where a newly-certified union seeking its first collective bargaining agreement with this employer submitted a proposed contract covering wages, hours and other terms and conditions of employment and including a clause establishing binding grievance arbitration during the life of the contract. The employer bargained for a time and agreed to a few of the union's proposals but met the bulk of the union's demands with a counterproposal for an extremely broad "management functions" clause. The clause stated that management had the sole right to hire and promote employees, to discharge and discipline for cause, and to maintain at its discretion most other terms of employment. The clause provided that machinery would be set up to handle union and employee grievances but vested final dispute resolution not in arbitration but in review by a top management official.

The NLRB found that the employer's insistence on this clause was a per se violation of § 8(a)(5) because, at the very least, the NLRA requires an employer to agree to fix in a collective bargaining agreement minimum standards for work schedules and other terms and conditions of employment during the life of the agreement. In this case management had offered no fixed standards but had demanded a clause giving it complete flexibility over the life of the contract. According to the Board, the clause could be requested by the employer but insistence upon it constituted a refusal to bargain.

The Supreme Court reversed. The Court emphasized that the NLRA is designed to promote collective bargaining without regulating the content of agreements or even compelling agreement itself. From this premise, it followed that the NLRB could not "either directly or indirectly, compel concessions or otherwise sit in judgement upon the substantive terms of collective bargaining agreements." There was nothing wrong with the employer stating its position directly. The error of the Board's decision was that it apparently condemned all management function clauses. Management function clauses have a permissible place in collective bargaining agreements and the duty to bargain issue is to be decided by the Board on the facts of each case, not by developing per se rules.

One view of the duty to bargain in good faith is that it implies a decision by Congress to take away management control over wages, hours and working conditions. Thus any employer who insists upon unilateral control over a condition of employment violates § 8(a)(5). *American National* rejects this view. An alternative meaning of the good faith bargaining duty is that it is satisfied by employer proposals fixing an employment term in the collective bargaining agreement, fixing it by joint employer and union action during the agreement, or leaving it to management discretion during the agreement. So long as the employer negotiates in good faith over these alternatives, insistence upon management discretion would not violate § 8(a)(5). If the employer insists on leaving every term to management discretion during the bargaining agreement and demands a clause to this effect, does *American National* stand for the proposition that the employer commits no unfair labor practice? Lower courts have not read *AmericanNational* so broadly and have looked at the complete history of bargaining in a particular case to determine whether the employer has met his obligation. A refusal to find any common ground with union proposals, together with an insistence on management discretion over every term and condition, may well lead the NLRB and a reviewing court to find a § 8(a)(5) violation. NLRB v. Reed & Prince Mfg. Co. (1st Cir.1953). *American National* might be distinguished because there the employer had engaged in some bargaining and its clause was in response to a union demand for grievance arbitration.

The relationship between good faith bargaining and the use of economic weapons was examined by the Court in NLRB v. Insurance Agents' Intern. Union (U.S.1960). During negotiations for a bargaining agreement, a union of insurance company district agents brought economic pressure against the insurance company by refusing to solicit new business or to follow reporting procedures, and by arriving late to work and refusing to attend business conferences. The union also picketed various company offices. The NLRB found that the union had a sincere desire to reach an agreement, but that its tactics constituted a refusal to bargain in good faith in violation of § 8(b)(3).

The Supreme Court disagreed. According to the Court, the NLRB had intruded into the substantive aspects of collective bargaining when it attempted to regulate the use of economic weapons. The Court found a dual congressional policy of government abstention from control over the terms reached in collective bargaining, and of government abstention from regulation of economic weapons. If the Board could regulate the choice of economic weapons, it could also dictate in large measure the terms of collective bargaining agreements.

The Board's theory in *Insurance Agents* was that use of a particular economic weapon during collective bargaining may so interfere with the bargaining process as to warrant finding a refusal to bargain in good faith even though the weapon is used to force a bargaining agreement on favorable terms. The Court's rejection of the argument in that case does not completely dispose of the issue. For example, in NLRB v. Truitt Mfg. Co.

(U.S.1956), the union's request for a 10 cents an hour wage increase met with an employer response that it could not afford to pay such an increase because it would put the firm out of business. The union demanded that the company produce documents supporting its claim of inability to pay but the employer refused.

The Supreme Court upheld an NLRB finding of a § 8(a)(5) violation and ordered the information supplied. The Court noted that there was no contention that the union's disclosure request was too broad, or that production of documents supporting the employer's claim would be an undue burden on the company. The information was highly relevant and once the employer put its inability to pay on the table, it was within the Board's power to find upon all the circumstances that the refusal to substantiate was evidence of bad faith bargaining.

The case should probably not be seen as Supreme Court condemnation of an economic weapon, but as the condemnation of a procedural device that so impedes collective bargaining as to render it less than an acceptable procedure for reaching agreement. While the Truitt Company desired to reach agreement on its terms, the claim of an inability to pay, if believed, may have an overwhelming impact on bargaining. What group of employees will hold out for wage increases if they believe an employer's claim that success will only deprive them of their jobs and their employer of its business? A union cannot judge the accuracy of the employer's claim without access to the information supporting it. The careful management lawyer counsels her client how best to phrase what is said in negotiations so as to avoid the *Truitt* case.

A similar theory was used by the Supreme Court in NLRB v. ACME Industrial Co. (U.S.1967), where it upheld a Board requirement that employers disclose wage data and other information necessary to permit the union to administer a collective bargaining agreement. With respect to these demands for information, no employer statement was necessary to trigger the duty to disclose. Such a holding is not surprising because, perhaps more obviously than in *Truitt,* a union cannot formulate its bargaining demands if it cannot determine present rates of pay. A union may not be able to gather such information from its membership if the bargaining unit is large.

The duty to provide the union with information relevant to collective bargaining is not unlimited, however. In Detroit Edison Co. v. NLRB (U.S.1979) the Court held that an employer need not turn over to the union a test battery and answer sheets that the company used for hiring and promotions. The company's concern for test secrecy prevailed in the Supreme Court, although it had not before the Board. The Court also held that individual test scores did not have to be divulged by the company in the absence of consent by the employee involved. The employee's privacy interest was paramount.

Other union requests for information continue to be controversial. For example, employers may be reluctant to divulge information that would assist the union in winning an arbitration award; that might support a suit against the employer alleging a violation of prohibitions against racial and sexual discrimination in employment; or that would interfere with the employer's ability to manage his work force.

In *Truitt* there was a violation of the duty to bargain even though the employer had a subjective desire to reach an agreement. Another instance of a statutory refusal to bargain even though the employer seeks to reach a bargaining agreement is where it institutes a change with respect to a term of employment without first bargaining collectively with the union representing his employees. NLRB v. Katz (U.S.1962).

In *Katz,* collective bargaining was underway when the employer made unilateral changes (changes neither agreed to by the union nor with respect to which impasse had been reached). The employer changed its sick leave policy and it was not clear whether the overall effect of the change was beneficial or harmful to bargaining unit employees. The Court condemned the change because some employees would see it as an improvement, others as a reduction in benefits, and this would undermine the union's ability to negotiate with respect to the change at the bargaining table. The employer also unilaterally increased wages. Although the parties were currently bargaining over wages, the wage system instituted unilaterally was more generous than that which had been offered to the union and rejected by it. In the Court's view, these facts were sufficient evidence of employer bad faith and justified finding a § 8(a)(5) violation. "[Even] after an impasse is reached [the employer] has no license to grant wage increases greater than he has ever offered the union at the bargaining table, for such action is necessarily inconsistent with a sincere desire to conclude an agreement with the union." The employer is permitted, after notice and consultation with the union, to institute a wage increase identical to one that the union has rejected as too low even though the employer does not have the agreement of the union.

The Court reaffirmed that the NLRB is not to pass judgment on the legitimacy of economic weapons, but it held that the facts in *Katz* showed more than an employer's resort to economic warfare: "[The] Board *is* authorized to order the cessation of behavior which is in effect a refusal to negotiate, or which directly obstructs or inhibits the actual process of discussion or which reflects a cast of mind against reaching agreement."

Thus both unilateral increases and unilateral decreases in employment terms violate § 8(a)(5). Employers contend that this puts them in a particularly difficult situation when, for example, they have granted wage increases every year on July 1st and this year finds them engaged in collective bargaining with the union on that date. To suspend the regular wage increase might be considered a unilateral change; but to the extent that the wage increases are discretionary in amount, granting the increases risks possible NLRA liability. It appears that an employer's best course is to grant wage increases if they are automatic but suspend them, pending bargaining, to the extent that they are discretionary in timing or amount. Some language in *Katz* supports this advice.

Once the bargaining agreement between the employer and the union has expired, there is no contractual commitment to maintain employment conditions. But the holding in *Katz* requires bargaining to impasse before changing employment terms. The Board has not held that every term of an expired collective bargaining agreement must be continued during bargaining, however. Employers have been permitted unilaterally to discontinue union-shop and check-off provisions, but have not been allowed to suspend superseniority for union officials or grievance procedures. NLRB v. Cone Mills Corp. (4th Cir.1967); Marine & Shipbuilding Workers v. NLRB (3d Cir.1963); Hilton–Davis Chemical Co. (NLRB 1970).

One bargaining tactic occupying many pages in NLRB and court of appeals reporters is the General Electric Company's tactic known as "boulwareism." General Electric Co. v. NLRB (2d Cir.1969). Reduced to its essentials, this bargaining tactic consists of the following elements. The company begins by soliciting input from its low-level supervisors regarding the desires of the work force, and the type and level of benefits that employees expect. These inputs are researched with respect to costs and other management values and a company proposal is formulated consisting of an entire package of bargaining agreement terms. This proposal is then released to the public in a major publicity campaign designed to convince the public in general, and General Electric employees in particular, of the wisdom and fairness of the proposal. At collective bargaining, the company puts its entire package on the table immediately and adopts a "firm, fair offer" position—that the company is not prepared to move from its proposal unless the union can show some error in the underlying data supporting the package.

Critics have attacked boulwareism on several grounds. It has been condemned because the company's public posture "paints itself into a corner" with respect to all bargainable matters, and the company comes to the table with a closed mind. It is also seen as bypassing the union to deal directly with the employees. And the company's better access to the data underlying its package makes the union a second-class participant in negotiations.

Those who would find boulwareism lawful have argued that it is no more than an innovation in collective bargaining: a refusal to engage in the ritual of beginning with a low (unacceptable) proposal and gradually bargaining until, at the final hour, a realistic proposal is made. The employer's publicity campaign is a permissible economic weapon, and arguably falls within § 8(c)'s guarantee of free speech. Section 8(d) of the NLRA states that the Board may not require concessions to be made in bargaining and this is deemed to protect the "firm, fair offer" approach of boulwareism.

While the General Electric Company no longer engages in boulwareism, consideration of boulwareism is useful because it requires one to examine the theories underlying the concept of good faith bargaining. It is difficult to say that any single element of the boulwareism tactic is or should be unlawful. Perhaps the most debated point is the "firm, fair offer" posture. A dissenting judge in the Second Circuit suggested that condemnation of boulwareism means that a union cannot demand that a new employer in the area sign the standard union collective bargaining agreement, and that this result would be unfortunate. Construction industry unions, for example, regularly take the position that they cannot permit a new employer in the area to obtain a bargaining agreement more favorable than the one negotiated with other area contractors, for that would give the new entrant an unfair competitive advantage. While many assume this tactic to be lawful, and it is supported by the unions' economic self-interests, others argue that it represents a closed mind in bargaining and thus violates § 8(b)(3).

B. Subjects of Bargaining

Absent a union, the implied terms of the unwritten employment contract between an employer and an employee give the employer absolute discretion over terms and conditions of employment. The firm may hire as it pleases and it may discharge for good cause, bad cause or no cause at all. This is the employment-at-will doctrine. While an increasing number of state court cases have protected some employees against discharge, these cases often arise in special circumstances, such as where the discharge offends some public policy. Under the employment-at-will doctrine, the employer's discretion extends (except as otherwise limited by law) to every matter that might affect an employee working for the firm.

Sections 8(a)(5) and 8(d) require the employer to bargain with his employees' union over "wages, hours, and other terms and conditions of employment...." Must the employer bargain with a union about every matter that might have an effect on its employees? That question was answered in the negative in the landmark case of NLRB v. Wooster Div. of Borg—Warner Corp. (U.S.1958). An employer refused to sign a collective bargaining agreement unless the agreement included a clause requiring a pre-strike secret vote of union and nonunion employees on the employer's last economic offer, and a recognition clause omitting as a party to the contract the international union that had been certified by the NLRB and substituting the international's uncertified local affiliate.

The NLRB held that for an employer to insist upon either of these clauses amounted to a refusal to bargain in violation of § 8(a)(5). The Supreme Court agreed; neither clause fell within the definition of a mandatory subject of bargaining under § 8(d), and thus an employer violates § 8(a)(5) by conditioning its assent to a bargaining agreement upon inclusion of either clause. The ballot clause was not mandatory because it concerned the relationship between a union and employees, and settled no term or condition of employment. (The Court did not see it as a form of no-strike clause.) It was also thought to be an interference with the union's right to represent the employees since it enabled the employer, in effect, to deal with employees rather than with the union. The recognition clause was not a mandatory subject since the NLRA required the company to bargain with the certified representative of its employees, a duty that the employer could not insist that the union relinquish.

Since it is most often unions that prefer to expand the scope of bargaining and thus limit management discretion, *Borg—Warner* confines the power of unions to expand subjects of bargaining. The case has been vigorously debated. The arguments in favor of its result are that it is required by the language of the statute (but statutory language is unclear) and that it makes agreements easier to reach by removing peripheral issues from bargaining. Further, it narrows the range of detrimental economic impact resulting from negotiations where either the employer or the union has overwhelming economic power.

Arguments against the *Borg—Warner* result are strong, however. It tends to drive bargaining topics underground at the expense of forthright discussion—a union whose proposal has been rejected as nonmandatory may thereafter take an intractable position on mandatory issues. Employers with sufficient economic power to resist a particular union demand may instead label it nonmandatory and thus needlessly invite NLRB litigation. The complaint has been made that the NLRB and the reviewing courts lack the expertise to characterize subjects as mandatory or nonmandatory since the agency and the courts are not staffed with people with sufficient practical experience in industrial relations. Nor, the argument goes, is the statute precise enough in its definition of mandatory subjects of bargaining to guide the Board and courts. The mandatory-nonmandatory dichotomy should be drawn differently depending upon the industry involved; and even with respect to a particular industry, the dichotomy should be flexible over time so as to reflect changes in matters of interest and importance to the parties. But because the NLRB is charged with the duty of declaring subjects mandatory or nonmandatory, the doctrine is not likely to be responsive to different conditions between industries, or within a particular industry over time.

The *Borg—Warner* decision is not sufficiently instructive on how the Board is to decide whether a particular bargaining demand is mandatory or nonmandatory. More guidance was given in the controversial case of Fibreboard Paper Products Corp. v. NLRB (U.S.1964). The issue there was whether the contracting out of part of the employer's work was a mandatory subject of bargaining. The facts were very appealing for finding the subject to be mandatory. The work that the employer sought to contract out without bargaining was maintenance work that had to be done in the employer's plant, and the employer was contracting it out in an attempt to save labor costs because the subcontractor's employees were paid less than bargaining unit employees. After the work was contracted out, the employer took the position that it had no further use for its maintenance employees and that negotiation of a new bargaining agreement for those employees would be pointless.

The Court relied on several factors to find the contracting out to be a mandatory subject of bargaining. First, it fell within the literal meaning of the phrase "terms and conditions of employment" in the statute. It was easy to reach that conclusion because the contracting out caused employee terminations. Second, declaring contracting out to be mandatory effectuated the purposes of the Act by "bringing a problem of vital concern to labor and management within the framework established by Congress [collective bargaining] as most conducive to industrial peace." Third, the Court looked to industrial practices of other employers and found that contracting out restrictions were common in many collective bargaining agreements. The Court was careful, however, to restrict its holding to contracting out that involves the replacement of employees in a bargaining unit with those of an independent contractor to do the same work under similar employment conditions, and the Court expressed an unwillingness to hold that the decision encompassed other forms of subcontracting.

Justice Stewart penned a concurrence which has proved to be more influential than the majority's opinion. Noting that many managerial decisions may affect the security of worker's jobs, the Justice stated that some decisions have only an indirect and uncertain impact upon job security. Citing examples of an investment in labor-saving machinery and a decision to liquidate assets and go out of business, the Justice stated, "Nothing the Court holds today should be understood as imposing a duty to bargain collectively regarding such managerial decisions, which lie at the core of entrepreneurial control. Decisions concerning the commitment of investment capital and the basic scope of the enterprise are not in themselves primarily about conditions of employment [and are not mandatory subjects]."

In First National Maintenance Corp. v. NLRB (U.S.1981), the employer was a firm that offered cleaning and maintenance service to commercial customers in New York City. The firm hired employees separately for each of its customers, and did not transfer employees between locations. One of its customers was Greenpark Care Center, a Brooklyn nursing home. Apparently First National was losing money on the Greenpark operation, for it gave Greenpark notice that it was terminating the contract.

Meanwhile, a union was successfully organizing First Maintenance's employees at the Greenpark location. Although the union was certified by the Board as the employees' representative, the firm neither notified the union nor bargained with it over the decision to discontinue the Greenpark contract. As a result of the termination of the Greenpark contract, these employees lost their jobs. The Board ruled that the firm had violated § 8(a)(5) and (1) by failing to bargain over the decision to discontinue the contract because that decision was a mandatory subject of bargaining. A court of appeals enforced the Board's order.

The Supreme Court reversed. Adopting its usual practice of not referring to the Board's expertise when it has decided to reverse the Board, the majority reasoned as follows. Some management decisions are clearly nonmandatory because of their indirect and attenuated impact on the employment relationship. These include choice of advertising, product design and type, and financing arrangements. Other decisions are clearly mandatory because they are almost exclusively an aspect of the relationship between employer and employee. These include order of succession of layoffs and recalls, production quotas, and work rules. A third type of management decision is one that has a direct impact on employment, but has as its focus for management a concern for economic profitability wholly apart from the employment relationship. Such a decision is like a decision whether to be in business at all, but it also is a "central and pressing concern to the union and its member employees."

The goal of the statute in this regard is to bring problems of vital concern to labor and management to the bargaining table, the Court reasoned. But such a goal is appropriate "only if the subject proposed for discussion is amenable to resolution through the bargaining process. Management must be free from the constraints of the bargaining process to the extent necessary for the running of a profitable business. It must also have some degree of certainty beforehand as to when it may proceed to reach decisions without fear of later evaluations labeling its conduct an unfair labor practice.... [B]argaining over management decisions that have a substantial impact on the continued availability of employment should be required only if the benefit, for labor-management relations and the collective bargaining process, outweighs the burden placed on the conduct of the business."

The Court then proceeded to apply these principles to the issue at hand. The union's interest in a
case of partial closing is largely to delay or halt the
closing. However, even if the closing is held a
nonmandatory subject of bargaining, the union is
not unprotected. It has a clear right to bargain
over the effects of a partial closing, and such a
closing motivated by anti-union animus is prohibited by § 8(a)(3). Managements' interests in such a
situation are more complex. "If labor costs are an
important factor in a failing operation and the
decision to close, management will have an incentive to confer voluntarily with the union to seek
concessions that may make continuing the business
profitable. . . . At other times, management may
have great need for speed, flexibility, and secrecy
in meeting business opportunities and exigen-
cies. . . . Labeling this type of decision mandatory
could afford a union a powerful tool for achieving
delay, a power that might be used to thwart
management's intentions in a manner unrelated to
any feasible solution the union might propose."

The Court then noted that provisions in existing
bargaining agreements rarely call for bargaining
over decisions of this sort. It rejected a test that
would turn on the economic necessity facing the
employer for such a test would not give employers
enough certainty respecting their bargaining obligations in situations when timing is likely to be
important.

An issue that has come before the Board several
times is whether a partial shutdown by an employ-

er presents a mandatory subject of bargaining. Otis Elevator Co. (NLRB 1984). At least when the decision is not motivated by labor costs, most Board members treat the subject as permissive only, but rationales vary. Some observers contend that carefully counseled employers can mischaracterize whether a decision to discontinue a department, for instance, turns on labor costs.

It is clear that the distinction between mandatory and nonmandatory subjects of bargaining is a major determinant of the impact of unions in the marketplace. In most instances, it is the union that would challenge the exercise of management discretion by demanding that the employer bargain over a discretionary act and the union that would bring economic pressure to bear if the employer either refuses to bargain or takes the position that he should retain his managerial discretion. A finding that the union's demand is nonmandatory means that the union may not insist upon bargaining over it, that the employer does not violate the statute if it refuses to discuss the matter, and that the union may not bring economic pressure (including picketing) to bear on the employer over this matter.

C. Multiemployer and Multiunion Bargaining

It is common for employers to bargain with a union on a multiemployer basis. The employers continue to be separate employers but they sit down together with the union and reach a common collective bargaining agreement applying to all the employers, although with perhaps minor variations to suit individual differences. Instances of multiemployer bargaining differ greatly in complexity and formality. Sometimes the negotiations set only general terms of the agreement and leave many details to be worked out between individual employers and the union. In other instances, all details of the agreement will apply to each employer. Occasionally, an exceptionally strong employer will reach an agreement with the union that serves as a pattern for other employers. This is not technically multiemployer bargaining, but the ultimate effect is the same: an agreement common to all the employers.

Commentators have suggested reasons why some employers and unions prefer multiemployer bargaining to single-employer bargaining. Multiemployer bargaining can offset the power of a particular union, especially by avoiding union "whipsawing" tactics—where a union strikes competitive employers one at a time in an effort to force each to yield for fear of a loss of business to the others during the strike. Employers may prefer multiemployer bargaining because it reduces the number of negotiations, and facilitates information exchange. Also, if one employer is a pacesetter in negotiations and the union is likely to insist that other employers adopt the same agreement, the smaller employers may have more input if they join with the pacesetter in multiemployer bargaining.

Another employer interest is in controlling competition between employers. Establishment of common wages, hours and working conditions means that employers with a common bargaining agreement will not compete in the labor market. And to the extent that the agreement is not subject to successful antitrust attack, various restrictions in a multiemployer bargaining agreement on the introduction of labor-saving machinery, for example, may control competition in the product market.

The NLRA does not speak to multiemployer bargaining except that § 8(b)(1)(B) makes it an unfair labor practice for a union to interfere with the employer's selection of its bargaining representative. The legislative history of this section suggests that it was intended to prohibit a union from coercing an employer into or out of multiemployer bargaining. The NLRB and reviewing courts have taken the position that multiemployer bargaining is consensual on both sides: it is an unfair labor practice for an employer or a union to coerce its trading party to engage in multiemployer bargaining. However, once consent has been given and negotiations have begun, neither an employer nor the union may withdraw without the consent of the other side absent "unusual circumstances." This prevents withdrawal from ongoing negotiations simply because those negotiations have taken an unfortunate turn.

In Charles D. Bonanno, Inc. v. NLRB (U.S.1982), the Court held that an impasse in collective bargaining between a union and a multiemployer group did not justify an employer's unilateral withdrawal from multiemployer bargaining. Whether an impasse in bargaining has occurred can be a difficult issue to resolve, especially if important legal rights turn on the question, but in *Bonanno* the parties conceded that there had been an impasse. After the impasse, the union called a strike against Bonanno but not against the other members of the multiemployer unit. The other employers then locked out the union, however. Bonanno hired permanent replacements for its striking employees, and then announced that it was withdrawing from the multiemployer unit. Soon afterwards, bargaining resumed between the union and the multiemployer unit and an agreement was reached. The union sought to bind Bonanno to the agreement by seeking an NLRB order that Bonanno's attempted withdrawal was a refusal to bargain and therefore ineffective.

The Court was sharply divided. The majority mentioned two reasons why it agreed with the Board that a bargaining impasse was not such an "unusual circumstance" as to justify a unilateral withdrawal from multiemployer bargaining. Impasse is a temporary condition, an agreement is usually reached at some later time. Also, an impasse can be deliberately brought about by one of the parties if it is to the party's strategic advantage.

When a union strikes a multiemployer group, it sometimes signs interim collective bargaining agreements with one or more of the firms in the group. In *Bonanno,* the Court held that the signing of an agreement that was truly interim—that would be replaced by any agreement reached in multiemployer bargaining—did not warrant unilateral withdrawal from multiemployer bargaining by another firm. Such a withdrawal would be permitted, however, if the union had fragmented the multiemployer unit by signing an agreement with one of the unit's firms that was to survive any agreement reached in multiemployer negotiations.

Justice Stevens, whose concurring vote was necessary for a majority, emphasized in a separate opinion that an employer is free to set conditions on its participation in multiemployer bargaining. Thus an employer could condition that participation on its ability to unilaterally withdraw after an impasse in negotiations, so long as the employer stipulated this condition prior to commencing negotiations.

Multiunion bargaining is less common than multiemployer bargaining. When multiunion bargaining is consensual on both sides, it is not a problem; however, some unions have brought representatives from other unions, or other bargaining units, to negotiations with an employer over the employer's objection. In General Electric Co. v. NLRB (2d Cir.1969), the union's use of several negotiators from outside the union (including representatives from other unions representing the employer's employees) was held not to be an interference with collective bargaining and did not justify the employer's refusal to negotiate further. The employer argued that the union had unlawfully attempted to expand the bargaining unit. The court recognized the danger that the negotiators might improperly attempt to expand subjects of bargaining to those of interest to other unions (tantamount to forcing the employer into multiunion bargaining), but was unwilling to condemn the union's use of outside negotiators unless and until improper expansion of bargaining agreement subjects was attempted.

Multiunion bargaining may have beneficial effects for both the employer and the unions. Where the employer is subject to seriatim strikes by various unions representing his employees, with each strike shutting down the entire operation because each employee group is critical to the operations or because all employees honor each union's picket line, bringing the unions together in common bargaining sessions may reduce the strike threats to a single threat. From a union point of view, if no one union can successfully shut the employer down by a strike, or if the effectiveness of a single union's strike depends on the honoring of its picket line by other employees, multiunion bargaining may increase the strength of the unions.

D. Bargaining During the Term of an Existing Agreement

Suppose an employer and a union have settled the terms of a collective bargaining agreement to last for a fixed period. While the agreement is in effect should the union be able to insist that the employer bargain over an additional union demand? In this, as in other matters, it is more important to understand the various policy considerations sometimes conflicting, than to be aware of the details of current NLRB case law.

With respect to one item there is agreement: the union may not make additional bargaining demands during the agreement's term over a subject written into the current agreement. This much is required by § 8(d) of the NLRA, which provides that the duty to bargain shall not require either party to discuss or agree to a modification of the bargaining agreement's provisions, during its term.

Differing views are held on the status of matters not written into the current agreement. One view is that a policy of contract stability demands that the parties realize that all bargaining demands must be laid on the table during negotiations and that neither party can go back for an additional bite of the apple while the agreement is in effect. Otherwise, neither side will be confident of the extent of its rights and liabilities under the contract. The problem with this view is that it requires the union to foresee every matter that will become important during the agreement. Second, such a view demands that the union raise potential problems that might never become actual problems or, by leaving them aside, forego the right to raise them if they do arise during the agreement. The employer seldom faces a similar problem, for in the absence of contract coverage the employer ordinarily will be deemed to have control over workplace issues.

Another policy consideration is that industrial peace will be promoted through open, on-going discussion between union and management even when that discussion must occur during the period of a bargaining agreement. Adherents to this view might take the position that further bargaining on a particular subject is foreclosed only when a written term of the agreement deals expressly with that subject and the additional bargaining demand would modify that term.

A compromise view would preclude midterm bargaining over issues that were "consciously explored" during collective bargaining even though no written provision resulted. One argument supporting the compromise view is that a bargaining demand laid on the table and thoroughly discussed but not agreed to is equivalent to an explicit rejection of the demand in the bargaining agreement.

The Board currently appears to adopt the compromise view. A subject will be foreclosed from bargaining during the term of an agreement if the subject matter is written into the agreement, or has been "fully discussed" or "consciously explored" and the union has "consciously yielded" or "clearly and unmistakably waived its interest in the matter." The Bunker Hill Co. (NLRB 1973); Proctor Manufacturing Corp. (NLRB 1961). The fullest discussions of these issues are found in Jacobs Manufacturing Co. (NLRB 1951), which found support for virtually every view in a badly split NLRB decision.

The parties during negotiations may stipulate that no further bargaining as to any issue can be demanded during the term of the agreement. This is accomplished through "zipper clauses" in which each side waives its right to further bargaining. The current NLRB view appears to be, however, that a zipper clause will constitute an effective waiver only if the clause expressly waives the right to negotiate over the particular subject matter in "clear and unmistakable" language. Thus general zipper clauses may be ineffective.

Even with respect to a matter over which the union can demand midterm bargaining, the union's economic power may be substantially curtailed by the applicability of a bargaining agreement's no-strike clause. Also, § 8(d) of the NLRA provides for a mandatory 60–day cooling-off period with notice to appropriate mediation agencies before the union can strike at the end of the bargaining agreement's term. A strike within this insulated period causes employees to lose their protected status and they may be discharged without the employer violating § 8(a)(3).

In NLRB v. Lion Oil Co. (U.S.1957), the Court held that where there is a formal contract reopener on one or more terms, the union may strike over a demand regarding the term without running afoul of § 8(d), even though the contract as a whole has not expired. The union must, however, give proper notice and wait for the passage of 60 days. There is no definitive authority on whether a similar rule would apply in the absence of a reopener, but on a matter subject to mid-term bargaining. There appears to be no reason, however, why the rationale of *Lion Oil* should not apply in this situation.

The Court held in NLRB v. Katz (U.S.1962) that an employer's unilateral change of a term of employment constitutes a refusal to bargain in violation of § 8(a)(5). Since a current collective bargaining agreement fixes terms of employment, should not a unilateral change in a bargaining agreement provision by the employer constitute a refusal to bargain? The answer is a qualified yes. To the extent that a unilateral change is a refusal to bargain, the employer can avoid violating § 8(a)(5) only by first obtaining the consent of the union to the change. But since § 8(d) of the NLRA prohibits either party from insisting upon a modification of the agreement during its term, bargaining to impasse with the union over the change is not enough. The union need not agree, and if not, the employer cannot make the change.

The Board members have been in disagreement over how to treat a plant closure or relocation that occurs during the term of a bargaining agreement. If an employer decides to relocate a department of the business in order to save labor costs and this decision comes when a bargaining agreement is in force, a finding that maintenance of the department is "contained in" the bargaining agreement means that even if the employer offers to bargain over the decision, the union may refuse under § 8(d). The employer is then barred from making the move. The Board so held in Milwaukee Spring I (NLRB 1982), but reversed itself in Milwaukee Spring II (NLRB 1984).

In Allied Chemical and Alkali Workers, Local One v. Pittsburgh Plate Glass Co. (U.S.1971), the Court held that a mid-term unilateral modification of a bargaining agreement provision constitutes a § 8(a)(5) violation only if the provision is a mandatory subject of bargaining. Thus an employer's assent in negotiations to a union demand on a nonmandatory subject of bargaining will not convert that demand into a mandatory subject in negotiations for a subsequent agreement, and neither does its assent to the demand create a duty to bargain before he engages in a mid-term modification of it. The modification probably breaches the bargaining agreement, and there is a breach of contract remedy, but it is not a § 8(a)(5) violation.

Assume the employer has signed a bargaining agreement that includes a provision whereby the employer agrees not to discharge an employee except for good cause. If it thereafter discharges an employee without good cause, hasn't it made a unilateral change in the collective bargaining agreement violating § 8(a)(5)? On this reasoning one can argue that every breach of a collective bargaining agreement constitutes a refusal to bargain. But Congress decided not to give the NLRB jurisdiction to enforce collective bargaining agreements. The issue is whether the Board can, or should, enforce agreements through its power to remedy violations of § 8(a)(5).

In NLRB v. C & C Plywood Corp. (U.S.1967), the collective bargaining agreement set wage scales and provided that the employer had the right to pay a premium rate above an established wage scale to an employee for some special skill. During the term of the agreement the employer unilaterally instituted a premium-incentive pay plan for employees in one job classification. The union filed § 8(a)(5) and (1) charges. The union argued, and the Board agreed, that the contract had not given the employer the power to institute the new wage plan, although the Board did not deny that an interpretation of the agreement was at the heart of the unfair labor practice charge. The Court of Appeals refused to enforce the Board's order because the unfair labor practice turned upon the correct meaning of the bargaining agreement.

The Supreme Court held that the Board had acted within its power. Pointing out the fact that there was no arbitration clause in the bargaining agreement, without explaining the significance of that omission, the Court emphasized that speedier adjudication was available before the NLRB than in a civil action for breach of contract. It also noted the difficulties of relegating the case to a civil action since damages appeared to be incalculable, being in the nature of an injury to the union's status as a bargaining representative. If an injunction were sought to vindicate the union's rights, the applicability of anti-injunction provisions of the Norris–LaGuardia Act would have to be faced. Perhaps only a declaratory judgment would be available in state or federal court. The Court ruled that while the Board has no jurisdiction to enforce collective bargaining agreements, the Board can construe an agreement in order to decide an unfair labor practice.

In NLRB v. ACME Industrial Co. (U.S.1967), a companion case to *C & C Plywood,* the union filed grievances under its collective bargaining agreement alleging that the employer was subcontracting work or transferring it to another location, either of which would breach the agreement. To enable it to prosecute its grievances, the union asked the employer to furnish it with information regarding the removal of certain plant machinery. The company refused and the NLRB found that the refusal violated § 8(a)(5).

The employer argued that it was for the arbitrator under the agreement to decide the relevance of the requested information, but the Supreme Court, upholding the Board's decision, disagreed. The Court reasoned that the Board was not making a binding construction of the contract, nor was it deciding the merits of the breach of contract claim. The Board was only aiding the arbitration process by mandating the transfer of information that would enable the union better to sift out unmeritorious claims.

The Supreme Court's cryptic comment in *C & C Plywood* that the bargaining agreement contained no arbitration clause might have been intended to suggest that where the speedy remedy of arbitration is available the NLRB loses its power to act. This would be a weak argument upon which to rest an ouster of NLRB jurisdiction and, in any event, later cases have held that the Board can act in this situation even though the bargaining agreement contains an arbitration clause. NLRB v. Huttig Sash and Door Co. (8th Cir.1967).

The fact that the Board has the power to decide breach of contract claims in § 8(a)(5) cases does not mean that as a matter of policy it should exercise that power. For more than twenty years, the Board has, in cases deemed appropriate, voluntarily deferred to existing arbitration awards where the awards effectively dispose of unfair labor practice issues. This deferral policy is popularly known as the *Spielberg* doctrine. Spielberg Manufacturing Co. (NLRB 1955).

As originally applied, the deferral requirements were that the unfair labor practice issue had been disposed of by an arbitration decision already rendered, that the arbitration was procedurally fair, that all parties were bound to the proceeding, and that the arbitrator's decision was "not clearly repugnant to the purposes and policies of the Act." Later in the doctrine's development, the Board held that it would not defer unless the arbitrator had considered the precise issue that would be before the Board, but the current rule appears to be somewhat less demanding. In Olin Corp. (NLRB 1984), the Board required for deferral only that there be a general factual similarity between the contract issue and the unfair labor practice issue, and that the arbitration award be susceptible to an interpretation consistent with the statute.

The Board has also held that it will not defer to an arbitration award involving the rights of an individual employee unless the employee's interests were adequately represented in the proceedings. Jacobs Transfer, Inc. (NLRB 1973).

If the Board is prepared to defer to an existing arbitration award, should it also defer when the unfair labor practice charge is filed before arbitration has run its course? In Collyer Insulated Wire (NLRB 1971), the employer unilaterally increased wage rates for two employee groups and directed that certain job tasks previously done by two employees would be done by a single employee. The employer contended that these actions were sanctioned by the collective bargaining agreement as interpreted in light of past practice. The union did not invoke the arbitration clause in the agreement but instead filed a § 8(a)(5) refusal to bargain charge. The Board, for the first time, held that it would defer to arbitration procedure even though there was no existing arbitration award.

In the view of a Board majority, several factors made the case appropriate for arbitration. The parties had a long, productive collective bargaining relationship and there was no claim that the employer was motivated by antiunion animus. The employer's claim of contract privilege was well suited to arbitration. Recognizing the risk that the arbitration procedure and ensuing award might not conform to the *Spielberg* standards, the Board held that it would defer to arbitration but would retain jurisdiction against the event that the arbitration award did not comply with those standards.

Collyer provoked controversy. Some argued that the NLRA's protection of public rights could not or should not be lost through private contractual undertakings. But perhaps the strongest criticism of the case has stemmed from its extension to new fact situations. In *Collyer*, the employer claimed a privilege under the contract to take the action challenged by the union as a refusal to bargain. If an arbitrator upheld the employer's contention, it would follow that the employer's action was not a unilateral change in conditions of employment. That is, a proper invocation of contract privilege would end the § 8(a)(5) case.

But consider the Board's decision in Radioear Corp. (NLRB 1972). The employer had given employees a small bonus each Christmas throughout the company's history. The company was then organized by the union and in negotiations for a new bargaining agreement the Christmas bonus practice was not mentioned. The agreement contained a broad "zipper clause." In a 3 to 2 decision the Board deferred to arbitration. This deferral is not within the scope of the *Collyer* rationale. Absent the deferral issue, the Board's test for a § 8(a)(5) violation is whether the Christmas bonus practice was "contained in" the bargaining agreement, either by contract language or by virtue of having been discussed in negotiations. On this test, the employer would seem to have violated § 8(a)(5) on the *Radioear* facts. An arbitrator viewing the dispute as a matter of contract interpretation might well rule that nothing in the bargaining agreement bound the employer to continue the Christmas bonus practice, a ruling consistent with the finding of a § 8(a)(5) violation by the Board. Unless the arbitrator found that the bonus termination was privileged by the zipper clause, the arbitrator's decision would not be ground for dismissing a refusal to bargain charge—if anything, it would support finding a refusal to bargain.

Another extension of the deferral policy occurred in National Radio Co. (NLRB 1972), where the employer was charged with violating § 8(a)(5) by imposing unilaterally a requirement that union

representatives record their movements in the
plant while processing grievances on company-com-
pensated time, and with violating § 8(a)(3) by discharging an employee for refusing to comply with
the reporting requirement. In another 3 to 2 decision, the Board announced the application of *Collyer* to § 8(a)(3) cases. Thereafter, an arbitrator
found that the discharge was neither antiunion in
motivation nor a contract violation. In the arbitrator's view, the employee was bound to comply
with the employer's rule and challenge it through
the grievance process. The arbitrator did not rule
on the question of whether the reporting clause's
unilateral adoption violated § 8(a)(5). The griev-
ant returned to the Board, which again declined to
consider the merits National Radio Co. (NLRB
1973).

The case is worth emphasis for two reasons. It
extends the pre-arbitration deferral doctrine to
§ 8(a)(3) cases. And, it is another case in which
the arbitrator's award does not necessarily dispose
of the unfair labor practice issues. It is arguable
that if the employer's reporting rule was unilaterally promulgated in violation of § 8(a)(5), its enforcement would violate § 8(a)(3) and (1) even without a showing of antiunion animus. The arbitrator
would have neither jurisdiction nor expertise to
adjudicate that NLRA issue.

Following a change in NLRB personnel, *National Radio* was overruled in General American
Transportation Corp. (NLRB 1977). Two NLRB
members voted to continue to adhere to *Collyer* in

its broadest applications. Two other Board members contended that the NLRB lacks the statutory power to "Collyerize" cases. Another Board member, casting the swing vote, held that deferral was proper in § 8(a)(5) and 8(b)(3) cases but not in cases alleging violations of § 8(a)(3), 8(b)(2) and 8(b)(1)(A), nor in cases where an unfair labor practice complaint alleges both a refusal to bargain and a violation of one of the other sections. In the final chapter of this sorry story of vacillation, the Board reversed *General American Transportation Corp.* and returned to *National Radio* in United Technologies Corp. (NLRB 1984).

E. Remedies for Refusals to Bargain

The most troublesome problem with respect to good faith bargaining is that the Board lacks, or has refused to adopt, adequate remedies for employer refusals to bargain. Consider the case of the unscrupulous employer willing to abuse NLRB and court processes to defeat a union's representation attempt. This employer realizes that union representation campaigns are in no small part emotional. A group of employees cannot be very excited about the prospect of a union representing them if they are fearful that the employer will punish the attempt, and they recognize that success, if achievable at all, is many years in the future. The employer may engage in conduct designed to prevent a union election victory without regard for whether the conduct violates any provisions of the NLRA, although the employer will try to avoid conduct that would support an NLRB bargaining order even absent a union election victory under the standards announced in NLRB v. Gissel Packing Co. (U.S.1969).

But even if a bargaining order issues as a result of the employer's unfair labor practices or a union election victory, the unscrupulous employer is likely to challenge either, on frivolous grounds if necessary. This forces the NLRB to initiate its § 8(a)(5) processes. An unfair labor practice hearing must be held, a Board decision must issue and, since the employer will not comply with that decision, court of appeals enforcement must be sought. This process can take years, during which time the employer does not have to bargain with the union.

Even when the Board is successful in the court of appeals, the only remedy will be a bargaining obligation beginning when the court of appeals enforces the order. If the money saved by the employer from ignoring the union during the period of litigation is greater than the attorney fees expended in litigating, the employer will be advantaged and the employees will be the losers. Another advantage of this delay to the employer is that court of appeals enforcement may come so late that employee interest in the union may have waned substantially. Thus when the employer is forced to bargain, a much weaker union sits across the table than would have had the employer fulfilled its bargaining obligations from the outset.

Another frustrating situation from the union's point of view is where the employer only goes through the motions of bargaining, making no real effort to reach an agreement. Even where the Board agrees that the employer has not fulfilled its statutory duty to bargain, there is no effective remedy. The Board will only issue a cease and desist order telling the employer to go back and bargain in good faith. In H.K. Porter Co. v. NLRB (U.S.1970), an employer newly organized by the union only went through the motions of collective bargaining and at one point refused to agree to a union request that he check off dues for employees requesting it. The Board found the employer's refusal to be in bad faith, and no more than an attempt to harass the union. It ordered the dues check-off provision to be adopted by the employer. The employer resisted the Board's order, relying on the provisions of § 8(d), which state that the good faith bargaining obligation does not compel either party to agree to a proposal.

The court of appeals held that the § 8(d) standard goes to the question of what factors the Board may consider in finding whether there is a violation, but does not go to the remedy issue. Since the Board had found employer bad faith in this case, § 8(d) did not prevent the finding of a violation or the remedy.

The Supreme Court reversed, holding that the NLRB has the power to require the parties to negotiate but is "without power to compel a company or a union to agree to any substantive contractual provision of a collective bargaining agreement...." Section 8(d) is an implied limitation on the Board's powers.

It is clear from the Supreme Court's opinion in *H.K. Porter* that a majority of the Court was unsympathetic to the Board's finding that there had been a refusal to bargain by the employer. While certiorari had not been granted on that issue, the Court appeared to see the employer's refusal more as an exercise of economic strength than as a refusal to bargain in good faith. It would have been preferable for the Court to have put the decision squarely on that ground rather than on a question of the Board's remedial power. To the extent that the opinion confuses an exercise of economic strength with a refusal to bargain, the result is that an effective remedy is denied in the single situation where it is most warranted: where the union lacks the economic strength to force the employer to bargain in good faith. If *H.K. Porter* means that there is no remedy in such a situation, then the requirement of good faith bargaining may be just a pious exhortation.

The Court of Appeals for the District of Columbia Circuit once attempted to pressure the Board into fashioning a remedy for employer refusals to bargain in instances where the employers have used administrative and judicial processes to avoid the bargaining obligation during the slow progress of litigation. The suggestion was that the NLRB should adopt a "make whole" remedy requiring companies to compensate employees for money lost on account of employer refusals to bargain. When an employer refuses to bargain in order to test the lawfulness of a union's election victory or other bargaining order, and a substantial delay ensues, the employer should be required to make the employees whole for the losses suffered in the delay. The court of appeals contended that the Board has the statutory power to impose such a remedy and that it should do so where the employer's refusal to bargain is based on grounds that are frivolous or in bad faith. No such remedy should be rendered where the employer's objections to the imposition of a bargaining obligation are "fairly debatable." IUE v. NLRB [Tiidee Products, Inc.] (D.C.Cir.1974).

The Board rejects the make-whole remedy. Those Board members who criticize the remedy urge that it exceeds the Board's powers under § 10(d) of the NLRA as construed by the Court in *H.K. Porter.* They also decline the use of the remedy as a matter of administrative discretion. In their view, the employers' position in these cases merits sympathy: The only way an employer can obtain review of a Board's order to bargain is by committing a technical refusal to bargain which is then appealed to a court of appeals. Conditioning this right to appeal on the possibility of a substantial damage remedy in favor of employees would approximate a punitive remedy. These Board members feel that the distinction between debatable and frivolous employer challenges to bargaining obligations is unworkable. Further, there is no way to compute the damage remedy. For these Board members only two special remedies are currently available: interim injunctions under § 10(j) of the Act, requiring the employer to bargain while the case proceeds through Board processes; and, in appropriate cases of flagrant employer violations, an order that the employer reimburse the NLRB and the union their litigation expenses, provide the union reasonable access to company bulletin boards, mail a signed copy of the Board's order to each employee, and make available to the union for a period of time the names and addresses of all employees currently employed. The Board will not order a union reimbursed for its organizational expenses, lost dues and initiation fees. Ex–Cello–O Corp. (NLRB 1970); Tiidee Products, Inc. (NLRB 1972).

A minority of NLRB members would award a make-whole remedy in appropriate cases. The statutory authorization of "affirmative action" in § 10(c) is sufficient to support the remedy. These Board members are not as sympathetic to the employers' position. After all, a union has no way of challenging a Board decision that an employer has no duty to bargain; why should the Board be insistent on protecting the employer's right to challenge such an order if the challenge visits substantial economic loss on employees? The amount of the make-whole remedy can be determined by looking at bargaining agreements at other plants of this employer, at the settlement pattern of other unionized employers in the same geographic area or industry, and at national averages.

It is apparent that only some kind of make-whole remedy, or other remedy more clearly punitive, will prevent some employers from calculating that they are economically advantaged by refusing to bargain and paying the attorney fees required to gain the delay. Injunctions under § 10(j) have not proved effective. Regional directors will seldom seek such injunctions, and district courts are, at times, reluctant to issue them. It is not clear what the status of any collective bargaining agreement reached during the pendency of such an injunction would be if the employer eventually prevailed on the duty to bargain issue.

It is not certain that the NLRB lacks the power to issue a make-whole remedy, but it is certain that a Board majority is opposed to its imposition absent a further statutory directive. This has caused unions to lobby in Congress for NLRA amendments that would give make-whole remedies in some refusal to bargain cases and would also provide for certain punitive remedies, such as debarment from government contracts and double back pay to discriminatorily discharged employees. These lobbying efforts have not been successful.

F. Terminating the Duty to Bargain

The contract-bar and election-bar rules developed by the Board (see Chapter III.B., *supra*) provide incumbent unions with certain protections against loss of the right to represent employees. The election-bar rules were given Supreme Court approval in Brooks v. NLRB (U.S.1954). If there is neither a contract-bar nor an election-bar, an incumbent union enjoys a rebuttable presumption of continued majority status.

There are several ways in which the right to continued representative status may be challenged. An employee, group of employees, or an individual or union on their behalf may file a decertification petition with the Board under § 9(c)(1) of the NLRA. This petition must be accompanied by a showing that 30 percent or more of the employees in the union's bargaining unit support decertification. The Board will then conduct a secret ballot election.

An employer is not permitted to file a decertification petition and commits a § 8(a)(1) violation if it instigates or assists a decertification petition. The Board has ruled, however, that an employer may refuse to bargain with the union while a decertification petition is pending. Telautograph Corp. (NLRB 1972). This rule is peculiar since the decertification petition, standing alone, only signifies that somewhat less than half of the employees fail to support the union. On the other hand, agreement on a new contract is unlikely if the employer believes ouster of the union is likely.

The employer is permitted by § 9(c)(1)(B) of the NLRA to file an election petition when presented with a request for recognition by a union. This includes a claim for continued recognition (e.g., for collective bargaining) by an incumbent union. The Board, fearing that unions would be put to the test of an election with the expiration of every bargaining agreement, which would disrupt bargaining, has held that it will entertain an employer's election petition only if the employer demonstrates by objective considerations that it has reasonable grounds for believing the union has lost its majority status. United States Gypsum Co. (NLRB 1966).

The employer's other option upon doubting the incumbent union's current majority status is to refuse to bargain with the union. Whether the employer commits a § 8(a)(5) violation by such a refusal produced disagreement among the Board members in Stoner Rubber Co. (NLRB 1959). There the employer had both refused to bargain with the union and had instituted unilateral economic changes. Two Board members reasoned that after the certification year expired the union enjoyed only a presumption of continued majority status. The burden of proof is initially on the employer to "produce sufficient evidence to cast serious doubt on the union's continued majority status." If the employer carries its burden, it is then up to the General Counsel to prove that, as of the refusal to bargain date, the union in fact represented a majority of the employees.

Another Board member would not find employer unilateral action to constitute a violation so long as the employer demonstrates a good faith doubt of the union's majority status. The other two Board members would permit an employer to withdraw recognition if the employer entertains a good faith doubt of the union's majority status, but would find a violation when unilateral action is taken before the union has "an opportunity to protect its established position and reaffirm its statutory entitlement to recognition." Such unilateral action would itself tend to undercut the union's majority status.

It is now clear that in the refusal to bargain case, as in the § 9(c)(1)(B) case, the employer's good faith doubt must be based on objective considerations. Terrell Machine Co. (NLRB 1969). Also, an employer will not be permitted to rely on a loss of majority caused by its own unfair labor practices. To establish a "good faith doubt based on objective considerations" employers have sometimes relied upon declines in union dues-payers, high employee turnover, polls of the employees, rumors of employee dissatisfaction, sudden changes in union bargaining posture, and failure of the union to communicate with the employer over a period of time. Employers have not always been successful.

There appears to be disagreement among the circuit courts on whether the employer's refusal to bargain should be found to have violated § 8(a)(5) when the employer establishes a good faith doubt of the union's majority status but the General Counsel proves that the union, in fact, enjoyed majority support. The Board's present view is that if the employer establishes a reasonably based doubt, the union's actual majority status is irrelevant. Arkay Packaging Corp. (NLRB 1976).

Employees who strike for economic benefits may be permanently replaced by their employer with new employees. NLRB v. MacKay Radio & Telegraph Co. (U.S.1938). If a substantial number of striker replacements are hired, the employer may claim the union no longer enjoys majority support and either petition for a new election or refuse to bargain with the union. Without more, this is not likely in the Board's view to justify a refusal to bargain because of the Board's principle that replacements for economic strikers are presumed to support the union in the same ratio as those whom they have replaced. Windham Community Memorial Hospital (NLRB 1977). This presumption was challenged in NLRB v. Curtin Matheson Scientific, Inc. (U.S.1990). A divided Court upheld the Board on the grounds that the Board had the authority to make an empirically based presumption, and that this presumption properly diminished an employer's ability to oust a union merely by precipitating a strike and then hiring replacements. Chief Justice Rehnquist, whose concurring vote was needed to make up the majority, argued that the Board's presumption might not be justified if Board rules also prohibited the employer from polling its workers regarding their union support in these circumstances.

In cases where the employer has a reasonably held doubt, § 9(c)(3) provides that the economic strikers are entitled to vote in an election if it is conducted within 12 months of the commencement of the strike. The replacements will also vote. Similarly, within that 12–month period, any attempt to show a reasonably held doubt of majority status must take the strikers into account. Pioneer Flour Mills v. NLRB (5th Cir.1970).

The right to representative status may also be lost through the doctrines of successorship and bankruptcy, examined in Chapter IX.C., *infra*.

CHAPTER VIII

LABOR AND THE ANTITRUST LAWS

The extent to which the activities of unions should be subjected to antitrust scrutiny has perplexed courts and scholars throughout the century. It is fairly easy to demonstrate that simple answers will not do. Consider a proposal to treat unions as any other enterprise and subject them to antitrust scrutiny. This would probably outlaw unions entirely because any strike by a union for higher wages, for example, is a concerted refusal to deal. Nor do the antitrust statutes tell us with helpful precision how union activities should be treated.

The Sherman Act, passed in 1890, was initially applied more often to unions than to employers and was regularly cited by federal courts as authority for striking down union-called boycotts. Even this statute, however, was not used to restrict union monopoly power, such as industry-wide unions, but was targeted at certain union practices.

The Clayton Act, passed in 1914, has language that attempts to limit the courts' application of antitrust laws to union activities. Section 6 provides that the "labor of a human being is not a commodity or article of commerce" and that the antitrust laws are not to be construed to forbid the existence of unions or to restrain them "from lawfully carrying out the legitimate objects thereof." Section 20 bars the issuance of injunctions in cases arising out of disputes "between employers and employees" concerning "terms and conditions of employment." Certain union activities such as quitting work are expressly deemed not to be violations of federal law. But the Clayton Act is run through by the use of words such as "lawful" and "unlawful."

The hopes of unions that the Clayton Act would provide a strong measure of antitrust immunity were dashed by Duplex Printing Press Co. v. Deering (U.S.1921), a case in which the Supreme Court condemned a secondary boycott on antitrust grounds. The Court held that § 6 of the Clayton Act conferred no antitrust immunity "where ... [unions] depart from ... normal and legitimate objects...." Nor was § 20 of any help to the union, in the Court's view, because it applied to "a case between an employer and employees, or between employers and employees," and this protected only workers in a proximate relation to the dispute—the employees of the primary employer. Thus it appeared that only primary union activity would be protected, and even that protection might be lost if the Court deemed the union's object "illegitimate."

Might a union's intent determine whether its activity should be struck down on antitrust

grounds? The results under such a test were illus-
trated in two cases decided three years apart involving the same parties. In United Mine Workers
v. Coronado Coal Co. (U.S.1922), a union shut down
the Coronado Coal Company's mine by violence
following the employer's lockout and attempted
nonunion operation. When the case first reached
the Court the evidence tended to show a local
motive of the union: an employee reaction to the
lockout. If this were so, the Court was ready to
find no antitrust violation. But on remand, evidence at the second trial showed that the union
that called the shutdown had viewed Coronado's
coal production as a serious threat to union wages
at other companies and to union organizing efforts
generally.

When the case again reached the Court in Coronado Coal Co. v. United Mine Workers (U.S.1925),
the Court found that the union's intent was
enough to establish antitrust liability. While a
strike with a "local motive" would ordinarily be
deemed merely an indirect obstruction to commerce, an intent to restrain or control the supply
entering interstate commerce, or the price of it in
interstate markets, was held to be a violation of
the antitrust laws.

Nor did it require a strike to expose the union to
antitrust liability. In United States v. Brims
(U.S.1926), the union obtained the agreement of
area building contractors that union carpenters
would not be required to work on nonunion mill

work. The union's reason for obtaining the agreement was that it was losing work to nonunion manufacturers paying lower wages. *Coronado* and the earlier decisions subjecting secondary strikes to antitrust liability were cited by the Supreme Court in finding the union's activity to be unlawful under the antitrust laws.

As of 1930, federal courts regulated national labor policy through application of the antitrust laws. The opinions were reminiscent of the "ends-means" test used in state tort law. The procedural device used to control union conduct was the labor injunction. All of this led to the passage in 1932 of the Norris–LaGuardia Act, which limited the federal courts' injunctive power in labor disputes and signalled to the courts a congressional belief that the antitrust laws were a poor vehicle for the formulation of national labor policy.

In 1935, the passage of the Wagner Act showed an even greater willingness by Congress to assume the role of labor policy maker and demonstrated that the Congressional policy was to be the encouragement of unionization and collective bargaining. Yet neither the Wagner Act nor the Norris–LaGuardia Act amended the antitrust laws.

The Supreme Court delivered a major decision in Apex Hosiery Co. v. Leader (U.S.1940). After organizing the company but being denied its request for a closed shop, the union called a sitdown strike, which became violent and stopped production for four months. The union prevented the shipment of finished goods into interstate commerce. There was no showing of a union purpose to prevent the company's goods from competing with union-made goods, so the *Coronado* cases ("local purpose") could have been used to reverse the lower court's award of treble antitrust damages. But in a long opinion for the Court, Justice Stone, reversing, attempted to state broad principles applicable to union antitrust cases.

Union activity does not violate the antitrust laws unless it was intended "to restrain commercial competition" or to control the product market. The opinion delivered a famous dictum: "Since, in order to render a labor combination effective it must eliminate the competition from union-made goods ... an elimination of price competition based on differences in labor standards is the objective of any national labor organization. But this effect on competition has not been considered to be the kind of curtailment of price competition prohibited by the Sherman Act."

Brims was quoted with approval, but was deemed to be a case of a labor organization being used by a combination of employers as a means for suppressing competition or fixing prices. The Court did, however, rely on the fact that the union's delay of shipments of Apex's products had not affected prices nor had it been so intended.

The precise contours of "commercial competition" were not explored. The *Apex* Court did not use the more familiar distinction between the labor market and the product market. While the categories in practice are nowhere near as neat as they often ... c. ...id ... owing kinds of ... s. ... .ight, through collective ... economic pressure on employers, directly manipulate the labor market without having a direct effect on the product market. An example would be a strike for higher wages which, if successful, will fix the wages for this employer, and, if done in multiemployer bargaining or by the union's imposition of the wages on other employers bargaining separately, may set an industry-wide wage scale. Other examples of such labor market restraints are when the union agrees with a group of employers that all shall adopt the same hours of work, pension benefits, methods of determining compensation, and the like. This control of the labor market will ultimately have its effect in the product market, but it is not considered a direct product market restraint.

Other kinds of union activity provide a direct benefit in the labor market but also constitute a direct product market restraint. Limitations on subcontracting or on the introduction of labor-saving materials, especially when agreed to by a multiemployer group, directly benefit employees in the labor market by increasing hours of work, for example. Such restraints also have a direct impact on the product market.

A final form of union restraint is a direct restraint on the product market yielding an indirect benefit in the labor market. An example is the setting of product prices through multiemployer bargaining which, to the extent that it increases employer profits, will provide more money that can be given to union members in the form of wages. The benefit of the labor market is available only because the employers are made more profitable. In that sense it is indirect.

The *Apex* distinction between restraints on commercial competition and those directed at the elimination of differences based on labor standards was short-circuited in United States v. Hutcheson (U.S.1941). *Apex* did not mention an exemption for union activities. Rather, it cut back on antitrust liability by restricting the substantive grounds on which unions were exposed. In *Hutcheson,* by contrast, an "exemption" from the antitrust laws was carved out for unions.

In that case the Attorney General of the United States had embarked upon a program of Sherman Act prosecutions of union bad practices. The case involved a jurisdictional dispute between the Carpenters and Machinists unions and a resulting strike against the primary employer, picketing of a secondary employer, and a call for a nationwide boycott of the primary employer's product. Justice Frankfurter, writing for the Court, reasoned that the Clayton Act had withdrawn certain specified union practices from the coverage of the Sherman Act. Case law development after the Clayton Act was said by many to have been inconsistent with the congressional intent to carve out freedoms for unions from antitrust restraint. Of particular significance was the passage of the Norris–LaGuardia Act in 1932. Although that Act by its terms only removed the injunctive remedy, Justice Frankfurter concluded that the question of whether union conduct violates the Sherman Act could only be decided by reading the provisions of the Sherman, Clayton, and Norris–LaGuardia Acts as a "harmonizing text."

Having found the three statutes to be "interlacing," the Justice declared a broad exemption (immunity) for unions from antitrust scrutiny: "So long as a union acts in its self-interest and does not combine with non-labor groups, the licit and the illicit under § 20 [of the Clayton Act] are not to be distinguished by any judgment regarding the wisdom or unwisdom, the rightness or wrongness, the selfishness or unselfishness of the end of which the particular union activities are the means...."

Hutcheson was criticized for the Court's interpretation of Congressional intent. Arguably, those people calling for passage of the Norris–LaGuardia Act secured its passage only by persuading Congress that the limited effect of the proposed statute was to deprive the federal courts of the power to use the labor injunction, which had fallen into considerable disrepute: the statute was not dealing with the issue of damage exposure of unions under the antitrust laws. In this view, *Hutcheson's* conclusion that the three Acts should be harmonized was improper; and Justice Frankfurter should have treated the Sherman and Clayton Acts as the central provisions, with Norris–LaGuardia only serving to withdraw a particular remedy.

But for those who believed that federal courts should leave labor policy issues to the Congress, *Hutcheson* was deemed to be a proper, and far reaching, decision. Determining the contours of "commercial competition," as *Apex* required, was unnecessary under *Hutcheson*. It declared a much broader exemption from antitrust scrutiny. But *Hutcheson* was not to be the last word.

In 1945, a very unappealing, from the union perspective, antitrust case reached the Supreme Court. In Allen Bradley Co. v. IBEW, Local 3 (U.S.1945), the union had organized New York City electrical contractors and obtained closed-shop agreements from them. The union then organized the city's electrical equipment manufacturers with promises of a sheltered market. Manufacturers and contractors agreed to do business only with New York City firms organized by the union. Firms from outside New York City were excluded from the market by union picketing and boycotts. Working with the union, the employers inflated prices and rigged bids. The scheme was originally policed by the union but later was taken over by employers' associations. Non–New York City manufacturers who had been excluded from the New York City market brought suit against the union, but did not name any of the employers as defendants.

The Court found a violation of the Sherman Act by incorrectly characterizing the scheme as a business conspiracy aided and abetted by the local union. In the absence of an antitrust exemption, a substantive violation was easily found on the authority of *Apex* : the scheme had restrained trade in and monopolized the New York City market, excluded equipment shipped from other states, directly controlled prices, and discriminated between would-be customers. In finding that the *Hutcheson* immunity did not apply, the Court stated,

> "employers and the union did here make bargaining agreements in which the employers agreed not to buy goods manufactured by companies which did not employ the members of Local No. 3. We may assume that such an agreement standing alone would not have violated the Sherman Act. But it did not stand alone. It was but one element in a far larger program in which contractors and manufacturers united with one another to monopolize all the business in New York City, to bar all other businessmen from that area, and to charge the public prices above a competitive level. It is true that victory of the union in its disputes, even had the union acted alone, might have added to the cost of goods, or might have resulted in individual refusals of all of their employers to buy electrical equipment not made by Local No. 3. So far as the union

might have achieved this result acting alone, it would have been the natural consequence of labor union activities exempted by the Clayton Act from the coverage of the Sherman Act. [Citing *Apex*]. But when the unions participated with a combination of businessmen ... a situation was created not included within the exemptions.... We know that Congress feared the concentrated power of business organizations to dominate markets and prices. It intended to outlaw business monopolies. A business monopoly is no less such because a union participates, and such participation is a violation of the Act...."

Given the facts of *Allen Bradley,* neither the loss of the exemption nor the finding of substantive liability is surprising. More difficult, however, has been the articulation of the test for the loss of the exemption. First, since the *Allen Bradley* scheme was initiated by the union, which was the driving force behind it, the case cannot apply only to sham arrangements: employers using a union as an excuse to control product markets. Second, condemning all schemes that bear similarities to business conspiracies not requiring union participation cuts too broadly. That might outlaw the setting of a wage rate by multiemployer bargaining groups. Indeed, in the eyes of some commentators, *Allen Bradley* rendered vulnerable multiemployer bargaining. Third, examination of actual bargaining in order to discover whether employers were resisting the union's demands or were secretly happy with a market restraint suggested by a union would only serve to punish bad acting and reward good acting.

Allen Bradley raised many difficult questions, but labor antitrust was quiet in the Supreme Court for the next twenty years. In 1965, two cases, decided at the same time, changed the direction of labor antitrust and found the Court deeply divided over the direction the law should take. In United Mine Workers v. Pennington (U.S.1965), trustees of the United Mine Workers Union Welfare and Retirement Fund brought suit against the Phillips Coal Company for royalty payments allegedly due under a collective bargaining agreement with the union. The company defended and crossclaimed alleging that the Fund trustees, the United Mine Workers Union, and certain large coal operators had conspired in violation of the Sherman Act. The allegations of the crossclaim were that the union had entered into a multiemployer bargaining agreement with large coal mine operators and that in order both to control overproduction in the coal industry and to permit modernization of methods, the union allowed modernization, received substantial wage increases, and agreed to impose these increases on smaller companies regardless of whether those companies were modernized or could afford the increases. It was further alleged that the union and the large companies had agreed upon other steps to exclude marketing, production, and sale of nonunion coal. One such step was a joint approach by the union and the company to the Secretary of Labor to obtain a minimum wage for employees of companies selling coal to the Tennessee Valley Association that was much higher than the minimum wage in other industries, and that would make it difficult for small companies to compete in the Tennessee Valley Association market.

In the district court, motions to dismiss the cross-claim were denied and a jury verdict was returned against the union for $90,000, which was then trebled under the antitrust laws. The trial court overruled the union's motion for a judgment notwithstanding the verdict or for a new trial. The court of appeals concluded that the union was not exempt from antitrust liability.

The Supreme Court reversed and remanded. The Court split into three groups of three Justices each. Justice White wrote an opinion for the Court joined by Chief Justice Warren and Justice Brennan. Justice Douglas concurred in a separate opinion joined by Justices Black and Clark. Justice Goldberg authored a dissent joined by Justices Harlan and Stewart.

Justice White's opinion deserves careful examination. Citing the *Allen Bradley* business conspiracy doctrine, the opinion argues that a multiemployer bargaining agreement that sets product prices is not exempt from the antitrust laws. It is a direct product market restraint yielding only the indirect labor benefit of a hope for better union wages. The exemption is also lost if the union is a party to a collusive bidding arrangement designed to drive smaller operators from the product market. The more difficult issue is presented by Phillip's claim that the union had agreed with larger operators that the union would impose a wage rate upon smaller operators regardless of the smaller operators' ability to pay. The union argued that such an agreement should be exempt from the antitrust laws because it concerns wage standards. Justice White reasoned that the exemption was more narrow. He specifically approved of an exemption for multiemployer bargaining over wages to be paid by the multiemployer group's members. The benefit to union members from such an agreement is direct, and the restraint on the product market results only from the elimination of wage competition, a restraint not intended to be proscribed by the Sherman Act. Furthermore, the union may later seek the same wages from other employers as a matter of its own policy without exposing itself to Sherman Act scrutiny.

But, according to Justice White, the fact that a multiemployer agreement involves a mandatory subject of bargaining does not compel antitrust immunity, nor are NLRB determinations of mandatory subjects controlling on the Sherman Act question. A union loses its exemption when it agrees with one group of employers to impose a wage scale on other employers. The union can, acting alone, vigorously seek a wage rate from an employer even though it cannot afford to pay the rate; and such a union effort, in Justice White's view, does not by itself support the finding of an

Allen Bradley conspiracy. But a union's agreement with one set of employers to impose a wage scale on another firm does not enjoy national labor policy protection because the union's best interest is served by maintaining its flexibility to engage in bargaining on a unit-by-unit basis. An employer has an interest in seeing that its wage scale is not undercut by other unionized employers, but the union may not agree to protect this interest—it is essentially anticompetitive rather than a regulation of the employer's own labor relations.

According to Justice White's opinion, the fact that the union surrenders its own freedom of action by agreeing to impose a wage rate on other employers compels the loss of antitrust immunity even without a showing of predatory intent or effect. Thus the lower court would have been correct in overruling the union's motion to dismiss in this case. The jury verdict against the union and the trustees was reversed, however, because the admission of evidence relating to the appeal to the Secretary of Labor was inconsistent with prior Supreme Court precedent that efforts to influence public officials cannot violate the antitrust laws even though those efforts are intended to restrain competition.

The concurring opinion authored by Justice Douglas differs from Justice White's opinion only with respect to the evidence required by plaintiff to make out a prima facie showing. The Douglas view is that an industry-wide bargaining agreement setting wages beyond the ability of some operators to pay would be prima facie evidence of an *Allen Bradley* conspiracy.

Justice Goldberg's dissent argued that the thrust of *Apex* and *Hutcheson* is to immunize collective bargaining over mandatory subjects. While the Justice would not defer entirely to NLRB decisions defining mandatory subjects, such decisions would be entitled to great weight in measuring labor's antitrust exemption. It is not clear, however, that Justice Goldberg was labelling the alleged agreement in this case a mandatory bargaining subject. An employer demand that the union impose a wage scale on another employer would not likely be held mandatory by the NLRB.

In bargaining over wages, an employer or multiemployer group will be concerned over a potential competitive disadvantage caused by a high wage agreement and will naturally undertake to elicit the union's position on the demands that will be made of the employer's competitors in the product market. The majority's test is mischievous, in the dissent's view, because it will have the effect of driving this natural and legitimate concern into underground conversations or, to the extent that they are prevented altogether, the union may have to resort to unilateral action, such as a strike for the higher wages. The dissent also criticizes what it sees as the majority's willingness to infer a prohibited agreement from the union's conduct.

Several points should be appreciated with respect to Justice White's *Pennington* opinion.
While Justice White is willing to say that the
allegations may make out an *Allen Bradley* business conspiracy, he is not ready to do so without
first squaring such a finding with national labor
policy. This will be significant in future cases.
His handling of national labor policy on the facts
of the case has generated criticism. He might
have said that an agreement with a group of employers to impose a contract term on another employer constituted a violation of § 8(b)(3) because it
required the union to approach the second employer with a closed mind. But instead the opinion
seems to suggest that Justice White knew better
than the union did what was in the union's best
interest. And the union's best interest apparently
defined national labor policy.

The *Pennington* opinions do not suggest that if
the antitrust exemption is lost, the market restraint would still be subject to an antitrust "rule
of reason." Perhaps only the issue of the exemption was thought to be before the Court. How the
rule of reason might apply is not clear. A court
might look only at the effect of the restraint on the
competitive market, or it might also consider labor's interest in removing wages from competition.

Amalgamated Meatcutters and Butchers Workmen, Local 189 v. Jewel Tea Co. (U.S.1965), was
decided at the same time as *Pennington,* and found
the Court divided into the same three groups of

three Justices each. Although the opinion of Justice White has had the greatest influence, in *Jewel Tea* only two Justices supported his reasoning. Three other Justices reached the same result on very different grounds, and another three Justices disagreed with the result.

Jewel Tea began with contract negotiations between a multiemployer bargaining group of Chicago grocery stores and seven unions representing butchers in the Chicago area. The multiemployer groups agreed to a bargaining agreement restriction on the marketing hours for fresh meat, a restriction that forbade the sale of meat before 9 a.m. and after 6 p.m. in both service and self-service markets. Jewel Tea initially rejected the restraint, arguing among other things that it was illegal, but under the duress of a union strike vote eventually signed the contract that had already been signed by the other employers. Jewel Tea then brought an antitrust suit against the unions seeking to invalidate the marketing hours provision in the collective bargaining agreement.

After a trial, the district court found that the "record was devoid of any evidence to support a finding of a conspiracy" between the multiemployer group and the unions to force this bargaining agreement restriction on Jewel Tea. The trial court also found that for service markets to sell meat before 9 a.m. or after 6 p.m. would require butchers to be present. Even in self-service markets removing the restriction would either inaugurate longer hours and night work for the butchers or result in butcher's work being done by others unskilled in the trade. The unions had imposed the marketing hours restriction on Jewel Tea to serve their own interest in conditions of employment, in the trial court's view, and were clearly within the labor exemption. The court of appeals reversed but did not disturb any of the lower court's fact-finding. The Supreme Court reversed and held the union's actions were entitled to an antitrust exemption.

Justice White's opinion was joined by Chief Justice Warren and Justice Brennan. His opinion first rejected any contention that this case was analogous to *Pennington.* The trial court had found no evidence of an attempt by the multiemployer group to have this restriction imposed on Jewel Tea, and the union was acting in its own self interest. Justice White then reached the surprising conclusion that although the parties to the agreement were but a single employer and the unions representing his employees, that fact did not compel immunity for the agreement: "We must consider the subject matter of the agreement in light of the national labor policy." He explained this no further, and he appeared to be saying that the immunity may be lost, but will not necessarily be lost, when the union signs an agreement with a single, unwilling employer who then becomes plaintiff in the antitrust action.

For Justice White, the test for the exemption is "very much a matter of accommodating the coverage of the Sherman Act to the policy of labor laws." That wages, hours and working conditions are mandatory subjects of bargaining weigh heavily in favor of an exemption for agreements respecting those subjects, a weight not warranted when the bargaining is over nonmandatory subjects. Under the labor laws the unions could not have insisted that Jewel Tea bargain over the prices to be charged for its products, Justice White wrote; and if Jewel Tea had reached an agreement with the union over product prices and had been sued by an injured party, it is unlikely that the agreement would be entitled to an antitrust immunity. The issue in this case, then, was "whether the marketing-hours restriction, like wages, and unlike prices, is so intimately related to wages, hours and working conditions that the union's successful attempt to obtain that provision through bona fide, arm's length bargaining in pursuit of their own labor union policies, and not at the behest of or in combination with nonlabor groups, falls within the protection of the national labor policy and is therefore exempt from the Sherman Act." It is not the form of the agreement (wages or prices) that controls, "but its relative impact on the product market and the interest of union members."

Justice White then hypothesized a restraint on the hours during which butchers would be required to work. Such a provision has an effect on competition, but it also involves a mandatory subject of bargaining and is of immediate concern to union members. Therefore, "weighing the respective interests involved," a union-employer agreement on when employees must work is subject to an antitrust exemption.

For Justice White the key consideration in this case was the conflicting contentions of the unions and the employer as to whether the night sale of meat in Jewel Tea stores was possible without the night employment of butchers, an impairment of the butcher's work jurisdiction, or a substantial effect on the butcher's work load. Were such operations possible without these effects, the case for antitrust exposure would be strong because the marketing hours restraint would go further than the restraint necessary to protect the union's legitimate interest. The lower court, however, had made a fact finding that evening operations would either require butchers to work or would mean that their work would be done by others unskilled in the trade. This finding, undisturbed in the court of appeals, meant that the unions had imposed on the employer the least restrictive bargaining agreement provision necessary to protect the unions' legitimate interests. A Sherman Act exemption was justified, and the question of whether the restraint was unreasonable under the antitrust laws need not be reached.

Justice Goldberg, joined by Justices Harlan and Stewart, concurred in the result but dissented from Justice White's opinion. Justice Goldberg criticized the opinion of the court of appeals for its holding that the union was subject to Sherman Act liability because the hours during which meat could be sold were a "proprietary" matter within the exclusive control of the employer and of no legitimate concern to the union. He criticized the dissenting opinion of Justice Douglas for condemning an agreement over selling hours merely because the agreement was reached through multiemployer bargaining. (Justice White's opinion did not treat the Jewel Tea contract as a product of multiemployer bargaining.) Justice Goldberg criticized Justice White's opinion for drawing lines among mandatory subjects of bargaining, and for permitting bargaining based on some mandatory subjects to be free from antitrust scrutiny while subjecting others to that scrutiny "presumably based on a judicial determination of [the subject's] importance to the worker...." In Justice Goldberg's view, "Congress intended that collective bargaining under the labor act [was not subject] to the antitrust laws...."

Justice Douglas, with whom Justices Black and Clark joined, dissented on the ground that the collective bargaining agreement between the multiemployer group and the unions in this case was evidence of a conspiracy among those employers and the unions to impose the marketing hours restriction on Jewel Tea by a strike threat from the unions—an *Allen Bradley* conspiracy.

Several points with respect to Justice White's opinion are worth considering. First Justice White poses a hypothetical agreement between a union and a single employer over prices to be charged for the employer's product. He appears to treat it as an agreement among competitors to set prices. If, as he seems to say, the case does not involve multiemployer bargaining considerations, it is not apparent why a union, acting alone and not at the behest of other employers, and a single employer with whom that union bargains should be considered engaged in a conspiracy of product market competitors.

Second, Justice White's test for determining whether union actions deserve antitrust immunity is not as clear as it might be. At one point, the opinion speaks of accommodating national labor policy and Sherman Act coverage and devises a test that might be described as a "least restrictive alternative" test: Did the union insist upon a restraint in the commercial market no greater than that necessary to preserve its legitimate interests in wages, hours and working conditions? But in other parts of the opinion, the Justice talks in terms of weighing respective interests. If this means that a lower court should weigh the legitimacy of the union's objectives against the magnitude of the competitive restraint, then it is arguably a return to the pre-Norris-LaGuardia Act practice of imposing a judge's personal views of good labor policy under the rubric of the antitrust laws. It must be conceded, however, that unlike that period, there are now over forty years of NLRA developments setting out the national labor policy.

Another decade was to pass before the Supreme Court cleared up some of the confusion. In Connell Const. Co. v. Plumbers & Steamfitters Local Union No. 100 (U.S.1975), the Court decided a labor antitrust case with substantial secondary boycott overtones. Local 100 represented workers in the plumbing and mechanical trades in Dallas and was party to a multiemployer bargaining agreement with a group of about 75 mechanical contractors. The union approached the Connell Construction Co., a construction industry general contractor, seeking an agreement that Connell would subcontract jobsite mechanical work only to firms that had a current collective bargaining agreement with the union. Connell's practice was to obtain work through competitive bidding and to subcontract all the jobsite plumbing and mechanical work. Connell followed a policy of awarding these subcontracts on the basis of competitive bids and favored neither union nor nonunion subcontractors.

While Connell's employees were represented by various construction industry unions, Local 100 had never sought to represent any of Connell's employees nor to bargain on their behalf. Connell refused to sign the union's subcontracting agreement and Local 100 picketed, causing a major construction project to come to a halt. Connell filed suit in Texas state court to enjoin the picketing as a violation of Texas antitrust law and Local 100 removed the case to federal court. At that point, Connell signed the subcontracting agreement under protest and amended its complaint to allege a Sherman Act antitrust violation. While this was going on, Connell also asked the NLRB's regional director to issue a complaint that the agreement violated § 8(e) of the NLRA, but the regional director refused.

The district court found that the subcontracting clause was authorized by the construction industry proviso to § 8(e) of the NLRA and that this federal legislation preempted the state's antitrust laws. The Fifth Circuit affirmed, finding that the union's goal was a proper one of organizing non-union subcontractors and that state law was preempted. The Supreme Court granted certiorari. It affirmed the ruling on state law preemption but held there was no federal antitrust immunity.

According to Justice Powell's opinion for the Court, the statutory immunity recognized in *Hutcheson* is lost whenever a union enters into a bargaining agreement with an employer. But there is a second, nonstatutory immunity stemming from "a proper accommodation between the Congressional policy favoring collective bargaining under the NLRA and the Congressional policy favoring free competition in business markets...." The source of the nonstatutory immunity is the Congressional policy of freeing unions to remove the competitive elements of wages and working conditions from business competition. While the union can promote this limited interest, it cannot directly restrain competition in the "business market."

Here the union's goal was to support its organizing efforts, but the union's restraint on the business market was too broad, the union had done more than simply take wages out of commercial competition. To demonstrate the breadth of the business market restraint, Justice Powell emphasized certain facts in the case. The agreement with Connell, and the similar agreements with other general contractors, excluded nonunion subcontractors from a substantial portion of the Dallas market even if those subcontractors gained their competitive advantage over unionized employers for reasons other than lower wages, hours and working conditions. A nonunion subcontractor with more efficient operating methods would be excluded from the market even though it paid union wages. Furthermore, the multiemployer bargaining agreement between Local 100 and Dallas mechanical contractors contained a "most favored nation" clause, which gave the mechanical contractors the right to insist on inclusion in their bargaining agreement of any favorable term which the union might negotiate with a new mechanical contractor. The mechanical contractors were thereby guaranteed that the union would give no new subcontractor any competitive advantages over existing signers of the union's bargaining agreement. Since such an agreement might well include nonmandatory items of bargaining, this effectuated a substantial potential restraint on the market. Furthermore, the Court worried that the union could create a sheltered market in Dallas, keeping out subcontractors by refusing to sign collective bargaining agreements with them.

While the Court conceded that the union's goal of organizing subcontractors was legal, the agreement with Connell enjoyed no such immunity: "This kind of direct restraint on the business market has substantial anticompetitive effects, both actual and potential, that would not follow naturally from the elimination of competition over wages and working conditions. It contravenes antitrust policies to a degree not justified by congressional labor policy, and therefore cannot claim a nonstatutory exemption from the antitrust laws."

Justice Powell reasoned that although there is a labor policy favoring collective bargaining and bargaining agreements, no such interest could be shown by the union in this case because it represented none of Connell's employees, nor did it seek to represent them, and so the bargaining agreement was not one protected by national labor policy.

Justice Powell then turned to the thorny issue of relating NLRA secondary boycott liability and the Sherman Act exemption. The union argued that the agreement with Connell was protected by the construction industry proviso to § 8(e) of the NLRA, or in the alternative, that if it were not within the proviso it then violated § 8(e), a violation for which the NLRA provided the sole remedy.

Justice Powell first scrutinized the clause for § 8(e) liability. He found that the congressional intent in enacting the construction industry proviso was to allow unions to protect their members from having to work along side of nonunion workmen on construction jobsites with resultant strife. But the union in this case represented none of the general contractor's employees, and the scope of the agreement was not limited to jobsites where the union's members would necessarily be working. Furthermore, the clause would not prevent the use of nonunion subcontractors in other trades. The union was using the clause to organize subcontractors by putting pressure on general contractors (called "topdown" organizing)—a purpose outside the congressional policy—and the Court was unwilling to construe the proviso as legitimatizing such conduct. The construction industry proviso "extends only to agreements in the context of collective bargaining relationships and ... possibly to common-situs relationships on particular job sites as well."

Having found the clause not to be protected by § 8(e), Justice Powell turned to whether NLRA remedies for secondary boycotts preclude Sherman Act scrutiny of those boycotts. The union showed that when Congress passed § 8(b)(4) and § 303 in 1947, some Congressmen had proposed that secondary activity be regulated by an expanded application of the antitrust laws. These suggestions were rejected and NLRA remedies were enacted instead. Refusing to decide the effect of this history, the

Court left open the question of whether conduct precluded by § 8(b)(4) is to be free from antitrust scrutiny because in the instant case the allegation was that the union's clause violated § 8(e). That section was enacted in 1959 when no legislative history suggested it as an alternative to the imposition of antitrust liability. Furthermore, the damage remedy available in § 303 of the NLRA could not provide the exclusive remedy in this case, for § 303 does not provide damages for § 8(e) violations.

In the court below, Connell had sought to enjoin further union picketing to coerce execution of the contract. Connell obtained a temporary restraining order against the picketing and thereafter signed the contract. There had been no further picketing at Connell's construction sites. The union argued in the Supreme Court that even if the contract clause violated the Sherman Act, the injunction remedy was withdrawn by the Norris–LaGuardia Act because there was a "labor dispute" between the parties. Justice Powell found it unnecessary to resolve this question since there had been no further picketing at Connell's construction jobsite and he did not anticipate that the union would resume picketing to compel adherence to an illegal agreement.

Justices Douglas, Brennan and Marshall joined a dissenting opinion authored by Justice Stewart. The dissent correctly noted that § 8(b)(4)(A) and § 303 combine to provide a damage remedy for an employer when a union strikes in order to force the employer to sign a bargaining agreement that violates § 8(e). The dissent saw Connell as having a fully effective private damage remedy in the circumstances of this case. Furthermore, any non-union mechanical contractor believing that its business had been harmed by the unlawful § 8(e) agreement secured by the strike would have standing to sue for damages under § 303. If, on the other hand, the union was correct in its assertion that its conduct was specifically protected by the construction industry proviso to § 8(e), that would be a clear indication that the conduct must be free from antitrust scrutiny. Even had Connell entered into an unlawful agreement absent union strike pressure, an excluded subcontractor would still have § 8(e) remedies available, although no § 303 damage suit could be sustained. The dissent suggested that had Connell voluntarily agreed to limit its subcontracting, that might well suggest an *Allen Bradley* antitrust business conspiracy.

The important parts of the *Connell* discussion are the definition of labor's exemptions to the antitrust laws, the tests for when the exemptions apply, and the relationship of the antitrust laws to the NLRA's secondary boycott provisions. As to the first, what could only be inferred from *Jewel Tea* is now explicit: The *Hutcheson* immunity is virtually a dead letter. Only if the union is acting unilaterally will this statutory immunity attach. An employer wanting to challenge unilateral union activity on antitrust grounds need only formally agree to the union's demand and then challenge the agreement on antitrust grounds, as was done in *Connell*.

The important consideration, then, is the nonstatutory immunity. As in Justice White's opinion in *Jewel Tea*, there is some suggestion in *Connell* that the Court is adopting a "least restrictive alternative" analysis. That is, the union can take economic action and reach agreements with employers to remove wages, hours and working conditions from business competition; but to the extent that the union's restraint on the business market affects a greater elimination of competition than is necessary to secure the removal, it is not immune from antitrust scrutiny. There is, however, also a suggestion in Justice Powell's *Connell* opinion that even the broader restraint might be entitled to the nonstatutory exemption if it is grounded in a policy sheltering collective bargaining agreements.

There is less suggestion in Justice Powell's opinion than in Justice White's *Jewel Tea* opinion that the lower courts are to balance union interests against antitrust interests. *Connell* seems to be saying that once an anticompetitive restraint is found, the national labor policy should be looked to for a determination of whether the union's conduct is justified.

Whether the policy favoring collective bargaining will actually shelter union conduct in other situations is an open question. Consider the union's insistence in National Woodwork Manufacturers Ass'n v. NLRB (U.S.1967) that its members should not be required to handle factory prefabricated doors on a construction job site. This was held not to be a secondary boycott on the grounds that it was work preservation and thus primary. Would it now enjoy Sherman Act immunity? On the one hand, the union has not adopted the least restrictive alternative: presumably, it might merely restrict job site importation of doors produced at a factory where union wages, hours and working conditions are undercut.

An alternative analysis is that the Supreme Court's *National Woodwork* opinion conclusively demonstrates that national labor policy in this context protects collective bargaining agreements that have resulted from the free hammering-out between unions and employers of inconsistent economic positions over work preservation and technological progress. Note that this is not the same as saying that the union's economic interest in job security is more important than freeing the product market from the union's restraint.

The *Connell* treatment of the relation between NLRA secondary boycott liability and antitrust liability is troubling on two grounds. First, it seems mischievous to suggest that if the union's conduct violates only § 8(e) then *treble* antitrust damages under the antitrust laws are available; but if the union also violates § 8(b)(4), then § 303 damages are the exclusive remedy. If the Court is ultimately forced to conclude that secondary boycott liability never precludes antitrust exposure, then § 303 damages are presumably unimportant because any § 303 plaintiff should now include a Sherman Act request for treble damages as a routine matter. Furthermore, if the nonstatutory exemption is lost whenever an antitrust restraint is not justified by congressional labor policy, as articulated in the federal labor statute, then isn't all unlawful secondary conduct by unions left without the benefit of the nonstatutory immunity because such actions are contrary to that labor policy?

An issue that has faced the lower courts several times after *Connell* is what antitrust liability standard to apply to a union secondary boycott once the statutory and nonstatutory exemptions are lost. The courts are split over whether to apply a rule of reason analysis or to find a per se violation. The argument for a per se violation is that group boycotts are so treated in other areas of antitrust law. Yet in antitrust law there are a host of exceptions to that statement. Moreover, if this was to be the rule, why did Justice Powell in *Connell* engage in so much additional analysis about the anticompetitive effects of the union's boycott?

In nonlabor antitrust cases, the rule of reason analysis consists of a full scale examination of the defendant's conduct, focusing on its anticompetitive effects and on its efficiency justifications. When lower courts have purported to apply a rule of reason in labor cases, however, they have focused on labor policy and the union's general interests rather than on efficiency justifications.

CHAPTER IX

ENFORCEMENT OF COLLECTIVE BARGAINING AGREEMENTS

A. The Role of Grievance Arbitration

The great majority of today's collective bargaining agreements provide for an impartial arbitrator to hear and decide grievances under the bargaining agreement. The details of grievance arbitration vary considerably among agreements. The handling of grievances at the lowest level in the plant ranges from highly formal to very informal. Agreements differ on who can file grievances; the union almost always is permitted to file a grievance, and sometimes the employer and individual employees are permitted to file as well. The power given to the arbitrator to decide grievances also varies considerably. An arbitrator may be empowered to decide any dispute arising during the term of the agreement, or the arbitrator may be limited to deciding disputes that relate to the meaning, application, or interpretation of the agreement. Some bargaining agreements withdraw specified matters from the arbitrator's authority, or put other kinds of limits on decisions that the arbitrator may reach.

Should either party to a bargaining agreement that provides for arbitration refuse to submit a grievance to arbitration, the other party may resort to federal or state court action to compel the submission or, in some cases, (with or without the agreement's authorization) may resort to economic coercion to force a submission to arbitration.

Some collective bargaining agreements designate a permanent arbitrator to decide grievances during the term of the agreement, but the majority of agreements call for ad hoc arbitration. In the latter situation, the parties will mutually agree on a particular arbitrator to decide one or more grievances that have occurred during the term of the agreement. This arbitrator may or may not have had prior experience with these parties.

Arbitration hearings are generally less formal than court trials. The rules of evidence are relaxed and the parties themselves may have a greater control over the form of the process than they would have in court. Sometimes transcripts are taken and legal briefs may or may not be filed. Arbitrators vary considerably in the length of time they require to prepare their opinion and award. Opinions and awards are usually in writing and contain a statement of the grievance, a summary of the evidence and the arguments on both sides, an explanation of the reasons why the arbitrator has reached her decision, and a statement of relief granted. Arbitrators normally charge on a per diem basis, and most often the costs of arbitration are shared by the parties.

If the losing party refuses to comply with an arbitration award, the winning party must either seek judicial enforcement in a breach of contract action, or resort to economic action to compel compliance with the award, with or without bargaining agreement sanction. A few agreements stipulate that arbitrators' awards shall be advisory only.

The jurisdiction of federal district courts to hear suits alleging breach of collective bargaining agreements, including failure to arbitrate and to comply with arbitrators' awards, came before the Supreme Court in Textile Workers Union v. Lincoln Mills (U.S.1957). In that case, the collective bargaining agreement contained a broad no-strike clause and a clause providing for arbitration as the last step in the grievance procedure. The employer refused to arbitrate a grievance and the union sought an injunction in federal district court ordering the employer to arbitrate. The district court assumed jurisdiction under § 301 of the LMRA, which by its terms gives district courts power to hear suits for breach of a bargaining agreement. However, in argument before the Supreme Court, the employer contended that the effect of this provision was to give a naked grant of jurisdiction to federal courts without a corresponding grant of substantive law to apply and that such a grant was unconstitutional because it exceeded the Article 3 power. The Court finessed this issue by holding that there is "no constitutional difficulty." The Court construed § 301(a) as directing the federal courts to develop a federal common law of collective bargaining agreement enforcement.

The employer also resisted the lawsuit by arguing that an injunction compelling it to submit the grievance to arbitration would violate the anti-injunction provisions of the Norris–LaGuardia Act. While the Court acknowledged that a literal reading of that statute might support the employer, it found that "the failure to arbitrate was not a part and parcel of the abuses against which the Act was aimed." The Norris–LaGuardia Act was thus no bar to the union's suit.

In subsequent developments the Supreme Court ruled that state courts have concurrent jurisdiction to enforce collective bargaining agreements, Dowd Box Co. v. Courtney (U.S.1962), but they must apply the federal common law of collective bargaining agreements and enforcement. Teamsters Local 174 v. Lucas Flour Co. (U.S.1962). Actions for breach of collective bargaining agreements brought in state courts may be removed to federal courts by defendants under the federal question removal jurisdiction. Avco Corp. v. Aero Lodge 735 (U.S.1968).

The contours of the federal common law of bargaining agreement enforcement were developed in three cases decided together in 1960, which have come to be known as the "Steelworkers Trilogy." Two of the cases dealt with the issue of what standard a federal court is to apply in determining whether a grievance should be ordered submitted to arbitration. The third case dealt with the standard to be applied when the winning party seeks enforcement of the award.

In United Steelworkers v. American Manufacturing Co. (U.S.1960), an employee left his work because of an injury and settled a Workmen's Compensation claim against the company on the basis that he was permanently partially disabled. Afterwards the union filed a grievance claiming that the employee was entitled to return to work by virtue of the bargaining agreement's seniority provision. The agreement provided that arbitration could be had of all disputes "as to the meaning, interpretation and application of the provisions of the agreement." The company, considering the grievance to be frivolous, refused the union's demand to arbitrate the grievance. The union sued in federal district court to compel arbitration and the case eventually reached the Supreme Court.

Justice Douglas, speaking for the Court, found in § 203(d) of the LMRA a congressional policy of giving voluntary settlement mechanisms under a collective bargaining agreement full play by the courts. The opinion expressly disapproved a case from New York, IAM v. Cutler—Hammer, Inc. (N.Y.1947), which had held that if the meaning of a bargaining agreement provision is beyond dispute, there is no issue to arbitrate and the contract cannot be said to provide for arbitration in such an instance. Justice Douglas pointed out that the bargaining agreement in this case called for the submission of all grievances to arbitration, and he would not construe this to mean merely those grievances a court deems to have merit. Furthermore, the agreement contained no exception to the "no strike" clause which is the *quid pro quo* for the grievance arbitration.

The courts are to stay out of the merits of the claim: "The function of the court is very limited when the parties have agreed to submit all questions of contract interpretation to the arbitrator. It is confined to ascertaining whether the party seeking arbitration is making a claim which on its face is governed by the contract." Even the processing of frivolous claims, in the Court's view, has a therapeutic effect on the plant environment.

The arbitration clause was more complex in a companion case, United Steelworkers v. Warrior and Gulf Navigation Co. (U.S.1960). There the employer contracted out to another company certain bargaining unit work, causing employee layoffs. The union grieved over the contracting out claiming that it constituted a partial employer lockout. The agreement had a broad no-strike clause, a no-lockout clause, and an exclusion from arbitration clause reading: "Issues ... which are strictly a function of management shall not be subject to arbitration under this section." Yet the agreement committed to arbitration "differences

[that] arise between the company and the union or its members employed by the company as to the meaning and application of the provisions of this agreement, or [with respect to] any local trouble of any kind...."

The union sued the employer in federal district court to compel the employer to submit the contracting-out dispute to arbitration. The district court held that contracting out was a management function and thus was excluded from arbitration. The court of appeals affirmed. The case served as a vehicle for Justice Douglas to comment generally on the nature of the collective bargaining agreement. In his view, a bargaining agreement is more than a contract, it is a generalized code to govern a variety of situations that the draftsman cannot or will not wholly anticipate. Given the complexities of industrial relations in a particular plant, a bargaining agreement cannot reduce everything to writing, and the nature of the labor relations process demands "a common law of the shop which implements and furnishes the context of the agreement."

Inevitably gaps will be left in such an agreement and many of the specific practices underlying the bargaining agreement may be "unknown, except in hazy form, even to the negotiators." At the heart of most collective bargaining agreements is the grievance and arbitration machinery. Arbitration serves as the forum for resolving disputes unforeseen by the bargaining agreement. Thus, a court asked to compel the submission of a grievance to arbitration is to do so freely: "apart from matters that the parties specifically exclude, all of the questions on which the parties disagree must ... come within the scope of the grievance and arbitration provisions of the collective agreement." Furthermore, the arbitrator is not confined to the express provisions of the bargaining agreement "as the industrial common law—the practices of the industry and the shop—is equally a part of the collective bargaining agreement although not expressed in it."

Arbitrators may consider factors such as the effect on productivity of a particular result, the decision's consequence to the morale of the shop, and the degree to which tensions will be either heightened or diminished by a considered result. The Court repeated its standard: "[the] judicial inquiry under § 301 must be strictly confined to the question whether the reluctant party did agree to arbitrate the grievance or did agree to give the arbitrator power to make the award he made. An order to arbitrate the particular grievance should not be denied unless it may be said with positive assurance that the arbitration clause is not susceptible of an interpretation that covers the asserted dispute. Doubts should be resolved in favor of coverage." Thus although the scope of an arbitration clause is normally for the court to construe, the standard to be applied leaves little room for exclusion.

In the instant case, Justice Douglas found the scope of the grievance procedure to be broad, including, as it did, "local trouble of any kind." Also significant was the fact that the no-strike clause contained no exceptions. The lower court was not to decide the merits of the grievance in the guise of determining arbitrability, even though the agreement excluded functions of management from arbitration; the meaning of that clause must be interpreted, said the Court, to refer only to those matters over which the contract specifically gives management complete control and unfettered discretion. Since contracting out is a typical subject for arbitration and was not specifically excluded from this arbitration clause, the union grievance had to be ordered to arbitration.

A dissenting Justice found in the record evidence that during negotiations the union had sought a restriction on management's right to contract out and had failed to secure it. This issue was taken up in a concurring opinion by Justice Brennan and two other Justices. According to that opinion, since a court can explore the collective bargaining agreement to see if contracting out is a management function, there is no logical reason why it could not examine bargaining history. But whatever logic might require, national labor policy demands that there be no such search into bargaining history. The possibility of error and of substantial intrusion by the courts is too great; the lower courts are only to search the bargaining agreement for any explicit provision excluding an item from arbitration.

Lower court cases since the *Steelworkers Trilogy* have generally applied the proper standard for sending a grievance to arbitration, but there have been exceptions. Union claims resting upon past practice that cannot be tied to any specific language in the agreement have occasionally fared badly in the lower courts. This is especially true where the agreement contains language (seen by many experienced observers as boilerplate) such as: "The arbitrator shall be bound by the provisions of this agreement and shall have no authority to add to, subtract from, amend or modify any of its provisions." See Boeing Co. v. UAW (3d Cir.1965).

Where the subject matter of a grievance is specifically excluded from arbitration, it logically means only that a court, rather than an arbitrator, should decide whether the action challenged by the grievance is a breach of contract. Nonetheless, it is clear that in the majority of cases where a subject matter is excluded from the bargaining agreement's arbitration clause, the exclusion is meant to vest absolute discretion over that term in one party, usually management.

The Supreme Court has ruled that where the contention is made that a grievance is not arbitrable because a procedural step in the collective bargaining agreement has not been complied with, that issue is for the arbitrator, not a court. John Wiley and Sons, Inc. v. Livingston (U.S.1964). Procedural issues are too often intertwined with the substantive merit of the grievance, and to permit a court to decide procedural issues in the first instance would enmesh the court in the merits of the grievance.

In Nolde Bros., Inc. v. Bakery Workers Local 358 (U.S.1977), the bargaining agreement provided for severance pay if the employment of certain employees was ended. After termination of the collective bargaining agreement, the employer permanently closed its bakery. Although employees received accrued wages and vacation pay due them under the terminated agreement, the employer refused to pay severance money and also refused to arbitrate the union's claim for severance money, contending that the employer's contractual commitment to arbitrate disputes had ended with the termination of the agreement. The union brought a § 301 suit to compel arbitration, and the Supreme Court ordered the dispute to be arbitrated. The union argued that the right to severance pay had vested under the terminated agreement, while the company contended that the right to severance pay and its obligation to arbitrate ended at the same time the bargaining terminated. The Court found that the parties' substantive disagreement turned on an interpretation of the bargaining agreement, an interpretation that would have been reserved for an arbitrator absent the agreement's termination. The company's argument, carried to its logical conclusion, would deny arbitration even when a dispute occurred during the agreement's term but arbitration was either not requested or completed prior to the agreement's termination. The Court found this result to be foreclosed by precedent and policy. Thus absent indications in the expired agreement of a contrary intent by the parties, a strong presumption favoring arbitration applies, and for such a dispute to be withheld from arbitration, "the presumption favoring arbitrability must be negated expressly or by clear implication."

The last case in the *Steelworkers Trilogy* involves the question of the scrutiny that courts asked to enforce an arbitrator's award should give to the merits of the award. In United Steelworkers v. Enterprise Wheel and Car Corp. (U.S.1960), a bargaining agreement clause provided that any disputes over the meaning and application of the bargaining agreement should be sent to final and binding arbitration. An arbitrator then found that the discharge of the strikers was not justified, although punishment of some sort was proper. He ordered the employees reinstated with back pay, with the deduction of ten days' pay for each and of any moneys earned by them elsewhere during their layoff. However, after the discharges and before the arbitration award was issued, the bargaining agreement expired. Nonetheless, the district court directed the employer to comply with the award. The court of appeals reversed, holding that the failure of the award to specify with precision the amounts to be deducted from the back pay rendered the award unenforceable and, in any event, that an award for back pay subsequent to the date the contract terminated could not be enforced. Reinstatement of the discharged employees was likewise unenforceable because of the agreement's expiration.

The Supreme Court reversed in an opinion by Justice Douglas. The same policy considerations that compel a court to order an employer to arbitrate even though the court sees no merit in the union's grievance also compels the court to abide by the arbitrator's decision and award even though it finds that award on its merits to be repugnant to logic and justice. In some circumstances the court is required to refuse to enforce an award, but the circumstances are limited: "Nevertheless, an arbitrator is confined to interpretation and application of the collective bargaining agreement; he does not sit to dispense his own brand of industrial justice. He may of course look for guidance from many sources, yet his award is legitimate only so long as it draws its essence from the collective bargaining agreement. When the arbitrator's words manifest an infidelity to this obligation, courts have no choice but to refuse enforcement of the award." An ambiguity suggesting that the arbitrator may have gone outside the collective bargaining agreement is not enough to warrant setting aside the award. Since arbitrators need not write opinions supporting their awards, scrutinizing those opinions for ambiguity might suggest to arbitrators that they should write no opinions at all, a result inconsistent with sound labor policy. The parties in the instant case bargained for the arbitrator's construction of the agreement, and that is the construction they should get, not the construction of the reviewing court.

The strong presumption in favor of the enforceability of an arbitration award was reaffirmed by the Supreme Court some 30 years after the *Steelworkers Trilogy* in United Paperworkers Intern. Union v. Misco, Inc. (U.S.1987).

Most lower court decisions since the *Steelworkers Trilogy* have applied Justice Douglas' standard of review of an arbitrator's award, but occasionally courts have been so offended by a particular award that they have found a way to reverse it. A celebrated example is Torrington Co. v. Metal Products Workers (2d Cir.1966). The employer publicly announced that it was discontinuing its practice of giving employees paid time off for voting. The practice had been consistently adhered to by the employer but was not mentioned in the bargaining agreement. Negotiating for a new bargaining agreement, the union demanded that the practice be reinstated, but the company refused and a strike ensued. The strike was settled and a new agreement was signed. The new agreement, like the old, however, made no mention of paid time off for voting.

When the employer next refused voting time pay, the union grieved and carried the dispute to arbitration. The arbitrator held for the union. Since during negotiations each side had submitted a proposal that incorporated its position with respect to the voting time pay, and since the company submitted the first written proposal that did not expressly insist that its position be put in the agreement, the arbitrator took this to be a removal of the company's position from bargaining. He found that the company had the burden of negotiating away a past practice and that it had not done so.

The Second Circuit set aside the arbitrator's award on the ground that he had exceeded his authority by reaching a result inconsistent with contractual language that forbade him to add to the collective bargaining agreement. Admitting that this involved the court in a consideration of the merits, the opinion argued that the *Steelworkers Trilogy* gave it authority to examine the question of the arbitrator's authority, and based its decision on that ground.

The *Torrington* court may have given itself away when it stated, "[W]e think more exhaustive judicial review of this question is appropriate after the award has been made than before the award in a suit to compel arbitration...." While perhaps that position should have been reached by the Supreme Court in the *Steelworkers Trilogy*, it was not. It is not clear that the parties to the agreement meant to signal more exhaustive judicial review by including language in their agreement such as "no additions or modifications." It seems more likely that such language is boilerplate.

The enforcement of a collective bargaining agreement sometimes involves overlap and conflict with the NLRA. The Supreme Court has had no particular difficulty where it has been alleged that a breach of the bargaining agreement is also an unfair labor practice. The breach of contract action may go forward although its maintenance will not affect the power of the Board to issue a remedy. Local 174, Teamsters v. Lucas Flour Co (U.S.1962); Smith v. Evening News Ass'n (U.S.1962). Presumably the Court was influenced by the fact that arbitration decisions are often reached more quickly than Board decisions and that to stay breach of contract actions would give parties an opportunity for dilatory maneuvers.

In recent years there has been vigorous disagreement within the arbitration profession over what an arbitrator should do when asked to sustain a grievance which, in the arbitrator's view, would force the losing party to commit an unfair labor practice or other violation of law. Some arbitrators contend that it demeans the arbitration process to issue an award which, because it directs a violation of law, is unenforceable. Other arbitrators take the view that an arbitrator is only the ultimate contract interpreter and that as a creature of contract the arbitrator has no business looking to external law unless the bargaining agreement itself directs the arbitrator to look to external law (incorporation by reference).

A similar issue can come before a court when it is petitioned to send to arbitration a grievance that the resisting party contends would compel a violation of law, or when a similar defense is raised against enforcement of an arbitrator's award. It may be appropriate for the court to examine the issue only after the arbitrator's award is rendered, since the claim that a grievance would compel a violation of law may be mooted by the arbitrator's refusal to find that the grievance is meritorious.

In W.R. Grace v. Rubber Workers Local 759 (U.S.1983), a case involving potential conflict between a collective bargaining agreement arbitration award and Title VII of the Civil Rights Act, the Court agreed that federal courts should not enforce awards that violate "explicit" public policy. The Court cautioned that "[s]uch a policy ... must be well defined and dominant, and is to be ascertained 'by reference to the laws and legal precedents and not from general considerations of supposed public interests.'" This test was reaffirmed by the Court in United Paperworkers Union v. Misco, Inc. (U.S.1987)

Occasionally a party who contends that an arbitrator's award will or does compel a violation of law is, in effect, attempting to avoid a procedural prerequisite to enforcing that law. For example, certain conduct can be prosecuted as an unfair labor practice only if the NLRB's General Counsel challenges that conduct (e.g., § 8(a)(3) and § 8(b)(2), while other conduct may be adjudged a violation without regard to the General Counsel's agreement to prosecute (e.g., § 8(e)). Sometimes a violation of law will not be remediable because of a procedural default; examples are an unfair labor practice barred by the six-month statute of limitations, and an asserted civil rights violation barred for lack of exhaustion with the Equal Employment Opportunity Commission. Arguably, in these situations at least, the arbitrator should not scrutinize a potential award by the standards of external law.

B. Enforcing the No–Strike Clause

Most collective bargaining agreements contain some form of no-strike clause. Many clauses broadly prohibit all strikes during the term of the agreement, others prohibit strikes over any grievance that the employer is bound to arbitrate. A few clauses expressly permit strikes under specified circumstances; the most common is a strike permitted over a grievance which the employer refuses to arbitrate, or over an arbitration award with which the employer refuses to comply.

Where the bargaining agreement does not contain a no-strike clause, the Supreme Court has held that in appropriate circumstances one may be implied. In Local 174, Teamsters v. Lucas Flour Co. (U.S.1962), the union struck in protest of the discharge of a worker even though the bargaining agreement provided for binding arbitration of disputes and contained a union promise not to suspend work "during such arbitration." There was no general no-strike clause. The employer sued to recover damages caused by the strike, and the

Supreme Court held that "a strike to settle a dispute which a collective bargaining agreement provides shall be settled exclusively and finally by compulsory arbitration constitutes a violation of the agreement...."

The Court relied on both ordinary contract principles and its notions of national labor policy, and said that a no-strike obligation is not to be implied beyond the area that is covered by compulsory binding arbitration. In Gateway Coal Co. v. United Mine Workers (U.S.1974), the Court again implied a no-strike obligation from a broad arbitration clause and held that the implied no-strike clause would support an injunction against the strike.

In Mastro Plastics Corp. v. NLRB (U.S.1956), the Court construed a broad explicit no-strike clause as not covering a strike in protest of serious employer unfair labor practices that undermined the union's representative status.

Section 301 of the NLRA gives district courts jurisdiction to enforce bargaining agreements, including no-strike clauses. If the grievance and arbitration clause of a collective bargaining agreement states that the employer shall arbitrate his claims against the union, then arbitration is the place for an employer's claim for damages caused by a union strike in breach of the agreement. If the agreement only permits the *union* to grieve and take a case to arbitration, the employer's damage action for union breach of the no-strike clause lies in federal district court or state court. Atkinson v. Sinclair Refining Co. (U.S.1962).

Even though the union may be found liable in damages for breach of a no-strike clause, the officers and members of the union are not personally liable for those damages. *Atkinson.* Nor can the employer sue individual employees directly for the breach of a no-strike clause even if they have engaged in unauthorized, individual action. The Court reached this conclusion in Complete Auto Transit v. Reis (U.S.1981), reasoning that there are other methods for controlling wildcat strikes. These include discharging or otherwise disciplining workers who have participated in a strike in breach of the agreement, or asking the union to institute internal union disciplinary procedures against the wildcatters. However, in the absence of an express contractual clause obligating it to do so, a union is not liable for damages when it fails to take all reasonable steps to prevent wildcat strikes in breach of a bargaining agreement. Carbon Fuel Co. v. United Mine Workers (U.S.1979).

Employers have sometimes declared a bargaining agreement to be terminated by a union's strike in breach of contract. The employers' theory rests on the common law rule that a material breach of contract excuses performance on the other side. The Supreme Court has expressly rejected this theory in the context of collective bargaining agreements. Drake Bakeries, Inc. v. Bakery Workers Local 50 (U.S.1962); Packinghouse Workers Local 721 v. Needham Packing Co. (U.S.1964).

Employers are not often satisfied with damage actions for breach of the no-strike clause; they want the strike enjoined. In Sinclair Refining Co. v. Atkinson (U.S.1962), the Supreme Court held that the anti-injunction provisions of the Norris–LaGuardia Act preclude a federal district court from enjoining a strike in breach of a no-strike clause. The Court held that § 301 of the NLRA did not expressly or impliedly repeal the Norris–LaGuardia Act in this context. Among other things, the Court relied on NLRA legislative history in which a House provision for repeal of the anti-injunction provisions of Norris–LaGuardia was dropped in conference. Subsequent to *Sinclair*, the Court held in Avco Corp. v. Aero Lodge 735 (U.S.1968) that a suit for breach of bargaining agreement brought in state court could be removed to federal court under the federal question removal jurisdiction. The Court left open the questions of whether state courts are bound by the anti-injunction provisions of Norris–LaGuardia and whether federal courts, after removal of a breach of contract action, are required to dissolve any injunctive relief that might have previously been granted by the state courts.

The application of Norris–LaGuardia to injunctions against strikes in breach of contract was taken up again by the Supreme Court in Boys Markets, Inc. v. Retail Clerks Local 770 (U.S.1970), where the Supreme Court reversed *Sinclair*. The Court held that federal courts are not precluded by the Norris–LaGuardia Act from enjoining a strike in breach of a no-strike clause where the strike is over a grievance that both parties are contractually bound to arbitrate. A court asked to issue such an injunction is to order the employer to arbitrate as a condition of obtaining the injunction. The enjoining court must also consider ordinary principles of equity in determining whether the injunction is warranted. These include whether breaches are occurring and will continue or are threatened, whether the strike will cause irreparable injury to the employer, and whether the employer will suffer more from the denial of an injunction than will the union from its issuance.

The majority opinion in *Boys Markets* handled the legislative history of the NLRA by ignoring it. Stare decisis was also brushed aside with little difficulty. The Court argued that Norris–LaGuardia had already given way to injunctions forcing employers to arbitrate on the ground that a refusal to arbitrate was not "part and parcel of the abuses against which the Act was aimed." The *Avco* and *Sinclair* decisions had combined to give unions the incentive to forum-shop by removing cases from state to federal courts, an incentive not contemplated by Congress and inconsistent with the policy of § 301 to expand remedies for breach of contract. Furthermore, if states were allowed to enjoin strikes when federal courts could not, there would be a lack of uniformity, with no base in any sound labor policy. Finally, the lack of an effective remedy against union strikes in breach of contract provides a disincentive to employers to agree to arbitrate and produces arbitration agreements that are less than effective. Damage remedies are often disruptive and are seldom an effective alternative to the injunction.

Thus the Court was willing to conclude that the literal terms of Norris–LaGuardia must be accommodated to the subsequently enacted § 301. Norris–LaGuardia was treated as responsive to a situation no longer existing; namely, the alliance of federal court judges with management interests to stifle union organization by the use of the injunction. By contrast, current application of the anti-injunction provision to breach of contract strikes frustrates national labor policy. Norris–LaGuardia is no longer to be a bar to such injunctions so long as the circumstances set out by the Court are met.

The result reached by the Court in *Boys Markets* is certainly congenial to what most would perceive as sound labor policy; that the Court's route to that decision was proper is subject to serious question. It is likely that unions had enough influence in Congress to prevent repeal of the Norris–LaGuardia Act, but no statute having the effect of barring injunctions against breach of contract strikes would likely be passed by Congress today. Faced with this legislative stalemate, the Court obviously stepped in partially to repeal Norris–LaGuardia.

The Court subsequently refused to expand the *Boys Markets* exception to the Norris–LaGuardia Act to reach every strike in breach of a collective bargaining agreement. In Buffalo Forge Co. v. United Steelworkers (U.S.1976), the union ordered its members to honor a picket line established by other employees around the employer's premises. The employer claimed that the refusals to cross the picket line constituted a sympathy strike in violation of the union's no-strike pledge in its bargaining agreement and sought to enjoin the sympathy strike. The union denied that a sympathy strike violated the agreement. In a 5 to 4 decision, the Supreme Court held that the injunction was barred by Norris–LaGuardia. The circumstances of this case did not satisfy the conditions required by *Boys Markets* because the strike was not over a dispute which the employer and the union had agreed to arbitrate; the only dispute subject to arbitration was the legality of the sympathy strike itself. The Court relied on the refusal of Congress to repeal Norris–LaGuardia when it enacted § 301 and reasoned that pre-arbitration relief would involve federal courts in the merits of factual and legal issues that should be left to the arbitrator. Court decisions in injunction actions would not always agree with the arbitrators' ultimate decisions and many arbitrators would be heavily influenced by a court's decision in an injunction action. The Court also noted that even temporary injunctions often permanently settle union-management disputes. Once the strike has been declared by an arbitrator to breach the agreement, an injunction would lie.

One result of the *Buffalo Forge* decision appears anomalous. If the employer wishes to retain its power to exercise discretion over a particular working condition, it is likely to demand that in addition to a contract term to that effect, the bargaining agreement shall also exclude any dispute over that working condition from arbitration. While this is the strongest guarantee that neither court nor arbitrator will interfere with the employer's discretion, it has the unintended effect of precluding an injunction against a union strike to interfere with an exercise of the discretion. The *Boys Markets* conditions have not been met, and the dispute is not subject to arbitration. However, an employer can enjoin such a strike after an arbitrator has ruled that the strike is in breach of contract and ordered it to cease. The employer can be expected to demand prompt arbitration of the contract legality of a union strike in such situations, and it would appear that if the union is recalcitrant in submitting to a quick arbitration, the employer might compel swift action by filing a § 301 suit and requesting court action ordering the union to arbitrate immediately.

It is not clear whether Norris–LaGuardia bars injunctions against employer breaches of bargaining agreements in situations where the union can show that the breach cannot be later remedied by arbitration. An example might be an injunction against the sale of a business where the seller is not complying with a guarantee in a collective bargaining agreement that the company will sell only to a buyer who agrees to assume the bargaining agreement. The union can argue that injunctions against employers were not contemplated by Norris–LaGuardia and that such injunctions were not "part and parcel" of the abuses at which Norris–LaGuardia was directed.

C. Contractual and Bargaining Obligations of Successor Employers

When a union has secured bargaining rights for the employees of an employer, and perhaps has negotiated a bargaining agreement, the union naturally hopes to maintain the bargaining rights and the agreement if that employer should be replaced by a second employer. Supreme Court cases on the rights of a union in successorship situations have traveled a twisted path reaching results that are often susceptible to manipulation by a successor employer who wants to rid himself of a union.

The path begins with the Supreme Court's decision in John Wiley & Sons, Inc. v. Livingston (U.S.1964). In that case, the original employer, Interscience, a publisher, was purchased by and merged with John Wiley & Sons, another publishing firm, and ceased to do business as a separate entity. Interscience employees were represented by a union that had a collective bargaining agreement that contained no provision to bind successor employers to the agreement. Wiley was larger than Interscience and its employees were not represented by a union. Wiley refused to recognize the union or to honor the collective bargaining agreement, and the union brought a § 301 action to compel Wiley to arbitrate its grievances under the Interscience agreement.

The Supreme Court held that the question of whether the arbitration provisions of the predecessor's bargaining agreement survived the merger is for the courts to decide. The union relied on state corporation law making the successor liable for the debts of the predecessor and on national labor policy favoring arbitration. The Court held that the change in ownership would not automatically eliminate the duty to arbitrate since such a result would frustrate national labor policy. Rather, a court in a suit to compel arbitration needs to balance the management prerogative to rearrange the nature of the business against the need of employees for continued protection. Noting that collective bargaining agreements are not completely the product of consensual undertakings, the Court held that Wiley could be bound to arbitrate even though it had not in fact consented to the agreement. But the duty to arbitrate does not survive in every case of change in ownership. The test is whether there is a "substantial continuity of identity in the business enterprise before and after a change." Furthermore, the union can lose its right to arbitrate by not making its demand known in a timely fashion.

The Court also pointed out the limited nature of the claims made by the union in this case. No question was raised as to the union's right to continue to represent employees following the change in ownership, nor was the union asserting that it had any rights independent of the predecessor's bargaining agreement. The union did not seek to negotiate a new agreement. The Court brushed over the potentially difficult question of how the union could secure any rights in the Wiley plant for a minority of employees without raising the issues that a "members-only" bargaining agreement ordinarily entails. The bargaining agreement with Interscience had expired, but the union only contended that certain rights under the expired agreement had accrued, or vested. The Court indicated that the union was not seeking to acquire new rights against Wiley by arbitration. Identification of which substantive provisions of the Interscience bargaining agreement survived the change in ownership was left to an arbitrator.

Wiley left open several difficult issues but the most perplexing was the question of standards for an arbitrator who must decide which provisions of the bargaining agreement carry over. This arbitration process resembles interest arbitration, where the arbitrator actually selects the terms and conditions of a bargaining agreement for consenting employers and unions, rather than the grievance arbitration given deference by the Court in the *Steelworkers Trilogy*. In any event, *Wiley* was not to survive intact for long.

In NLRB v. Burns Intern. Securities Services, Inc. (U.S.1972), the Wackenhut Company provided plant guard services under a contract with Lockheed Aircraft at a California location. Wackenhut lost its contract with Lockheed when it was underbid by Burns International Securities Services. When Burns began providing guard services, it employed 42 employees of which 27 had previously been employed by Wackenhut. Burns refused both to bargain with the union that had represented Wackenhut workers and to honor the union's collective bargaining agreement with Wackenhut. Unlike *Wiley*, where the union had sought to compel arbitration in a § 301 suit, the union in *Burns* filed an NLRB charge that Burns had refused to bargain in violation of § 8(a)(5).

The Board held that the security guards at the Lockheed location constituted an appropriate bargaining unit, thus rejecting Burns' argument that the only appropriate unit was a California-wide unit of Burns employees. The Board then found that Burns had violated § 8(a)(5) and (1) by refusing to recognize the union, and by refusing to honor the collective bargaining agreement that the union had negotiated with Wackenhut. The Supreme Court granted certiorari on the bargaining agreement and recognition issues, but declined to review the question of unit appropriateness.

The Court upheld the Board's refusal to bargain finding. Crucial to the 5 to 4 majority on the question of the union's right to continued recognition was the fact that the Board had found the bargaining unit to be still appropriate, and that a majority of the workers hired by Burns had been employed by Wackenhut. It was undisputed that Burns knew all the relevant facts concerning Wackenhut's labor status before Burns took over the security operations at Lockheed.

On the issue of representation, four dissenting Justices argued first that the appropriateness of the bargaining unit was fairly in doubt and that the Court's result prevented Burns' employees from having the free choice guaranteed them by the NLRA. Although 27 of Burns' 42 employees were formerly Wackenhut employees, there was nothing in the record to indicate how many of these employees had approved of being represented by the union when they were employed by Wackenhut, or whether considerations that might have influenced some of them to vote for the union at Wackenhut would still pertain after Burns had taken over.

The Court was unanimous in rejecting a duty of Burns to honor the collective bargaining agreement. The Court relied on the congressional policy of non-interference with collective bargaining agreements as evidenced by § 8(d) of the NLRA, and found this case to be a departure from prior Board precedent, distinguishing *Wiley* on several grounds. First, *Wiley* was brought as a § 301 suit in which there is no § 8(d) limitation. Second, it rested on a preference for arbitration and left the ultimate decision of which contract provisions survived to a labor arbitrator. Third, *Wiley* involved a merger with a state law background that the surviving corporation is liable for the debt of its predecessor; whereas in *Burns* there was no buy-sale arrangement, nor any contact between the two employers. The policy of avoiding strife and securing industrial stability is not the only labor policy worth protecting, especially where, as in *Burns*, there was no voluntary assumption of the bargaining agreement. Forcing the agreement on the new employer might impede the sale of businesses and might also disadvantage the union, which would be unable to take advantage of changes in circumstances. Furthermore, it would mean that the new employer could not replace his predecessor's employees with new employees of his own choosing. The Court held out the possibility that the successor employer might voluntarily assume the provisions of a bargaining agreement or that with respect to other forms of sales and exchanges of capital, the Board might find such an assumption as a matter of law.

The Court turned finally to the Board ruling that Burns could not deviate from Wackenhut's collective bargaining agreement without first bargaining to impasse with the union—unilateral action would violate § 8(a)(5). The Court agreed that Burns had a duty to bargain but held that Burns was not necessarily required to continue the terms and conditions of the Wackenhut bargaining agreement pending current bargaining. Such an obligation turns on whether the new employer plans to retain a majority of the employees in the unit. If it is clear that the firm will retain a majority, then it is appropriate for the firm to consult the union before it fixes employment terms. But where continuity of the predecessor's work force will not be apparent until the successor's full complement of employees is hired, it has freedom to set unilaterally the initial terms and conditions of employment.

Many commentators after *Burns* concluded that the *Wiley* decision was dead, mainly for the reason that none of the grounds upon which it was distinguished by the Court seemed persuasive. Other commentators saw *Burns* as not a successorship case at all and deplored the effect that *Burns* was likely to have on sale-and-purchase of assets cases. However, in Golden State Bottling Co. v. NLRB (U.S.1973), the Court signaled the continuing viability of *Wiley* when it held that an NLRB order remedying an unfair labor practice could run against a purchaser of the enterprise who took with notice of the outstanding NLRB order. The Court relied on *Wiley* and rejected an argument that *Wiley* is applicable only in merger situations.

In Howard Johnson Co. v. Detroit Local Joint Executive Bd. (U.S.1974), the Grissom family operated a motel and restaurant under a Howard Johnson franchise. The Grissoms' collective bargaining agreement with the union provided for the arbitration of disputes and purported to bind any successors to the employer. During the agreement, the Grissoms sold all the personal property involved in the enterprise and leased the real property to the Howard Johnson Corporation. Howard Johnson fired all of the Grissoms' employees and supervisors and hired new employees, only a few of whom had been with the Grissoms. The union filed suit to compel Howard Johnson to arbitrate its dismissal of the Grissoms' employees, relying on *Wiley*.

The Supreme Court held that Howard Johnson had no duty to arbitrate and distinguished *Wiley* on three grounds. First, the parties in *Wiley* knew of the existence of state law making the successor liable for the debts of the predecessor. Second, in the instant case the predecessor still existed as an entity available for relief, although the particular relief requested by the union, continued employment for the employees, was admittedly unavailable. Third, and most important, in *Wiley* all of the predecessor's employees had been hired by the successor whereas here only a few had been rehired. Thus, there is no duty of a successor to arbitrate unless there is continuity in the work force.

The Court suggested some circumstances where this result might not be reached. One is where the successor is the "alter ego" of the predecessor. Another is where the change in ownership is "a paper transaction without meaningful impact on the ownership or operation of the enterprise." The Court also cryptically suggested that the union might have attempted to secure presale injunctive relief, ignoring the difficulty that unions ordinarily have in discovering pending sales prior to their effectuation.

Howard Johnson offers an important incentive for employers, upon taking over another's business, to discharge present employees and make sure that the new employee complement is not substantially comprised of employees of the predecessor. The new employer cannot avoid hiring the old work force if that work force has expertise required by the new employer and lacked by available replacements. But if new employees are readily available, the employer can probably insure the lack of work force continuity by interviewing actively on the open market. Furthermore, although the Court in *Howard Johnson* noted that the employer cannot avoid successorship by discriminating against the predecessor's employees, it did not seem to appreciate how difficult it would be for the union to prove such discrimination and how easy is it for the predecessor to accomplish it. Standards for new hires are usually vague, and unlike many cases where a hiring employer does not know the union affiliation of an applicant, a successor will know from an application form whether an applicant was an employee of the predecessor. Some commentators have argued that continuity of the work force should be controlling only where the successor makes a basic alteration in the operation requiring a change in the composition of the work force or a reduction in the work force. The kind of wholesale discharge that the Howard Johnson Company accomplished with Supreme Court approval is, in these commentators' view, no different than the mass discharge of employees by an employer out to destroy a union's majority status.

In the last important successorship to come before the Court, Fall River Dyeing & Finishing Corp. v. NLRB (U.S.1987), a textile dying and finishing plant fell on hard financial times. It laid off all its production employees, disposed of most of its assets, and hired a professional liquidator to sell the rest. Before this was accomplished, a former employee and a former customer formed a partnership and purchased the remaining assets and inventory. The company then advertised for employees and supervisors. Its initial hiring goal was 50 to 60 workers. In October, the company had hired 21 employees, 18 of whom had been with the original firm. The union that had represented workers in the original firm demanded recognition. By the following January, the company had 55 employees, 36 of whom had been with the original firm. In April, the company had grown to 107 employees, and 52 had been with the original firm. The company refused to bargain with the union, claiming that the company was not a successor employer. According to the Board, the critical period for testing successorship was when the firm had a "representative complement" of workers, which was in January. The union's November request for recognition was held to be a continuing request, thus the company violated § 8(a)(5) when, without recognizing the union, it reached a representative complement in which a majority of the workers had been employed by the original firm.

The Supreme Court first held that where a majority of a firm's employees have worked for the firm's predecessor, there is a conclusive presumption of majority status even if the union was not recently certified, as the union had been in *Burns*. The test for successorship is two-fold: there must be substantial continuity between the two enterprises, and a majority of the successor's employees must have been employed by the predecessor. "Substantial continuity" was described as "whether the business of both employers is essentially the same; whether the employees of the new company are doing the same jobs in the same working conditions under the same supervisors; and whether the new entity has the same production process, produces the same products, and basically has the same body of customers."

The Court then held that the Board was justified in finding substantial continuity in this case notwithstanding a business hiatus. The Court also approved the Board's "substantial complement" and "continuing demand" rules.

An employer's bankruptcy is another form of successorship situation, although the incumbent managers may remain, as the firm is controlled by the debtor-in-possession under supervision of the bankruptcy court. In NLRB v. Bildisco & Bildisco (U.S.1984), the Court addressed whether a debtor-in-possession may reject a collective bargaining agreement as it can other executory agreements, and whether unilateral rejection or modification violates the NLRA's duty to bargain requirement.

The Court held that a bankruptcy court should permit rejection of a collective bargaining agreement "if the debtor can show that the collective agreement burdens the estate, and that after careful scrutiny, the equities balance in favor of rejecting the labor contract." The Court then held that a collective bargaining agreement is not an "enforceable contract" under § 8(d) of the NLRA from the time that the firm files a bankruptcy petition, and so a unilateral termination or modification cannot be prevented by the Labor Board.

Bildisco was soon modified by Congress. The bankruptcy statute was amended to require court approval before a debtor can reject a collective bargaining agreement. Rejection should be allowed only if the union has refused the debtor's proposed contract modifications "without good cause" and if the balance of equities clearly favors rejection of the union contract.

D. The Duty to Represent Fairly in Bargaining and Contract Enforcement

A union with the status of exclusive bargaining representative under the NLRA is charged with the responsibility to represent fairly each of the employees for whom it is the bargaining agent. This duty was first announced in a Railway Labor Act case, Steele v. Louisville & Nashville Railroad (U.S.1944), where the Supreme Court struck down a bargaining agreement that discriminated against black members of the bargaining unit. The Court found embedded in the principle of exclusive representation an implied obligation to represent employees in bargaining fairly, and without hostile discrimination. The duty is no less exacting than the duty the Constitution imposes upon a legislature to give equal protection to those for whom it legislates. A wide range of discretion in bargaining is permitted the union but it must exercise that discretion "fairly, impartially, and in good faith." The same duty was read into the representation provisions of the National Labor Relations Act. Syres v. Oil Workers, Local 23 (U.S.1955).

The union's duty of fair representation under the NLRA is enforceable in a § 301 court suit. In Miranda Fuel Co. (NLRB 1962), enforcement denied (2d Cir.1963), the Board found that a breach of the union's duty violated § 8(b)(1)(A) and 8(b)(2) regardless of whether the breach was influenced by an employee's union activity. Union instigation of employer action against an employee in such circumstances violates § 8(b)(2), and the employer action itself violates § 8(a)(1). Although the Board's holding was rejected by the Second Circuit, the Board has persisted in its view and has been supported by several other circuits. The result is peculiar, not as a matter of policy, but as a matter of statutory interpretation, because the duty is implied from the representation provisions of the Act (§ 9), suggesting that the duty must have existed prior to the Taft–Hartley Act. But prior to Taft–Hartley there were no union unfair labor practices listed in the NLRA.

The duty of fair representation issue was presented to the Supreme Court in a different context in Vaca v. Sipes (U.S.1967). Employee Owens, who had been in the hospital on sick leave, attempted to return to work after getting the approval of his doctor. However, the employer's doctor said that continued work by Owens would endanger his health due to his high blood pressure. When Owens attempted to return he was discharged. The union grieved on Owen's behalf but refused to arbitrate his grievance when an examination by a doctor at the union's expense produced an opinion in agreement with that of the company's doctor. Owens then brought suit in state court attacking the union's refusal to take his case to arbitration. A verdict in favor of Owens was granted in state court but reversed by the Supreme Court.

The Court first held that federal courts, and state courts exercising concurrent jurisdiction over federal claims, have jurisdiction to hear fair representation cases notwithstanding the Board's assertion of jurisdiction in this area. The Court then outlined the contours of the fair representation doctrine in the context of grievance arbitration.

The Court seemed to reject views at both ends of the spectrum: that the union must carry all contract grievances to arbitration, or that the union can always refuse to go to arbitration unless the refusal is impermissibly motivated by racial discrimination or personal hostility. In the view of the Court, not all grievances must be submitted to arbitration lest arbitration become so expensive that its usefulness is ended. But notwithstanding the fact that it has considerable discretion, the union may not arbitrarily ignore a grievance or handle it in a perfunctory fashion. The union must act honestly, in good faith, and in a nonarbitrary manner. A court is not to second-guess the union on the merits of whether a grievance warrants arbitration, however. In this case, since there was no evidence that any union officer was personally hostile to Owens or that the union acted at any time in other than good faith, no breach of duty by the union was made out.

The state court's decision was faulty on another ground. It had charged the union with the entire measure of damages suffered by Owens. The Supreme Court held that courts cannot charge a union with damages that result from an employer's breach of contract. Damages must be apportioned between the employer and the union according to the fault occasioned by each. Those damages caused by the employer's breach of contract are properly chargeable to it, and any increase in the injury suffered by the employee on account of the union's breach of its duty to represent fairly are properly chargeable to the union.

When an employee sues the employer directly, the union's duty of fair representation plays an important role. The Court had already held that § 301 grants jurisdiction to federal courts to hear breach of bargaining agreement actions brought against employers by individual employees. Smith v. Evening News Ass'n (U.S.1962). According to *Vaca*, the employer in such a case may defend against the suit on the grounds that the employee failed to exhaust his contractual remedy of arbitration; the employee will be excused from exhausting the arbitration remedy if the union failed to represent him fairly. Thus the union's performance of its duty of fair representation may be litigated in a breach of contract action even though the union is not a party to the action.

Several judicial remedies are available when an employee sues the employer, and perhaps the union as well, in a breach of bargaining agreement and breach of fair representation suit. If the union is found to have breached its duty, the court may order an employer to arbitrate, the remedy called for by the bargaining agreement, but the court may also decide itself whether the bargaining agreement has been breached and can award damages. According to *Vaca*, availability of the latter alternative is required by sound policy because in some cases a portion of the damages will be attributable to the union's default and the normal arbitration award will not encompass those damages. Also, issues involving the merits of the breach of contract claim may have been completely litigated in the lawsuit and it would be inefficient for the court to not render a decision on those issues.

The Court held in Hines v. Anchor Motor Freight, Inc. (U.S.1976) that even an arbitration award in favor of an employer will not bar an employee suit against it for breach of bargaining agreement if that award is infected by the union's breach of its duty to represent the grieving employee fairly. In that case, the plaintiff employees alleged that evidence favorable to them had not been presented in the arbitration hearing because the union had handled their case in bad faith. There was no allegation that the employer contributed to the union's breach of duty.

In Bowen v. United States Postal Service (U.S.1983), without adequate explanation the union failed to take a grievance to arbitration, thus violating its duty to represent fairly an employee who had been discharged. The trial court apportioned damages between the union and the employer. The employer was charged with lost wages from the time of the discharge to the time an arbitrator would have ordered the employee reinstated, a time estimated by the court. The union was charged with the lost pay for the period after the employee would have been reinstated by the hypothetical arbitration.

Calling the union's decision not to invoke contractual arbitration a "waiver," the majority opinion in the Supreme Court agreed with the trial court's apportionment of damages. The majority emphasized the need to protect the employer's reliance interest. Dissenting Justices suggested that the result will force unions to arbitrate more often because of the risk of greater damage verdicts if they fail to arbitrate.

Many lower courts have required employees seeking to bring fair representation actions against the union, or who would rely on a union breach of fair representation to justify proceeding individually against the employer, to exhaust their internal union remedies. In Clayton v. United Automobile Workers (U.S.1981), the Court held that lower courts have some discretion in deciding whether to require employees to exhaust internal union remedies. The relevant factors are whether union officials are so hostile to the employee that he could not hope to obtain a fair hearing on his claim; whether the internal union procedures are adequate to offer the employee full relief; and, whether exhaustion of internal procedures would unreasonably delay the employee's opportunity to secure a judicial hearing on the merits of his claim.

Lower court cases dealing with the duty of fair representation have covered widely variant fact situations, yet several broad issues have emerged. First, is there a difference in the contours of the duty depending on whether the union's action takes place during collective bargaining or while deciding whether to send a grievance to arbitration? It has been argued that the union should be given more discretion during bargaining because in that process hard choices between competing interests cannot be avoided. On the other hand, with respect to grievance arbitration, the union has an external standard, the collective bargaining agreement, against which it can and must compare its actions.

Second, is the "arbitrary" standard meant to have meaning independent of notions of personal hostility and bad faith? If so, a union's honest attempt to reach a correct decision may be overturned by a court if the result reached by the union falls short of what the court thinks it should have been, or if the union has taken into account considerations that the court thinks are extraneous.

Finally, what notions, if any, of procedural due process are inherent in the duty to represent fairly? *Vaca* requires that a grievance not be handled in a perfunctory fashion, but the duty could also grant an employee the right to a fair union hearing before a union refuses to send his grievance to arbitration. A group of employees might have a similar right to a hearing before their bargaining demand is sacrificed by the union in favor of the demand of another group. A right to a fair union hearing would probably trail with it other due process rights, such as the right to notice and the right to confront adverse witnesses. In a plant employing many workers, and perhaps where labor-management relations are poor, the number of grievances, major and minor, sought by workers to be arbitrated may be substantial. The requirement of a fair union hearing on grievances that the union refuses to arbitrate would place a heavy administrative burden on the union. To require a hearing on "major," but not "minor," grievances seems an unmanageable distinction. If the requirement of a fair union hearing is thus rejected, are there other notions of procedural due process that might be considered? Some cases have found a breach of the duty where the union "misplaced" a grievance (query if that meets the *Vaca* standard if only good faith negligence was involved), but other than those instances of "perfunctory" handling, cases raising procedural due process in fair representation actions have been rare.

Jenna Elfman, top, stars with Richard Dreyfuss in "Krippendorf's Tribe"

CHAPTER X

FEDERAL PREEMPTION OF STATE LEGISLATION

A. Conduct Arguably Protected or Arguably Prohibited by the NLRA

It is a familiar principle of labor law preemption that the supremacy clause of the Constitution authorizes Congress to oust the states of their power to regulate labor relations. Yet the NLRA nowhere states the extent to which state regulation is preempted. It has been for the Supreme Court to declare when the states may and may not act respecting labor relations. Two principles are clear: not all state laws affecting labor relations are preempted by the federal statutes, and conduct actually protected by the federal statutes is immune from state regulation. For example, arson in a union organizing campaign may be subjected to state criminal and civil sanctions; and, a strike (in an industry subject to the NLRA) to gain better wages cannot be prohibited by the state. Aside from these principles, much is in doubt.

Two early Supreme Court cases established many of the policies applicable to preemption questions. Garner v. Teamsters Local 776 (U.S.1953) involved recognitional picketing prior to the passage of § 8(b)(7) of the NLRA. The question was whether a Pennsylvania state court could enjoin recognitional picketing because it was coercive. The Supreme Court held that it could not. The Court developed a "primary jurisdiction" rationale for preemption. The controlling consideration was the existence of the NLRB with power to adjudge the same controversy that was before the state court. The NLRA promotes uniformity of procedures, standards and remedies, thus avoiding diversities and conflicts that would arise if local procedures and attitudes were also brought to bear on labor-management conflict. Such diversities and conflicts would occur even though the substantive state law matched federal law, and so the Court was not willing to permit the state to supplement federal remedies. Supplementation would risk inconsistent fact-findings and perhaps conflicting remedies. Furthermore, the fact that the NLRA specifies the kinds of picketing that are to be federally regulated implies that picketing falling outside the federal prohibitions is to be left to be regulated by the economics of the marketplace.

While the Court may have been thinking about problems of scheduling hearings, and of conflicts in procedural matters between the NLRB and state courts, it seems clear that these sorts of conflicts would not justify ousting states of their power to act. Two other theories suggest that the states cannot supplement remedies for federal prohibitions. First, conduct is more or less prohibited depending upon the remedy provided. Federal law provides injunctions, cease and desist orders, and actual damages for secondary boycotts, but it provides only cease and desist orders and injunctions for recognitional picketing. As an extreme example, it is clear that criminalization of recognitional picketing by a state would interfere with the federal scheme. Second, while the state may attempt to be guided by federal laws prohibiting certain union and employer conduct, it is possible that the state will mistakenly deem conduct to be prohibited when it is actually protected by the federal statute.

If a state attempts to prohibit conduct protected by the federal laws, or otherwise federally preempted, there is no easy mechanism for a federal court to intervene. A private party may not petition a federal court to enjoin state court action, such a petition is prohibited by 28 U.S.C.A. § 2283. Amalgamated Clothing Workers v. Richman Bros. (U.S.1955). The NLRB, however, can sue in federal court to block state court action even though no unfair labor practice charge is pending. NLRB v. Nash—Finch Co. (U.S.1971). The normal route, then, for a litigant subject to a state court order that he believes to be preempted is to appeal the case through the state court system and seek a writ of certiorari from the United States Supreme Court. While one Supreme Court case declared that "a state court is without power to hold one in contempt for violating an injunction that the state court had no power to enter by reason of federal preemption," thus suggesting that a defendant is free to ignore a state court order if he is willing to take the risk that she will prevail on the preemption issue, the current view appears to be that the defendant must honor the order until it is held preempted upon pain of being held in contempt. Compare In Green (U.S.1962) with Walker v. City of Birmingham (U.S.1967).

The best known Supreme Court preemption case is San Diego Bldg. Trades Council v. Garmon (U.S.1959), which adopts the same policy considerations as did the *Garner* case. In *Garmon*, the state court entertained a suit for damages brought by an employer against a union for picketing directed at its customers and suppliers. The picketing had the purpose of pressuring the employer into establishing a union shop. The Court rejected the proposition that preemption could be decided on a case by case basis. General rules are necessary and the NLRB and Congress, not the Supreme Court, are the ones to decide the impact of labor activity on the scheme of federal policy and administration. Central to federal preemption is a concern with the labor activities being regulated, not a concern with whether state regulation is accomplished through state legislative policy or judge-made law, nor with whether the mode of state regulation is by general law or by laws specifically directed at labor relations. While federal law does not preempt matters of mere peripheral concern to the federal scheme or matters deeply rooted in local feelings, the extent of federal preemption is broad. First, "when it is clear or may fairly be assumed that the activities which a state purports to regulate are protected by § 7 of the National Labor Relations Act, or constitute an unfair labor practice under § 8," state regulation is preempted. And even where it is not clear that the activity is protected or prohibited, the determination of the status of other activity is to be made by the agency declared by Congress to have special competence, the NLRB. This led to the second part of the *Garmon* test: "When an activity is arguably subject to § 7 or § 8 of the Act, the states as well as the federal courts must defer to the exclusive competence of the NLRB. . . ."

The fact that the conduct is neither arguably protected nor arguably prohibited does not end the inquiry, for Congress may have intended the particular conduct to be left to the economics of the marketplace. Nor will the fact that the state is giving a remedy not provided for by the federal scheme permit the state to act. Finally, the Court did not see the facts in *Garmon* as raising a question of breach of domestic peace permitting the state to act.

While *Garmon* lays down an extremely broad test for federal preemption, the decision was effectively 5 to 4: four Justices rejected the broad test and concurred in the result on the narrow ground that the union's activity in this case could fairly be considered protected under the NLRA.

The *Garmon* test for preemption was controversial and there were hints in later cases that some Justices were prepared to retreat from it. It

came before the Court again in Amalgamated
Ass'n of Street Employees v. Lockridge (U.S.1971).
A union caused one of its members to be discharged from his employment. The union contended that the member had failed to remit his
dues in a timely fashion and had thereby forfeited
his right to continued employment under a union
security clause. The member, Lockridge, argued
that under a proper construction of the union
constitution he had remitted his dues in a timely
fashion. If Lockridge was correct in his construction of the union constitution, then his discharge
violated § 8(a)(3) and § 8(b)(2) of the Act. Those
sections might also have been violated if the union
was using his dues default to hide another reason
for securing his discharge. If the union's construction of its constitution was correct, those sections
of the NLRA permitted the union's collective bargaining agreement with the employer to provide
for an employee's discharge. Lockridge filed a
state court action against the union stating a will-
ful breach of the union constitution. He recovered
over $32,000 in lost wages and was restored to
union membership. The Supreme Court held that
the state court action was preempted.

Justice Harlan, who had disagreed with the
broad test announced in *Garmon,* undertook to
write the defense of the *Garmon* test for the Court.
Noting that the conduct in this case was both
arguably prohibited and arguably protected under
the NLRA, thus falling squarely within the *Garmon* principle, the majority opinion rejected alter-

native rationales suggested by the state court. First, a state cannot regulate arguably protected or arguably prohibited conduct even though it is applying its common law of contract, a law not designated to regulate labor relations. It does not matter that the state law is "general" law. Nor was it true in this case that different conduct (breach of the union constitution) was subject to scrutiny in state court than would be at stake in NLRB proceedings—the ultimate issue in both forums was Lockridge's dismissal from employment. The Court reiterated the primary jurisdiction rationale for federal preemption and emphasized that "this Court is ill-equipped to play [the role of declaring preemption on a case by case basis] and the federal system dictates that [the preemption] problem be solved with a rule capable of relatively easy application, so that lower courts may largely police themselves in this regard."

In *Lockridge,* the Court was unwilling expressly to reverse the prior case of International Ass'n of Machinists v. Gonzales (U.S.1958), and sought to distinguish it. *Gonzales* allowed a state court to award damages for loss of employment to a union member expelled in violation of his union constitution, and to order his reinstatement to union membership. The Court's rationale was that the state court was only filling out the remedy of membership reinstatement (concededly a state matter) with a damage remedy for the union's refusal to refer the member to employment. The state court's focus was not that the union had caused an employer to discriminate against the employee, which was the evil that the Board would have dealt with in an unfair labor practice action.

Prior to *Lockridge,* the rationale of *Gonzales* had been recast by subsequent Supreme Court cases as involving activity that was of "peripheral concern" to the NLRA. In *Lockridge,* the Court distinguished *Gonzales* on the ground that in the instant case the possibility of state and federal conflict was real and immediate, whereas in *Gonzales* it was tangential and remote. The reasons for Gonzales' deprivation of union membership had nothing to do with the employment relationship. By contrast, Lockridge's state court action was based solely on the procurement of his discharge from employment. Furthermore, in *Lockridge* the key to the state court action was a construction of the collective bargaining agreement's union security clause, a matter of equal relevance to the NLRB; in *Gonzales,* construction of the union constitution would not have been a matter of NLRB scrutiny.

The Court also rejected the argument that *Lockridge* involved a suit to enforce a collective bargaining agreement, or was a claim for a breach of the duty of fair representation, either of which would have been subject to state court jurisdiction.

The final word on *Garmon*'s "arguably prohibited or arguably protected" test came in Sears, Roebuck and Co. v. San Diego Cty. Dist. Council of Carpenters (U.S.1978). The union, in a dispute with Sears, picketed Sears' property. Sears first threatened to seek a state court remedy and then secured a state court injunction against the picketing on the ground that its location was a trespass. The Supreme Court held that the injunction was not preempted.

As a matter of federal law, the picketing was both arguably prohibited and arguably protected. It might have been prohibited as a jurisdictional dispute or as recognitional picketing, and it might have been protected as picketing for area standards.

The Court emphasized that the right to picket had not been attacked in state court, only its location. That the picketing was arguably *prohibited* did not, in the Court's view, justify preemption because the controversy in the state court was not the same controversy that would be heard by the Board. Before the Board, the controversy would have been over the lawfulness of the content of the picketing. The state court, however, was not concerned with the content of the picketing, but only with its location, a matter that would not have been relevant to the Board's determination of the picketing's prohibited status.

The Court also rejected the argument that the matter was preempted because the union's location of the pickets on Sears property was arguably *protected.* Acknowledging that there was some risk that state regulation would interfere with NLRB regulation—both the Board and the state court would decide whether the picketing's location

was actually protected under the NLRA—the
Court thought it determinative that the Board had
had no opportunity to decide this particular dispute, thus obviating the risk of interference. The
employer could not bring the issue of the protected
status of the picketing before the NLRB, since the
Board has not assumed declaratory judgment power; and the employer could not file an unfair labor
practice charge against itself. The union had chosen not to charge the employer before the Board.

The failure of the union to bring the unfair labor
practice charge against the employer did not end
the inquiry, however. A state court, in deciding
whether it is preempted from acting, is also to look
at the strength of the union's argument that its
conduct is actually protected by the NLRA. In
examining the argument for actual protection in
this case, the Court noted that instances of trespass
are rarely held to be protected under NLRB decisions.

Finally, the Court held that the state court will
be preempted unless, prior to bringing the state
court action, the employer threatens the union
with state court or state police action. This provides the basis for the union to file an unfair labor
practice charge against the employer. Absent such
a threat, the Board might be without jurisdiction
since the Board has held that an employer's resort
to state court action does not violate § 8(a)(1).

The majority opinion in *Sears* did not decide an
issue that will regularly face state courts in similar

situations. Suppose between the time of the employer's required "threat" and the seeking of a
state court injunction by the employer, the union
files an unfair labor practice charge. One concurring Justice expressly read the majority opinion as
declaring that the state court action will be
preempted if the union files an unfair labor practice charge and that the action will remain
preempted until either the General Counsel declines to issue a complaint, or the Board declares
the conduct to be actually protected. Another
concurring Justice expressly read the majority
opinion as declaring that there is no preemption
even if the union files an unfair labor practice
charge; preemption will attach only when the
Board declares the union's picketing to be protected. One might expect the Board's regional directors to act promptly on the unfair labor charges
in these kinds of cases.

B. Preempted Regulation Neither Arguably Protected Nor Arguably Prohibited

The *Garmon* test is most easily applied to exercises of economic weapons by unions and employers. It is more problematic to refer to provisions of
collective bargaining agreements as being "protected." In Local 24, Teamsters v. Oliver (U.S.1959),
local unions signed a multiemployer bargaining
agreement with motor carriers that provided for a
minimum fee rental whenever a motor vehicle was
leased to one of the signatory carriers by an owner-

driver (not represented by the unions) working for the carrier. An owner-driver affected by this agreement attacked it in state court as a price-fixing violation of state antitrust law. The state court enjoined the enforcement of the bargaining agreement and the Supreme Court reversed, holding that state court regulation was preempted.

The Court found that the object of the collective bargaining agreement provision was to protect the negotiated wage scale of union members from being undercut by owner-drivers who might lease their vehicles at a rate less than that necessary to defray their actual operating costs. In the Court's view, this was equivalent to a wage agreement and as a mandatory subject of bargaining was immune from state nullification.

The Court expressly noted that this was not a "case of a collective bargaining agreement in conflict with a local health or safety regulation...." Presumably the states will not be preempted from regulating items of concern to state safety policies, such as safety equipment for workers, even though they are mandatory subjects of bargaining.

An economic weapon that is neither arguably protected nor arguably prohibited nonetheless may be immune from state regulation. In Teamsters Local 20 v. Morton (U.S.1964), a union peacefully persuaded a secondary employer not to do business with the primary employer with whom the union had its dispute. The state court prohibited this persuasion and assessed damages against the union. It was an easy case for the Supreme Court to find preemption, even though the employer argued that the state could regulate the conduct since it was neither arguably protected nor arguably prohibited. The issue, as the Court saw it, was whether Congress had so occupied this field as to close it to regulation by the states. Since NLRA legislative history and prior Supreme Court precedent had described the peaceful appeal to a secondary employer as an economic weapon to be left to the economics of the marketplace, such a union appeal was permitted but not protected by federal law. The state was precluded from outlawing this self-help weapon and thus altering the balance of power between labor and management.

The *Morton* principle was relied on by the Supreme Court to find preemption in Lodge 76, Machinists v. Wisconsin Employment Relations Com'n. (U.S.1976). A union had pressed its economic demands on an employer by a concerted refusal to work overtime. The NLRB's General Counsel refused to go to complaint on an employer § 8(b)(3) charge, relying on a Supreme Court precedent denying the Board the power to regulate economic weapons. A state agency and a state court, however, prohibited the union's refusal to work overtime, finding the conduct to be neither arguably protected nor arguably prohibited by the NLRA and relying on the earlier Supreme Court decision in Automobile Workers v. Wisconsin Employment Relations Bd. [Briggs–Stratton] (U.S.1949). That case held that the state agency was not preempted from prohibiting quickie strikes called by the union in order to bring economic pressure on the employer during collective bargaining.

The Court reasoned in *Lodge 76* that in addition to conduct protected and conduct prohibited by the NLRA, Congress envisioned that certain employer and union conduct would be entirely free from legal regulation. Relying on Court NLRA case law that took away the NLRB's power to regulate economic weapons, except as specifically provided by the NLRA, the Court held that the state may not prohibit the use of such weapons nor add to employer or union legal obligations in collective bargaining. In the instant case, national labor policy would clearly be frustrated were the state prohibition permitted to stand: the state cannot alter the labor-management balance of power in the guise of filling in a gap left by federal regulation. *Briggs—Stratton* was overruled.

Two Justices, necessary to make up a majority, concurred, stating that "neutral" state statutes or judge-made law—those "not directed toward altering the bargaining position of employers or unions but [only having] an incidental effect on relative bargaining strengths"—were not to be preempted. State laws would not be regarded as neutral "if they reflect an accommodation of the special interest of employers, unions, or the public in areas such as employee self-organization, labor disputes, or collective bargaining."

The Court was asked to hold that state granting of unemployment benefits to strikers was preempted in New York Telephone Co. v. New York State Department of Labor (U.S.1979). Relying on both federal legislative history (of the Social Security Act) and on preemption theory, a majority of the Court held the state could pay the unemployment benefits to strikers. Members of the Court were in sharp disagreement over the importance of the argument that the state law granting unemployment benefits was one of general application and thus not intended to alter the balance of power between labor and management. The Court was also divided over whether the effect of unemployment benefits on the underlying labor dispute required preemption.

In Belknap, Inc. v. Hale (U.S.1983) a union argued that state contract law was preempted because it affected the balance of power in labor-management disputes and made those disputes more difficult to settle. In this case the union had gone on strike and the employer had made offers of permanent jobs to replacement employees. The strike was settled and part of the settlement was the employer's agreement to reinstate the strikers. When the newly hired employees were discharged to make room for the returning strikers they sued the employer in state court for damages for breaching their contract for permanent employment. A divided Supreme Court held that the breach of contract action was not preempted.

The Supreme Court decided an important case respecting state protection of workers from discharge in Lingle v. Norge Division of Magic Chef., Inc. (U.S.1988). The state of Illinois gives a state cause of action to workers who have been discharged for filing a state workmens' compensation claim. When employee Lingle was fired after she filed such a claim, she brought a state court action. The union representing her filed a grievance under the collective bargaining agreement alleging Lingle had been discharged without good cause. Although the Court conceded that both the state court claim and the arbitration claim would adjudicate the same facts, the Court rejected the contention that the state court action was preempted. Where the state law is "designed to provide minimum substantive guarantees to individual workers," and where the state action does not require the interpretation of the collective bargaining agreement, federal law does not preempt.

C. Exceptions to Traditional Preemption Analysis

Several areas of labor-management relations are free, to some extent, from traditional federal preemption doctrines. For example, while federal courts have jurisdiction under § 301 of the NLRA to enforce collective bargaining agreements, state courts have concurrent jurisdiction to enforce bargaining agreements. The state courts must apply federal law. Dowd Box Co. v. Courtney (U.S.1962); Teamsters Local 174 v. Lucas Flour Co. (U.S.1962).

Although the Supreme Court first developed the doctrine that a union has a duty to represent fairly employees for whom the union is exclusive bargaining representative, the NLRB thereafter ruled that a breach of the union duty constitutes an unfair labor practice. Miranda Fuel Co. (NLRB 1962). It was subsequently argued in Vaca v. Sipes (U.S.1967), that unfair labor practice liability for breach of the duty preempts the states from acting and precludes federal district courts from acting under § 301 by a primary jurisdictional rationale. The Court held that both federal and state courts retain their breach of contract jurisdiction to hear fair representation cases notwithstanding the Board's assertion of jurisdiction.

The broadest exception to preemption is in the area of internal union affairs. Although Title I of the Labor–Management Reporting and Disclosure Act sets out a bill of rights for union members enforceable in federal courts, § 103 of that title preserves state court remedies. It is clear that states may impose greater restrictions on unions vis-a-vis their memberships than does Title I. State courts also retain the power to hear suits for breach of union constitutions, an original jurisdiction that federal courts do not have. Several other titles of the Labor–Management Reporting and Disclosure Act do preempt state law, however, especially where enforcement responsibilities are given to the Secretary of Labor. This is the case with respect to most of the provisions of Title IV, covering union elections of officers.

An employer engages in at least arguably prohibited conduct if the employer attempts to prevent employees from engaging in an economic strike, but if the employer prevents the employees at gun point is there federal preemption of state criminal law? Presumably not, and the example points up the fact that Congress was not writing on a clean slate when it passed federal labor legislation. Certain areas of state regulation must have been intended, although not explicitly so, to remain fully operative. Thus it is clear, for example, that the state may assume jurisdiction over violence or threats of violence in labor disputes. Automobile Workers v. Russell (U.S.1958).

Other cases have adopted what might be seen as a partial exemption doctrine; the states' power to regulate is not completely ousted but is reshaped by the Supreme Court's declaration of federal law. In Linn v. United Plant Guard Workers (U.S.1966), a representative of an employer brought suit contending that the union and two of its officers had issued a statement defaming him in violation of state law. The Court conceded that the NLRB might have found the circulation of these statements to have been an unfair labor practice under § 8, or to have been campaign propaganda that warranted setting aside the pending representation election. But the Court found that the intentional circulation of defamatory materials was not protected by the NLRA, and recognized an overriding state interest in protecting residents from malicious libels. Consequently, the Court held that a state is not preempted from applying its libel laws to statements made in the context of labor-management relations so long as the state applies a standard no more inclusive than that announced in New York Times Co. v. Sullivan (U.S.1964): that the defamatory statements must have been published with knowledge or reckless disregard of their falsity, and that a plaintiff can recover damages only upon proof that the statements caused actual injury. The Court also suggested that an excessive damage remedy might be preempted.

A similar recasting of state law under a preemption rationale occurred in Farmer v. United Bhd. of Carpenters (U.S.1977). Plaintiff union member alleged that because of a disagreement between him and local union officers, the union refused to refer him out of the union hiring hall and reacted to his complaint against this discrimination with "a campaign of personal abuse and harassment in addition to continued discrimination in referrals." Several precedents confronted the Court, among which was Plumbers v. Borden (U.S.1963). There the Court had held preempted a suit by an employee who claimed that the union's arbitrary refusal to refer him for employment constituted a tortious interference with his right to contract and a breach of an implied term in the union constitution. The Court in *Borden* relied on the considerable possibility that state regulation would interfere with Board regulation of discriminatory union hiring hall practices, and applied its preemption bar. The *Farmer* Court declared *Borden* to be distinguishable because "outrageous conduct" is not protected by the NLRA, and the state has a police power interest in prohibiting it. Although plaintiff's challenge of the union's refusal to refer him for employment risks interference with the NLRA, this risk does not overbalance the substantial state interest in protecting its citizens from the union's conduct. In its hearing, the Board would not consider the union's conduct that allegedly caused emotional distress and physical injury. Furthermore, the state court action could be adjudicated without considering the merits of the underlying labor dispute.

The Court cautioned that "it is essential that the state tort be either unrelated to employment discrimination, or a function of the particularly abusive manner in which the discrimination is accomplished or threatened rather than a function of the actual or threatened discrimination itself." The jury is to be instructed that the employment discrimination issue should play no part in its determination of liability for damages, and the conduct complained of must be "outrageous," mere robust language or the clash of strong personalities is not enough to sustain state court jurisdiction. Finally, the state trial courts have the responsibility to assure that the damages awarded are not excessive.

CHAPTER XI

NLRA REGULATION OF INTERNAL UNION AFFAIRS

A. Union Security Devices

A union security clause is a provision in a collective bargaining agreement that describes the obligations of employees to support the union. The legality of various types of clauses is widely misunderstood. An "agency shop" is established by a clause that requires every company employee to pay to the union an amount equal to the union's customary initiation fees and monthly dues. It does not require any employee to become a formal member of the union, to be a member before being hired, to take any oath or obligation, or to observe any internal rules and regulations of the union except with regard to dues.

In NLRB v. General Motors Corp. (U.S.1963), the Court held that an employer does not violate § 8(a)(3) of the NLRA by agreeing to include an agency shop clause in a bargaining agreement. Although the Wagner Act allowed more pervasive forms of union security agreements, the Taft–Hartley amendments to the NLRA narrowly limited the forms of union security clause that could be put in a bargaining agreement. First, there is a 30–day grace period before any employee needs to pay union dues and fees. Second, even initiation fees and dues may not be required of an employee unless membership is available to the employee on the same terms as it is to others. Third, no employee may be discharged from employment for failure to comply with a union security clause if there is reasonable ground to believe that the employee's union membership was denied or terminated for reasons other than the failure of the employee to tender the periodic dues and initiation fees uniformly required as a condition of acquiring or retaining membership. This last provision nullifies union security clauses more stringent than the agency shop clause. It also gives the union a reasonable response to the free-rider problem; that is, the willingness of some employees to accept the benefits of union representation while refusing to pay the costs voluntarily. According to the Court, the term "membership," as it is permitted by § 8(a)(3), "is whittled down to its financial core."

Two other forms of union security clauses are thus prohibited by § 8(a)(3) and § 8(b)(2) of the NLRA. A "union shop" clause requires an employee to become a *member* of the union in order to retain a job, although no one needs to be a member in order to be hired, and every newly hired person has a prescribed period of time to become a member. A "closed shop" clause obligates the employer to hire only union members and to discharge any employee who drops union membership.

The only effect of state "right to work" legislation, which is permitted by § 14(b) of the NLRA, is to permit states so legislating to prohibit even the initiation fees and dues obligations of agency shops, and to permit employees who do not voluntarily pay dues and initiation fees to be free-riders. Unions in these states continue to be obligated by the NLRA to fully represent all employees, including free-riders.

The distinction between the obligation to pay initiation fees and dues and the obligation to become a full member of the union is important. Many unions require members to conform to union rules of conduct and assess fines for infractions. These fines are not considered union dues and the member does not risk discharge from employment by nonpayment. Electric Auto–Lite Co. (NLRB 1950). However, the fines may be enforceable in state court. An employee who pays dues but refuses to take out full union membership is not subject to these internal union rules and sanctions. Unfortunately, while the law is clear, it is seldom communicated to employees. Most collective bargaining agreements speak in terms of requiring union "membership" after the mandatory waiting period and they do not spell out that this means only the payment of dues and initiation fees. Neither the union nor the employer has an economic incentive to educate employees on the limited nature of their obligation.

Another widely misunderstood union device is the union referral to employment, often done through a union hiring hall. The most favorable view of a union hiring hall is that it serves as a central clearinghouse for jobs, and job seekers avoid time-wasting and duplicative job searches. It permits employers to have mobility in and out of the product market by relieving them of the responsibility of maintaining a permanent work force, and by freeing them of the time delay in recruiting workmen for particular jobs.

Union hiring halls and other union referral mechanisms surely encourage membership in labor organizations in that they enhance the reputation and apparent power of unions, but in Local 357, Teamsters v. NLRB (U.S.1961), the Court held that the operation of a union hiring hall is unlawful under the NLRA only if this encouragement of union membership is accomplished by discrimination. The collective bargaining agreement in that case specifically provided that applicants would be referred from the hiring hall without regard to their union membership.

It violates § 8(b)(2) and 8(b)(1)(A) for a union to refuse to refer someone from a hiring hall because she is not a union member. Similarly, it violates § 8(a)(3) and 8(a)(1) for an employer to participate in such discrimination. When a hiring hall has been operated in a discriminatory fashion, the current Board remedy is to award back pay to discriminatees and to require that various records and reports be retained for the regional director on the operation of the hiring hall for a period of time after the finding of unlawful discrimination. In addition, unions have been required to place referral registers in public view in the hiring halls for easy access and inspection by job applicants upon the completion of each day's entry of job referrals in the hope that disappointed applicants will police the use of the hiring hall.

Another form of union security device has received considerable recent attention. Some collective bargaining agreements provide for job preferences of one kind or another for union "stewards," employees designated by the union to handle union business at the workplace. In a series of cases, a sharply divided Board has held that stewards may lawfully be given seniority preference, limited to lay-offs and recalls, in a collective bargaining agreement. This device is thought necessary to ensure continuation of collective bargaining agreement administration. However, employment preference for stewards in other respects has been disapproved. See Dairylea Cooperative, Inc. (NLRB 1975). The protection is only available to union officials whose duties relate directly to administering the bargaining agreement. Gulton Electro–Voice (NLRB 1983).

B. Union Membership Policy

Many unions actively seek new members through organizing drives, and the like, but other unions limit their membership and become "closed locals." Why would a union limit its membership?

The answer depends in part on whether the law against job discrimination by unions is effective. A union with a restrictive admission policy and a practice of only referring members to jobs can distribute its monopoly gains to its current members, but it must exclude nonunion employees found elsewhere by the employer. However, discriminatory job referrals violate § 8(b)(2) and 8(b)(1)(A). If a union trains its members in the skills of the job, by apprenticeships, for example, then restricting union membership may keep down the number of qualified workers and ensure more job opportunities for members. The cost of obtaining similar training by nonunion workers may be higher than the cost of the training that the union provides. This is a lawful mechanism for controlling jobs. Also, a union might want to restrict membership policy in order to control collective bargaining, since nonmembers cannot vote on bargaining agreement ratification, etc., without the consent of the union, which is rarely given. However, under § 8(b)(2) a union could not demand dues (on pain of discharge) of an employee to whom membership in the union is not available on the same basis as it is to other employees. If that section is enforced, it would seem that this rationale for restricted membership policy must fail.

Prevailing law in state courts treats union membership the same way as it treats membership in churches and social clubs. Membership is the organization's affair and there are only isolated instances of state courts ordering someone admitted

to membership. Nor does the NLRA require unions to admit applicants to union membership. In
one case, however, a federal circuit court held that
because a union refused to admit blacks into membership, it was disqualified from NLRB certification in a bargaining unit where the union had won
a representation election. Such a certification
was, in the court's view, tantamount to judicial
enforcement of private discrimination, which im-
plicates governmental action under the Fifth
Amendment. NLRB v. Mansion House Center
Management Corp. (8th Cir.1973). The court's rationale on the difficult constitutional issue of governmental action was, at best, cryptic. The Board
was initially persuaded to accept the circuit court's
view but later reversed itself and held that the
certification of a union does not involve governmental action so as to constitutionally require the
Board to examine the union's membership policies.
Handy Andy, Inc. (NLRB 1977); Bell & Howell Co.
(NLRB 1977). The Board examines racial and sex-
based discriminatory union practices under its fair
representation doctrine, but it will not permit employers to raise alleged racial and sex-based discriminatory union practices in order to block a
union's certification or as a defense to a refusal to
bargain charge.

Inroads into restrictive union membership policies have been made under the civil rights laws,
principally Title VII of the Civil Rights Act of
1964. Section 703(c) of that Title prohibits a union
from discriminating on the basis of race, color,

religion, sex, or national origin with respect to admission to membership and treatment of members. In addition, the federal government has barred employment discrimination on construction projects paid for in whole or in part with funds obtained from the federal government, or obtained pursuant to a federal guarantee of a grant, contract, or loan. As a part of this program, the Department of Labor has required affirmative hiring of minorities in the construction industry upon the threat of barring contractors from government contracts for noncompliance.

C. NLRA Regulation of Union Discipline of Its Members

In addition to protecting employees who engage in protected concerted activity, § 7 of the NLRA protects employees who refrain from concerted activity. Section 8(b)(1)(A) declares that it is an unfair labor practice for a union to restrain or coerce employees in the exercise of § 7 rights, but it also provides that the section shall not impair the right of a union to apply its own rules with respect to the acquisition or retention of union membership. In NLRB v. Allis—Chalmers Mfg. Co. (U.S.1967), employees challenged under § 8(b)(1)(A) union imposition of, and state court enforcement of, fines against members who crossed the union's picket line and went to work during an authorized strike against their employer. The employees argued that § 8(b)(1)(A) was the union equivalent of § 8(a)(1). Perhaps willing to concede that their activity subjected them to expulsion from membership under the proviso to § 8(b)(1)(A), the employees' contention was that any discipline other than expulsion, such as a fine enforceable in court or by expulsion, violated that section.

The Supreme Court disagreed. Congress had engaged in extensive regulation of internal union affairs when it passed the Landrum–Griffin Act in 1959, and the Court found it unlikely that Congress had intended in the 1947 Taft—Hartley amendments to accomplish "an even more pervasive regulation of the internal affairs of unions." Nor was the Court persuaded that the apparent protection of the expulsion sanction accomplished by the proviso in § 8(b)(1)(A) was intended to provide sufficient protection for union control over its internal affairs. It reasoned that when the union is weak, membership is of little value and expulsion is not a viable union control mechanism; and when the union is strong and membership valuable, loss of membership is a harsher remedy than a union fine.

The Court interpreted the proviso to § 8(b)(1)(A) to mean that a union can impose fines on its members as a lesser penalty to expulsion, and it can expel for non-payment of the fine. Section 8(b)(1)(A) does not preclude the union from seeking direct enforcement of union fines in state court.

Justice White concurred in the result but suggested that there might be some internal union rules that the union could not enforce consistently with the NLRA. Four other members of the Court dissented. While they would permit a union to expel a member who violated a rule against working behind the union's picket line, they would not permit the union to fine a member for such conduct and enforce the fine either by court action or by the sanction of expulsion.

It was not clear from *Allis—Chalmers* whether the Court was holding that state court enforcement of union fines was not "coercive" under § 8(b)(1)(A) or that a union's regulation of its internal affairs was immune from that section's scrutiny. In any event, subsequent cases were to clarify the Court's rationale.

In NLRB v. Marine Workers (U.S.1968), a union member filed unfair labor practice charges against his union without first exhausting all the remedies provided for in his union constitution. This failure to exhaust violated a rule in the union constitution and the member was found guilty of violating the rule and was expelled by the union. He then filed a § 8(b)(1)(A) charge challenging his expulsion and was upheld by the Supreme Court. Describing *Allis–Chalmers* as a case assuring "a union freedom of self-regulation where its legitimate internal affairs are concerned," the Court held that "any coercion used to discourage, retard, or defeat [access to the NLRB] is beyond the legitimate interest of a labor organization," and thus violates

§ 8(b)(1)(A). Even a direct expulsion not involving a fine may violate § 8(b)(1)(A).

In Scofield v. NLRB (U.S.1969) the union imposed a workplace rule on its members. Members were paid by the employer on a piecework or incentive basis. The union feared that if employees regularly produced at a sweat-shop rate, the employer would establish that rate as the minimum acceptable. The union therefore established a ceiling on production: employees could produce more than the ceiling rate, but were forbidden to demand immediate payment for production above that rate. They could only "bank" the excess production against the day when the ceiling rate was not reached because of machine breakdown or other causes. A member violating this rule was subject to a union fine and a refusal to pay that fine could result in expulsion.

In the case reaching the Court, the union had sought to enforce several such fines in state court. Members challenged the union's court enforcement of the fines as a § 8(b)(1)(A) violation, but the Supreme Court disagreed. It described the approach of *Allis—Chalmers* and *Marine Workers* as "[leaving] a union free to enforce a properly adopted rule which reflects a legitimate union interest, impairs no policy Congress has imbedded in the labor law, and is reasonably enforced against union members who are free to leave the union and escape the rule." Since in the case before it there was no showing that the fines were unreasonable, or "the mere fiat of a union leader, or that the membership of petitioners in the union was involuntary," the fines escaped NLRA scrutiny. Enforcement of the union rule had not been carried out by unlawful methods (e.g. employment discharge), and the rule itself had been bargained for with the company, avoiding the charge of a § 8(b)(3) refusal to bargain. Noting the union's economic reasons for adopting the rule, the Court admitted that the rule was "intended to have an impact beyond the confines of the union organization," but it refused to find any "impairment of a statutory labor policy."

Under *Scofield*, then, union discipline of its members may violate the NLRA if the union rule being enforced is inconsistent with declared congressional labor policy. The limitations of such a rule sometimes have not been obvious to the NLRB. In Carpenters Local 22 (Graziano Construction Co.) (NLRB 1972) the NLRB set aside on § 8(b)(1)(A) grounds the fining of a union member in circumstances that apparently violated the Labor–Management Reporting and Disclosure Act of 1959, a statute the NLRB has no jurisdiction to enforce. The Board has also held that a union violates § 8(b)(1)(A) by fining a member for refusing to participate in a strike later found to be a secondary boycott, although one court has found no violation where the union expels a member for refusing to honor an illegal secondary picket line. Compare Longshoremen's Local 30 (NLRB 1977) with NLRB v. Local 18, Operating Engineers (6th Cir.1974).

In several of the cases, the Supreme Court referred to "reasonable" union fines, but in NLRB v. Boeing Co. (U.S.1973) the Court held that the NLRB is not to test union fines for reasonableness of amount. The Court also restated its interpretation of § 8(b)(1)(A): "The underlying basis for the holdings of *Allis—Chalmers* and *Scofield* was not that reasonable fines were noncoercive under the language of § 8(b)(1)(A) of the Act, but was instead that those provisions were not intended by Congress to apply to the imposition by the union of fines not affecting the employer-employee relationship and not otherwise prohibited by the Act." Since the relationship between a member and his union is generally considered to be contractual in nature, and state courts are both willing and able to treat the issue of the reasonableness of union fines, the states, not the Board, are to decide the issue.

What of an employee who does not join the union, or who resigns membership and, in either instance, violates an internal union rule? In NLRB v. Granite State Joint Board, Textile Workers Union Local 1029 (U.S.1972), the Court held that a union violates § 8(b)(1)(A) when it fines for strike-breaking members who have effectively resigned from the union. In Booster Lodge 405, Machinists v. NLRB (U.S.1973), the Court refused to imply into a union constitution a commitment prohibiting members from strike breaking after effective resignation from union membership. Finally, in Pattern Makers' League of North America v. NLRB (U.S.1985) the Court held that § 8(b)(1)(A) reasonably may be construed by the Board as prohibiting a union from fining members who have tendered resignations invalid under the union constitution. The union had sought, through its constitution, to impose fines on members who sought to resign during a strike or when a strike was imminent. The union's constitutional provision was found to "impair the policy of voluntary unionism [in the NLRA]."

The power of the union to regulate by union discipline conduct of union members who are also workplace supervisors has raised interpretative problems under § 8 of the NLRA. Section 8(b)(1)(b) makes it an unfair labor practice for a union to coerce an employer in the selection of its representatives for the purposes of collective bargaining and the adjustment of grievances. The language suggests a limited scope, and the legislative history indicates that it was enacted to prevent unions from forcing an employer into or out of a multiemployer bargaining group.

The Board has expanded the reach of the section in a doctrine beginning with San Francisco—Oakland Mailers' Union No. 18 (Northwest Pub., Inc.) (NLRB 1968). The Board found in that case that the union violated § 8(b)(1)(B) by expelling three member-foremen because they assigned bargaining unit work in violation of the bargaining agreement. In later cases, the Board extended the doctrine to encompass union discipline of a supervisor whenever she was engaged in management or supervisory activities, even though collective bargaining or grievances adjustment duties were not involved. Finally, in Florida Power and Light Co. v. IBEW Local 641 (U.S.1974), the Board applied § 8(b)(1)(B) to forbid union discipline of members who, as supervisors, performed rank-and-file work at a time when the union was on strike. The employer argued that union discipline of supervisors who are performing bargaining unit work during a strike would effectively deprive the firm of the loyalty of those supervisors. The Supreme Court rejected this argument and held instead that union discipline of a supervisor-member "can constitute a violation of § 8(b)(1)(B) only when that discipline may adversely affect the supervisor's conduct in performing the duties of, and acting in his capacity as, grievance adjuster or collective bargainer on behalf of the employer." The Court ruled that the Board had extended its *Oakland— Mailers* doctrine too far in this case.

Since supervisors are excluded from the definition of "employee" in § 2(3) of the NLRA, employers are free to demand that supervisors refrain from union activity and from taking out union membership. The employer may discharge a supervisor for either of these without violating § 8(a). This is the extent of the employer's explicit protection under the NLRA. *Florida Power* was cut back somewhat by the Supreme Court, however, in American Broadcasting Co. v. Writers' Guild of America West, Inc. (U.S.1978) where the Court upheld, by a 5 to 4 margin, a Board decision that a union violated § 8(b)(1)(B) when it disciplined supervisor-members who crossed the union picket line to perform supervisory functions. The Board has also held that union fines are unlawful when they are levied against supervisors who do bargaining unit work during a strike. Chicago Typographical Union Local 16 (NLRB 1975); United Bhd. of Carpenters (Skippy Enterprises) (NLRB 1975).

CHAPTER XII

LMRDA REGULATION OF INTERNAL UNION AFFAIRS

A. Free Speech and Assembly

The Labor Management Reporting and Disclosure Act (LMRDA, or Landrum–Griffin Act) was passed in 1959 to establish rights of union members with respect to their union. Title I of the LMRDA sets out a bill of rights for union members. This Title was hastily drafted and was not debated in congressional committee.

Section 101(a)(2) of the LMRDA sets out a right of free speech and assembly for union members and adds a proviso that nothing within the section should be construed to impair the union's right to "enforce reasonable rules as to the responsibility of every member toward the [union] as an institution and to his refraining from conduct that would interfere with [the union's] performance of its legal or contractual obligation." This section has not been subjected to Supreme Court scrutiny, but several cases in the courts of appeals have had considerable influence.

An early free speech case was Salzhandler v. Caputo (2d Cir.1963), where a local union member was convicted by a trial board of union members of having libeled union officers when he publicly accused the officers of having embezzled union funds. After giving Salzhandler notice of the charges and permitting his representation by a fellow union member, the union trial board found that the libel violated the union constitution. It ousted Salzhandler from his office of financial secretary and ordered that he not be permitted to attend union meetings for a period of five years. Salzhandler brought suit in federal district court pursuant to the grant of jurisdiction under § 102 of the LMRDA to enforce his rights guaranteed by § 101(a)(2).

The district court found Salzhandler committed libel and held that libel was an exception to the free speech guarantee of Title I, just as it is an exception to the First Amendment's free speech guarantee. The Second Circuit reversed, finding a § 101(a)(2) violation. First Amendment cases were distinguished because a finding of libel by a court guarantees the accused a disinterested tribunal whereas a union tribunal is not competent to decide a "delicate problem of truth or falsehood, privilege, and fair comment...." It was not important to the Second Circuit, however, that the district court in this case had also sustained the libel charge because Congress had not contemplated trials *de novo* of union discipline in district courts. Thus neither union nor court were competent to try the union member.

The court found in § 101(a)(2) congressional recognition of a public interest in encouraging union members to ferret out financial wrongdoing by union officers. The court concluded that Salzhandler's accusations of the officers were not condemned by the proviso to that section, which relates to the responsibility of union members towards the union, for it reasoned that it was in the union's best interest to permit challenges such as those raised by Salzhandler. Since Salzhandler's accusations related to the handling of union funds and the management of the union, the falsity of his statement was irrelevant to his protection under the LMRDA. The union officers might have sued for libel in a civil tort action, but the union was precluded from prosecuting a disciplinary action.

Perhaps, from the union's perspective, a more serious turn was taken by the Second Circuit in Farowitz v. Musicians Local 802 (2d Cir.1964), where a union member was expelled by the union for publicly urging the membership to refuse to pay union taxes assessed by the union, and which the member thought were being collected in violation of federal law. Claiming that his expulsion from membership violated § 101(a)(2), the member sought reinstatement and money damages. The court of appeals found that the member's statement fell within the protection of § 101(a)(2). Cryptically commenting that there might be "some situations in which a union member would not be protected against disciplinary measures if he were to urge other members to forego paying their dues," the court held that a member cannot be disciplined for challenging a course of union conduct that he reasonably believes to be illegal.

Farowitz is subject to criticism on two grounds. First, there is a strong argument that the responsibility of a member towards the union as an institution, contained in the proviso to § 101(a)(2), includes an obligation to refrain from recommending self-help in challenging an action of the union. Second, although the Second Circuit did not discuss it, presumably Farowitz could have been lawfully disciplined for refusing to pay the tax, as could other members who similarly refused. If not, then the union is effectively at the mercy of a minority of its members; but if so, it yields the anomalous result of a member being protected when he calls for action which, if taken by his audience, would result in lawful discipline.

One influential free speech case instructs that a union member's right of free speech is not to yield to the exceptions set out in the proviso, but is rather to be balanced against those exceptions. In Airlines Maintenance Lodge 702, Machinists v. Loudermilk (5th Cir.1971), a union fined member Loudermilk and sought to enforce the fine in state court. Loudermilk removed the action to federal district court and there contended that enforcement of the fine would violate his free speech rights under § 101(a)(2). Loudermilk had been fined because he joined and became president of a rival union that then tried to oust plaintiff union

as the bargaining representative in a bargaining
unit of an employer other than Loudermilk's.

In applying its balancing test, the court relied on
the fact that Loudermilk was compelled to join the
union under an agreement between his employer
and the union. The court also relied on the fact
that plaintiff union did not choose to expel Loudermilk or bar him from meetings, which the court
described as defensive action. Instead, the union
sought to compel Loudermilk's allegiance through
a fine. The court failed to discuss, if it appreciated
at all, the fact that Loudermilk had the option of
limiting his union membership to the payment of
dues, and thus could have avoided the union's
power to fine him. The court seemed persuaded
that if the union had the power to fine a member
in this circumstance, it could effectively foreclose
any challenge to its right to represent employees.
It is true, of course, that had the court decided
differently, a member would not be free both to
challenge his union's right to represent employees
and simultaneously to enjoy full participation in
union affairs. Presumably the court did not intend to rule that Loudermilk must continue to be
accorded full membership rights, including the
right to attend strategy meetings planning opposition to his attempts to replace the union as a
bargaining representative. Holding that the proviso only requires a balancing process provides a
mechanism to give the court more flexibility in
determining the scope of free speech protection.

A free speech issue unlike those typically arising under Title I was presented in United Steelworkers v. Sadlowski (U.S.1982). The union in that case had adopted a rule that forbade candidates for union office from accepting campaign contributions from nonmembers. The Court upheld the union's rule against a contention that it interfered with rights protected by § 101(a)(2). The Court described the rule as being "rationally related to the union's legitimate interest in reducing outsider interference with union affairs."

Whether union officials, elected or appointed, should have the same free speech rights as other union members has caused considerable controversy. On the one hand, it may be that a viable challenge to entrenched union leadership can only come from a union member with an independent power base, and this often requires service as a union official. This is especially true where national union office is at stake and the power base required to challenge the incumbent must have some national scope. The business agent of a powerful city local union may be relatively unknown in union locals in the rest of the country, but a representative of the national union who has national duties or travels widely in the course of her office may be able to put together sufficient support to mount a campaign.

On the other hand, union officials serve as the government of the union. Arguably, no set of union officers should be required to entrust the carrying out of their policies to one in active opposition to them and who would unseat them from office.

Sections 101(a) and (2) provide that every member of a labor organization shall have equal voting rights and the rights of free speech and assembly, and § 609 provides that it is unlawful for a union "to fine, suspend, expel, or otherwise discipline any of its members for exercising any right to which he is entitled under the provisions of this Act." Also, § 101(a)(5) provides that no member of a labor organization may be fined, suspended, expelled, or "otherwise disciplined" unless certain procedural rights are provided. Does removal from union office fall within the term "otherwise discipline" in § 609, and if so, does it also fall within the same term in § 101(a)(5)? A difficulty with ruling that it falls within the latter section is that it would then seem that union officers could not be removed from office by the membership before a hearing, yet there is evidence that Congress intended that a union could remove an officer summarily.

Three variables in removal-from-office cases are: how the officer was removed (e.g., vote of the membership, action of a superior officer), why the officer was removed, and whether the officer was elected or appointed. In Finnegan v. Leu (U.S.1982), plaintiffs were appointed business agents who (naturally) campaigned on behalf of the union president's bid for reelection. When the incumbent president lost, the newly elected president discharged plaintiffs, pursuant to power accorded his office in the union constitution. The Supreme Court held against plaintiffs.

The Court resolved the case not by construing the words "otherwise discipline," but by an interpretation that relied on the word "member" in the relevant statutory sections. The Court reasoned that the protection of § 609 extends only to actions that affect a union member's rights or status *as a member* of the union. Removal from union employment is not an interference with a membership right. Section 101(a)(5) was construed in similar fashion.

The Court acknowledged that this construction raised another issue. Section 102 of the Act gives union members the right to sue if "any rights secured by the provisions of this title have been infringed...." Plaintiffs argued that removal from office had interfered with their free speech rights and that they could sue under § 102 without being required to make out a violation of § 609. The Court rejected this argument by holding that the removal from office in the present circumstances was not within the intent of the free speech guarantee. A newly elected president should have the right to select her own staff. The Court hinted that a different result might be called for if the removal from office were shown to be "part of a purposeful and deliberate attempt ... to suppress dissent within the union."

In Sheet Metal Workers Intern. Ass'n v. Lynn
(U.S.1989), the Court's pivotal distinction turned
on whether the official was appointed or elected.
Lynn, an elected business agent of a local union,
was removed by an official of the parent international union who was acting as trustee of the local.
The international had placed the local in trusteeship, enabling the international to exercise day-to-
day control over the local. Lynn was removed for
speaking against a dues increase proposed to the
local membership by the trustee. The Court held
the removal from office violated § 102. The removal of an elected official for making policy-
oriented public remarks interferes with the rights
of the members who voted for the official and chills
their free speech rights. A concurring Justice expressed doubt that the Court will adhere to and
elected/appointed distinction in future cases.

B. The Meaning of "Discipline"

The meaning of "discipline" raises difficult problems under Title I, in addition to those raised by by
Finnegan and *Lynn, supra.* Two cases illustrate
these problems.

In Detroy v. American Guild of Variety Artists
(2d Cir.1961), an employer contended that a union
member had breached the union's collective bargaining agreement with the employer. The question was submitted to arbitration and an award
was issued in favor of the employer and against the
union member, but the union member would not

abide by the award. The union then placed the
member on its "unfair list," which was a directive
to other employers not to hire the union member.
The member brought suit in federal district court
under § 102 of the LMRDA contending that his
procedural rights under § 101(a)(5) had been violated by the blacklisting. The union raised two de-
fenses: that the union member had not exhausted
his internal union remedies, and that the blacklisting of this employee was not "discipline" under
§ 101(a)(5).

Section 101(a)(4) of the LMRDA provides that a
union may not limit the right of a member to sue
the union or its officers but that a union member
may be required to exhaust reasonable hearing
procedures, not lasting in excess of 4 months, before instituting proceedings against the union or
its officers. The *Detroy* court held that although
this proviso was applicable to other sections of
Title I, it imposed no absolute duty on a union
member to exhaust remedies. Looking at the development of state law on this subject, the court
noted that there are many exceptions to the exhaustion requirement. In this case, exhaustion
was not required because an appeal from the arbitration award would not have raised the issue of
the appropriateness of the union's blacklisting.
Furthermore, there was no procedural opportunity
given the plaintiff to argue mitigation on his own
behalf, or to argue that the blacklisting exceeded
the union's constitutional powers. It was also unclear that there was an adequate union remedy

even if the union's decision had been reversed on internal appeal. Finally, there was no clear exhaustion procedure set out in the union constitution.

The court rejected the union's claim that the blacklisting did not constitute discipline. It relied on the fact that forcing members to adhere to collective bargaining arbitration awards promotes stability within the industry and thus protects all the members of the union. "In thus furthering its own end the union must abide by the rules set down for it by Congress in § 101(a)(5), and any member against whom steps are taken by the union in the interest of promoting the welfare of the group is entitled to these guarantees...."

The *Detroy* case was distinguished in Figueroa v. National Maritime Union (2d Cir.1965). There the union refused to refer several union seamen for employment when it came to light that many years ago they had been convicted of unlawfully possessing narcotics. The collective bargaining agreement with the employers stated that the union was not required to register seamen whom the union did not consider suitable for employment. The illegal possession or use of narcotics was expressly listed as one factor in passing upon suitability. No procedural rights were accorded the seamen by the union. The court cited *Detroy* with approval and stated that union interference with employment opportunities could constitute discipline within the meaning of § 101(a)(5). But it held that this case did not involve discipline because "unlike *Detroy* where the union acted unilaterally in blacklisting the plaintiff member, the refusal to register and refer was pursuant to the terms of a collective bargaining agreement and in compliance with the declared policy of the shipowners that they will hire no seamen known to have a narcotics conviction. This was no more 'discipline,' once appellees admitted their conviction and the applicability to them of the terms of the collective bargaining agreement, than it would have been to turn down an applicant who admitted that he lacked a physical requirement for the job...." If the seamen had disputed the fact of their conviction, they would have been entitled to a § 101(a)(5) hearing. The court also noted that no claim of breach of the duty of fair representation had been made in this case.

The court's suggestion that there was no need for a § 101(a)(5) hearing in *Figueroa*, and that therefore it was not required, is mistaken. Certainly the seamen would have wanted to argue for clemency, or that their conduct fell outside the spirit and the requirements of the collective bargaining agreement.

But treating the union's actions in both *Detroy* and *Figueroa* as § 101(a)(5) discipline would create its own set of problems. It would not be wise policy to require a union to grant a procedural hearing each time it decides, for example, not to arbitrate a union member's grievance with an employer. And certainly a decision to seek a wage increase for one group of employees rather than another should not necessitate a § 101(a)(5) hearing. Arguably, required hearings in either situation would swamp the union with procedural requirements. It might not be overly burdensome to require a union to grant a procedural hearing to an employee who wants his discharge carried to arbitration by the union, although a penal-type hearing may not be the appropriate procedure in that circumstance. But however that issue is resolved, employee grievances often involve issues much less serious than discharge, such as complaints of minor mistreatment by foremen in the plant. If failure to carry a grievance to arbitration is § 101(a)(5) discipline, then all of these grievances would require a hearing, for there is no exception in § 101(a)(5) for minor discipline.

The distinction between *Detroy* and *Figueroa*, that one implicated a collective bargaining agreement while the other did not, could serve as a basis for different treatments. Perhaps union misfeasance when an employer is involved (grievance handling and bargaining choices) should be handled under the fair representation doctrine, and only matters not involving an employer should require a § 101(a)(5) hearing. While this would settle some of the difficulties, it seems inconsistent with the notion that a fair hearing requirement goes to different policies than does the fair representation requirement: with respect to the former, a member is given a right to be heard and to argue his cause, whereas the latter protects an employee from arbitrary substantive treatment.

C. Exhaustion of Internal Union Remedies

Section 101(a)(4) contains a proviso stating that a union member may be required to exhaust union remedies before instituting a suit against a union or its officers. Courts have held that exhaustion of remedies may be required in any Title I case, and some have required employees who would prosecute fair representation actions against the union to show that they have exhausted their internal union remedies. Clayton v. United Automobile Workers (U.S.1981). State courts have developed many exceptions and they have been adopted by federal courts as well. Included are requirements that internal remedies must be reasonable, sufficiently communicated to employees, and must not be futile. These standards give a great deal of flexibility to a court.

The Supreme Court has ruled that the proviso to § 101(a)(4) applies to a *court* requirement of exhaustion of union remedies and not to a *union* constitutional requirement. Thus union discipline against a member for bringing suit without exhausting internal union remedies will be a violation of § 101(a)(4). NLRB v. Marine Workers (U.S.1968); Ryan v. IBEW (7th Cir.1966).

D. Procedural Rights in Discipline Cases

Section 101(a)(5) provides that before a member can be disciplined by a union (except for dues default), she must be served with specific written charges, given reasonable time to prepare a defense, and afforded a full and fair hearing. The concept of a "full and fair hearing" is necessarily vague, but it has been fleshed out by courts to mean that the member must be permitted to be present during the taking of evidence and to cross examine witnesses. She need not be given the right to be represented by a lawyer. Union constitutions regularly forbid representation by lawyers but permit representation by fellow union members. Whether the member is entitled to make a transcript of the hearing is unsettled.

The extent to which a federal court under § 101(a)(5) is entitled to examine a union disciplinary hearing for sufficiency of evidence or to examine the constitution for adequate authority to discipline, was considered in International Bhd. of Boilermakers v. Hardeman (U.S.1971). The Court held that a lower court in a § 101(a)(5) case may examine a union disciplinary hearing to decide whether "some evidence" at the hearing supported the charges made against the defendant. That is the only standard of court review of sufficiency of the evidence in a union disciplinary hearing.

The Court also held that a court in a § 101(a)(5) action cannot examine the union constitution to determine whether a provision authorizes the imposition of discipline. A state court can make that examination under state law, but the legislative history of § 101(a)(5) indicates that although the section requires that a member be served with specific written charges prior to any disciplinary hearing—charges that spell out and give adequate notice of the conduct for which the member is subject to discipline—there need be no prior union constitutional prohibition of the charged conduct. The Court in *Hardeman* stated, "and if a union may discipline its members for offenses not proscribed by written rules at all, it is surely a futile exercise for a court to construe the written rules in order to determine whether particular conduct falls within or without their scope."

This rationale is troubling if it means that a union member can be disciplined for conduct that he, in good faith, did not believe constituted a violation of union rules, or that prior to the bringing of charges would not have been a violation of union rules. Perhaps the defense could be grounded on a breach of the union constitution. Federal courts, having no jurisdiction to enforce a union constitution as such, must leave this issue to state courts.

In Hall v. Cole (U.S.1973), the Court held that an award of attorney fees is proper in a suit under § 102 of the LMRDA that establishes a violation of the free speech rights of Title I. The theory is that a vindication of free speech rights bestows a benefit on all union members, who will no longer be chilled from exercising their own free speech rights. The fact that the recovery of attorney fees is expressly authorized in two other titles of the LMRDA, while § 102 is conspicuously silent on the question, did not, in the Court's view, demonstrate a congressional purpose to preclude § 102 attorney fees. There appears to be no way to distinguish violations of § 101(a)(5) from the *Hall* rule awarding attorney fees, for presumably vindication of a single member's procedural rights in a discipline case will work to the benefit of all members subject to future discipline.

E. Election of Union Officers

Title IV of the LMRDA requires and regulates election of officers by local and national unions. While state courts are permitted to enforce the constitution and bylaws of a union even though such enforcement may affect election issues, any challenge to an election already held must be accomplished through procedures set out in Title IV. Indeed, prior to the holding of an election, even federal district court jurisdiction under other titles of the LMRDA may be affected by Title IV.

Title IV fixes the terms during which union officers hold office; requires that elections be by secret ballot; regulates the handling of campaign literature; requires reasonable opportunity to nominate candidates; authorizes reasonable qualifications, uniformly imposed, for candidates; and attempts thereby to guarantee fair elections in unions. Except for § 401(c), which permits a candidate for union office to enforce rights to equal treatment in the distribution of campaign literature and access to membership lists, the exclusive method for enforcing Title IV rights is through the Secretary of Labor after the election. Section 402 permits an individual member to file a complaint with the Secretary of Labor alleging election misconduct that may have affected the outcome of the election. The Secretary of Labor is the only party who may sue to set an election aside, and the Secretary can act only if there is a complaint by a union member who has satisfied certain exhaustion requirements set out in § 402(a).

In Calhoon v. Harvey (U.S.1964), the union's bylaws deprived a member of the right to nominate anyone but himself for office. The bylaws also provided that no member was eligible for nomination to a full-time elective office unless he had been a member of the national union for five years and had served 180 days or more of sea time in each of two of the preceding three years on vessels covered by collective bargaining agreements with the national union or its locals. Three union members filed a complaint in federal district court alleging that these bylaws deprived them of their equal right to nominate candidates established by § 101(a)(1). They asked that the union be enjoined from proceeding with the election until they were given full rights to nominate.

The Supreme Court held that jurisdiction under § 102 of Title I depends entirely upon whether the complaint shows a violation of rights guaranteed by § 101(a)(1). Jurisdiction cannot be upheld by allegations that in substance charge violation of the § 401(e) requirement that every member in good standing shall be eligible to be a candidate and to hold office, subject to reasonable qualifications uniformly imposed. In this case everyone had an equal right to nominate (one could nominate only oneself). The fact that the combined effect of that self-nomination right with the restrictive eligibility requirement arguably denied a meaningful opportunity to nominate was not to be considered under Title I. Whether the union's rules constituted "reasonable qualifications uniformly imposed" was subject to the procedures of Title IV only.

Title IV may be a member's exclusive remedy for an election infraction, and if the Secretary of Labor refuses to bring suit, the member may have no recourse. Thus a Title I suit will be barred if it "basically relates" to eligibility or charges "in substance" that a member has been denied the right to run for office. Driscoll v. Operating Engineers, Local 139 (7th Cir.1973). That court was prepared, however, to recognize two exceptions to *Calhoon*'s rule of the primacy of Title IV: "The complaint does not allege that the candidacy requirement is part of a purposeful program of suppressing any expression of dissent by plaintiff. Nor does it appear that the eligibility requirement is a discriminatory ad hoc device calculated to perpetuating certain individuals in office."

In Hodgson v. Steelworkers Local 6799 (U.S.1971), a union member exhausted his internal remedies with respect to several grounds challenging a union election, but added a new ground when he filed with the Secretary of Labor. The Supreme Court held that the Secretary was precluded from challenging the election on the newly raised ground because the member had not exhausted his internal union remedies.

If the Secretary of Labor decides not to bring suit, the results of the election appear to be immune from challenge. However, in Dunlop v. Bachowski (U.S.1975) the Court held that a complaining member was entitled to a statement of reasons from the Secretary of Labor supporting a decision not to file a Title IV suit. A district court then has jurisdiction to determine whether the Secretary's decision "is so irrational as to constitute the decision arbitrary and capricious." Where the statement is inadequate, the Court suggested that the Secretary should be given leave to supplement the statement. The Court expressly left open the question of whether a district court would have the power to order the Secretary to bring suit in an appropriate case.

If the Secretary does sue to set aside the election, there will be two issues: was there conduct violating Title IV, and might that conduct have affected the outcome of the election? On these issues, affected union members may intervene under 24(a) of the Federal Rules of Civil Procedure for the limited purpose of presenting evidence and argument in support of the Secretary's grounds for setting aside the election, but no additional grounds may be raised by the intervenor. Trbovich v. United Mine Workers (U.S.1972).

If the Secretary proves a violation of § 401, it will be considered prima facie evidence that the violation "may have affected" the outcome of the election, and the burden will then shift to the union to prove that the violation did not affect the election result. Wirtz v. Hotel, Motel and Club Employees (U.S.1968). Wrongful disqualification of a candidate will establish a prima facie case, and while that does not automatically prove that the violation affected the election result, it is not clear how a union could establish a sufficient rebuttal.

A controversial substantive issue under § 401(e) has been the extent of a union's right to set qualifications for a union office. In Steelworkers Local 3489 v. Usery (U.S.1977), the Secretary of Labor brought suit challenging the attendance rule eligibility requirement of the Steelworkers union. The union's rule required that eligibility for local union office was limited to members who had attended at least one-half of the regular meetings of the local union for three years prior to the election (unless prevented by union activities or working hours). The union argued that the rule was proper because it encouraged attendance at union meetings and promoted the election of qualified members with a demonstrated interest in union affairs. The Secretary of Labor showed that in this local union, 96.5percent of the members were ineligible to hold office because of this restriction. The union responded that, regardless of the percentages, every member had it in her own power to comply with the rule.

The Court found the rule to be an unreasonable qualification on union office seekers. It described the high percentage of disqualifications as a severe restriction on the free choice of the membership in selecting their leaders, and was unconvinced that the rule had the effect of encouraging attendance since at this local union's meetings only an average of 47 members attended out of a total membership of approximately 660. To the argument that the requirement helped ensure qualified, interested candidates, the Court responded that qualifications and interest were best left to be decided by the membership in open democratic elections. Nor was the Court convinced that a member was completely free to comply with the rule since any member planning to run for office would have to attend union meetings at least 18 months in advance of the election, when the issues motivating her to seek office might not yet have arisen. It thus appears that any union restriction on office seeking is likely to be struck down by the courts when it disqualifies a high percentage of the membership, as did the Steelworkers' attendance rule.

F. Trusteeships

The relationship between a national union and its constituent local unions is controlled by the constitution of the national union. When a local union does not abide by that constitution or refuses to follow the lawful orders of its parent union, a variety of control devices are available. One traditional device is the trusteeship. A trusteeship is accomplished by sending in a representative of the national union to direct the affairs of the local. Often the union treasury is put solely at the trustee's direction and democratic procedures are suspended. Officers may be ousted or are likely to serve only at the pleasure of the trustee. The trustee may also take over the process of collective bargaining and sign bargaining agreements binding the local.

The history of the American labor movement has shown instances of severe abuse of the trusteeship device. In some unions, locals were in trusteeship for decades while national officers controlled the locals' affairs and used this power over the trusteed locals to cement their own power base. Because of these abuses, Congress undertook to regulate the trusteeship device in Title III of the LMRDA.

In addition to reporting requirements, Title III provides that a trusteeship can be established only if it is in accord with the parent union's constitution and bylaws. Even then, it must be for one of the following specified purposes: correcting corrup-

tion or financial malpractice, assuring the performance of collective bargaining agreements or other
duties of a bargaining representative, restoring
democratic procedures, or otherwise carrying out
the legitimate objects of a labor organization. The
Secretary of Labor is given the power to bring suit
to void a trusteeship; but any member of the
trusteed union may bring a civil action in district
court without requesting the Secretary to do so,
even in the event that the Secretary decides not to
sue. However, if the Secretary does sue, that suit
becomes the exclusive vehicle for setting aside the
trusteeship.

Any trusteeship established in conformity with
the procedural requirements of the parent union's
constitution and bylaws, and authorized or ratified
after a fair hearing before the parent's executive
board or such other body as is provided in that
constitution, is presumed by Title III to be valid for
a period of 18 months from the date of its establishment. The presumption prevails except as
against clear and convincing proof that the trusteeship was not established or maintained in good
faith for a purpose allowable by Title III. After 18
months expires, the trusteeship is presumed invalid unless the union comes forward with clear and
convincing proof that the trusteeship's continuation is necessary for one of the allowable purposes.
There is some disagreement whether a trusteeship
established without a hearing either before, or soon
after, its imposition is unlawful under Title III, or

if it merely fails to enjoy the 18 months of presumptive validity.

Even if the trusteeship is lawful, the parent union is not allowed to count the votes of delegates from a trusteed local unless they have been chosen by a secret ballot in an election in which all the members in good standing were eligible to participate. Nor is the parent permitted to transfer funds from the trusteed local to the parent except at the same rate of per capita tax and assessment as is payable by local unions not in trusteeship.

Section 301 of the Labor–Management Reporting Act, which gives district courts jurisdiction over contracts "between ... labor organizations," has a part to play in the trusteeship context. Section 301 jurisdiction has been held to extend to suits brought by a national union to impose or enforce a trusteeship and also to suits by a trusteed union to set aside a trusteeship alleged to be established contrary to the union constitution. Parks v. IBEW (4th Cir.1963); Brotherhood of Painters v. Local 127 (N.D.Cal.1966).

Two issues that have vexed the courts with respect to Title III are what forms of control by a national union over a local union constitutes a trusteeship, and what purposes will be deemed to fall within the allowable statutory purposes for imposing trusteeships.

The revocation of a union's charter and the establishment of a new local union in the same geographical area would not seem to constitute a trusteeship. However, if all the members of the old local are granted membership in the new local, so that the only effect of the revocation and new charter is to remove the existing slate of local union officers, and perhaps to give the national union an opportunity to tamper with the local treasury during the transition, a federal court might be well advised to find that a trusteeship has been imposed.

A leading case on the range of allowable purposes permitted to a national union in establishing a trusteeship is United Bhd. of Carpenters v. Brown (10th Cir.1965). There the president of the national union ordered a local to affiliate with a union district council comprised of other local unions in the territory of the council, and ordered the local to raise membership dues as required by the district council's bylaws. The national union's purpose was fully to utilize the state's union membership on various missile sites in the area and to supply contractors on those sites with an adequate work force of union carpenters. If the state's local unions fully participated in the district council, a member of any local union could go anywhere in the territory of the council without being required to pay a journeyman's permit fee or a service permit fee to the local union with jurisdiction over the missile site. If a small local union were to find itself with a major job in its territorial jurisdiction, it might want to staff that job with members of outside locals while enhancing its own treasury with the collection of considerable service fees.

In *Brown,* the local union initially complied with the directive but some members became unhappy with the dues increase and the local's membership voted to withdraw from the council and rescind the increase. The national union imposed a trusteeship and individual members of the local sued to set it aside. The circuit court held that the trusteeship was void because it was not specifically authorized by the union constitution, and the court would not infer such a power from the more general provisions of that constitution. But the court went on to say that the parent union had no permissible purpose for a trusteeship in any event, relying on the fact that the local union's will had been made clear through a membership vote and that the trusteeship would thus interfere with the right of the local union to carry out the results of a democratic vote of the membership. Even the 18–month presumption would not help the union in this circumstance.

Brown's discussion of the legitimacy of the union's purpose seems indefensible. Virtually any action of a local union going against the command of the parent national union can be couched in terms of a membership vote. There is nothing in Title III suggesting that the results in Title III cases should turn on the presence or absence of such a vote. The circuit court did not see the parent union's purpose as one of those listed as allowable in Title III, but the staffing of the missile site project should have been deemed a part of "the performance of collective bargaining agreements or other duties of a bargaining representative," or at least considered a legitimate object of a national labor organization. Since this local union and others in the area were in a clear conflict of interest, democratic voting procedures within one local cannot be counted upon to reach an orderly accommodation. The national union, if authorized by its constitution, is the logical instrument for finding a just solution.

A vote of the membership will not always be meaningful in Title III cases. In Carpenters Local 1302 v. United Brotherhood of Carpenters (2d Cir. 1973), a local Carpenter's union had joined with 11 other craft unions in a trades council that had exclusive bargaining rights for 8,000 shipyard employees. The council had exercised these rights for over 25 years. The Carpenter's local union represented about 400 of the shipyard employees. The local's membership voted to sever its relationship with the trades council and filed a representation petition with the NLRB for separate certification of a unit of shipyard carpenters. The local's parent national union, complying with its constitutional procedures, put the local in trusteeship for refusing an order from the national to refrain from filing the NLRB petition. The trustee withdrew the NLRB petition and the trades council signed a new collective bargaining agreement with the shipyard. The trusteeship was then lifted but the national indicated that a trusteeship would again be imposed if the local sought separate bargaining rights.

The local filed suit under Title III for an injunction against the national union's interference, and the Second Circuit upheld the trusteeship. In the court's view, separate certification by the Carpenter's local union would delay the execution of the collective bargaining agreement with the shipyard and might well lead to attempts by other local unions to disaffiliate from the trade council representing shipyard employees, thereby undermining the council's position as bargaining representative. The trusteeship was deemed proper to prevent the destruction of the existing bargaining unit and to preserve the status of the certified bargaining representative. These were considered "legitimate objects" within the meaning of Title III. This result is not consistent with *Brown,*, and *Carpenters Local 1302* is the better reasoned decision.

G. Fiduciary Duties of Union Officers

Title V of the LMRDA declares that union officers stand in a fiduciary relationship to their unions. Section 501 is designed to provide a civil damage remedy to union members to enable them to restore pilfered funds to the union treasury. Yet there have been surprisingly few such suits. A union member bringing such a suit will have her attorney fees paid out of the recovery, but if there is no recovery, the member will have to stand her own litigation expenses. There is no direct reward to a member bringing such a suit, for any recovery will go into the union treasury. Plaintiff's per capita share is likely to be small and, in any event, is not capable of being withdrawn. In addition, a member bringing such a suit risks the displeasure of the defendant officers, which may be a substantial impediment. For these reasons, it is not surprising that many § 501 suits have been filed by plaintiffs with a personal political stake in the litigation. Almost without exception, such plaintiffs are potential or disappointed office-seekers apparently hoping to embarrass incumbent union officers. These plaintiffs have often looked to recover for actions which they deem an abuse of officer power even though few would agree that the acts, if proved, constitute pilfering.

The Second Circuit has held that § 501 shows on its face that it applies a fiduciary standard only with respect to the money and property of the union and "that it is not a catch-all provision under which union officials can be sued on any ground of misconduct with which the plaintiffs choose to charge them." Gurton v. Arons (2d Cir. 1964). However, other circuits have held that the legislative history shows a clear congressional intent to apply the fiduciary standards to all exercises of officer power, even when not relating to money or property. Stelling v. IBEW Local 1547 (9th Cir.1978); Johnson v. Nelson (8th Cir.1963).

One line of cases has held that a union officer violates his fiduciary duty when he acts outside of the authority given him by the union constitution, and the cases have imposed the courts' own inter-

pretation of union constitutional provisions. In
Morrissey v. Curran (2d Cir.1970), the president of
a national union gave a pension to several other
union officers pursuant to what the president believed was express authority in the union's constitution and bylaws. A disappointed office-seeker
sued the national president, among others, alleging
that the pension grant was the product of an
incorrect reading of the constitution and was therefore a fiduciary breach.

A panel of the Second Circuit split, two to one.
The dissent thought that the union president had
correctly interpreted the union constitution and
was authorized in paying the pension benefits.
The majority disagreed with the president's interpretation of his authority and found a fiduciary
breach. It declared that if the president was unable to recover the pension payments, he would be
personally liable to the union for the resultant
damage. Neither the majority nor the dissenting
opinions considered whether there might not be a
difference between a misinterpretation of one's authority under the union constitution and a fiduciary breach. A federal court would have no jurisdiction over a breach of the union constitution
unless it otherwise implicated the LMRDA.

Nor did the court consider whether the presence
or absence of personal gain should be a factor, or
whether a good faith interpretation of authority by
an officer charged with carrying out the daily
affairs of a union should be subject to deference by

a reviewing court. A Ninth Circuit case appears to have broken with this line of precedent. *Stelling, supra.* The unfortunate outgrowth of cases like *Morrissey*, assuming they have any effect at all, is that either union officers will be reluctant to accept office in light of the risk of substantial monetary liability for a good faith mistake in interpreting their authority or that union memberships will be prompted to give these officers expansive power to act so they may avoid liability.

Another line of cases imposes liability on a union officer by striking down the officer's constitutional authority on policy grounds and then holding the officer liable on fiduciary grounds for an unauthorized act. The first such case, and the most compelling, was Highway Truck Drivers and Helpers, Local 107 v. Cohen (4th Cir.1960), where union officers were charged with a fiduciary breach for using union funds to defend themselves against state charges of corruption in office. Payment of their attorney fees was authorized by a vote of the union membership but the court in a § 501 action found that the approval by the membership of the funds' dispersal was inconsistent with the policies of the LMRDA (although not with any specific provision thereof) and that the dispersing officers had thus committed a fiduciary breach.

While unarticulated, it seems clear that the court was concerned that unscrupulous union officers may so dominate their membership that any proposition submitted by them to the membership will be passed. This is a real concern, but a standard as vague as "inconsistent with the policies of the LMRDA" gives federal courts substantial power to strike down, as a fiduciary breach, policies that are not congenial to the judges. Membership ratifications of officers' acts have been struck down on the same ground, and also on the ground that they constitute prohibited "exculpation."

Another illustration in this line of cases is Johnson v. Nelson (8th Cir.1963). Political opponents of incumbent union officers had earlier brought suit under Title I of the LMRDA to enjoin disciplinary action by the local union. That suit was ultimately settled and following the settlement the plaintiffs secured a membership vote directing that their attorney fees be paid from local union funds. Incumbent officers had this vote rescinded by the membership at the next meeting and the parent national union then intervened. Acting upon a proposed method to settle the controversy, the membership voted to pay the attorney fees of both plaintiffs and defendants in the settled Title I suit, but the incumbent officers refused to pay plaintiffs' attorney (and their own) and instead appealed the vote to the national union. The national union relied on its broad constitutional authority to declare a policy against paying plaintiffs' attorney fees in such a situation, unless the local's officers were directed to do so by a secret mail ballot of the entire local membership. The local union officers were bound by the national union's constitution to follow this policy directive. They obviously were happy with the outcome.

At this point, the disappointed plaintiffs filed a § 501 suit alleging that the local officers were violating their fiduciary duty in withholding payment. The circuit court agreed. There was no theory available that would have supported an argument that a refusal to reimburse attorney fees to plaintiffs in a settled Title I suit violated any provision of the LMRDA. The circuit court, however, held that the action of the national union was irrelevant and that the local officers had violated their fiduciary duty by allowing "their personal feelings toward [plaintiffs in the prior Title I suit] to interfere with their duties as officers." The appeal to the national union by the local's officers was itself a fiduciary breach. The vote of the membership was also relied upon by the court to support its finding of a § 501 violation. The case suggests that in some federal courts if the judges are sufficiently offended by what local union officers do, a fiduciary breach may be found.

A similar case is Pignotti v. Local 3, Sheet Metal Workers (8th Cir.1973), where the forcing of a pension plan on a local union by the president of the national union was set aside as a fiduciary breach. The circuit court relied on the fact that members of the local had voted against the imposition of the pension plan, and that the president of the national had allowed his "personal feelings" to interfere with his duty as an officer. There was no suggestion that the national president exceeded his constitutional authority, or that he sought or received any personal gain by his actions. Why his judgment as to the pension plan that would be most appropriate for the local (in a case where the union membership was bitterly divided) should constitute an illicit "personal feeling" was not explained in the opinion.

*

INDEX

References are to Pages

---

†